A TRANSLATOR'S HANDBOOK ON PAUL'S LETTERS TO THE THESSALONIANS

Helps for Translators Series

Technical Helps:

Old Testament Quotations in the New Testament
Section Headings for the New Testament
Short Bible Reference System
New Testament Index
Orthography Studies
Bible Translations for Popular Use
The Theory and Practice of Translation
Bible Index
Fauna and Flora of the Bible
Manuscript Preparation
Marginal Notes for the Old Testament
Marginal Notes for the New Testament
The Practice of Translating

Handbooks:

A Translator's Handbook on the Book of Joshua
A Translator's Handbook of the Book of Ruth
A Translator's Handbook on the Book of Amos
A Translator's Handbook on the Books of Obadiah and Micah
A Translator's Handbook on the Book of Jonah
A Translator's Handbook on the Gospel of Mark
A Translator's Handbook on the Gospel of Luke
A Translator's Handbook on the Gospel of John
A Translator's Handbook on the Acts of the Apostles
A Translator's Handbook on Paul's Letter to the Romans
A Translator's Handbook on Paul's Letter to the Galatians
A Translator's Handbook on Paul's Letter to the Ephesians
A Translator's Handbook on Paul's Letter to the Philippians
A Translator's Handbook on Paul's Letters to the Colossians and to Philemon
A Translator's Handbook on Paul's Letters to the Thessalonians
A Translator's Handbook on the Letter to the Hebrews
A Translator's Handbook on the First Letter from Peter
A Translator's Handbook on the Letters of John

Guides:

A Translator's Guide to Selections from the First Five Books of the Old Testament
A Translator's Guide to Selected Psalms
A Translator's Guide to the Gospel of Matthew
A Translator's Guide to the Gospel of Mark
A Translator's Guide to the Gospel of Luke
A Translator's Guide to Paul's First Letter to the Corinthians
A Translator's Guide to Paul's Second Letter to the Corinthians
A Translator's Guide to Paul's Letters to Timothy and to Titus
A Translator's Guide to the Letters to James, Peter, and Jude
A Translator's Guide to the Revelation to John

HELPS FOR TRANSLATORS

A TRANSLATOR'S HANDBOOK
on
PAUL'S LETTERS TO THE
THESSALONIANS

by

PAUL ELLINGWORTH

and

EUGENE A. NIDA

UNITED BIBLE SOCIETIES

London, New York,

Stuttgart

Printed in the United States of America

Books in the series of Helps for Translators may be ordered from a national Bible Society or from either of the following centers:

United Bible Societies
European Production Fund
D-7000 Stuttgart 80
Postfach 81 03 40
West Germany

United Bible Societies
1865 Broadway
New York, New York 10023
U.S.A.

ISBN 0-8267-0146-9

ABS-1985-700-4,700-CM-4-08526

PREFACE

The judgment and advice of the translations consultants of the United Bible Societies, as a result of their experience with translators using earlier volumes in this series of Translator's Handbooks, have led to the introduction of certain special features into the present volume.

At the beginning of each section of the present Handbook, the text under consideration is given in two English translations: Today's English Version (TEV) and the Revised Standard Version (RSV). These translations differ considerably from each other, since they are based on different principles of translation and are intended to serve different purposes. RSV replaces the old-fashioned language of earlier translations by more modern expressions, but it generally follows as closely as possible the form and structure of sentences in the original Hebrew and Greek. TEV also uses modern language, but differs from RSV in reproducing as closely as possible, not the grammatical form of the original Greek text, but rather its meaning. This often involves changing the structure of the original text and using forms which fulfill in English the same function and convey the same meaning as the (often very different) grammatical forms of Hebrew and Greek.

Obviously, the two translations are printed in this Handbook for quite different reasons. TEV is a model of translation into the kind of English used by most ordinary native speakers of average education today. RSV, however, reproduces more closely the form, though not necessarily the meaning, of the original language. Neither of these English translations is intended to be retranslated into any other language. Every translation should be made by, or at least in close cooperation with, scholars having a good knowledge of the original languages. A translation of another translation is at best only second rate, for inherent in the process lurks the danger that any distortions which occur in the first translation will be compounded in the second.

As in Volumes 14 (Handbook on Romans) and 15 (Handbook on Ruth) of this series, the TEV running text is presented twice: first, in paragraph form, so as to facilitate the discussion of important features of the discourse structure; and second, verse by verse, to call attention to some of the detailed problems of grammatical and lexical structure. In earlier Handbooks the RSV was used for the running text, and in more recent volumes TEV has served the same purpose. The present Handbook is the first in which both the RSV and the TEV texts are given.

Reference is frequently made to translations of the letters to the Thessalonians in various European languages, especially English, Dutch, French, German, and Spanish. Sometimes these translations are quoted in a fairly literal English retranslation. Our purpose in citing these translations is not to suggest that European languages are in any way more developed, or that translations in them are better, than those in other parts of the world. Rather, we use them in two main ways: first, to illustrate how different interpretations of the Greek text affect the translation; and secondly, to provide examples of how the meaning of the Greek text has been expressed in particular translations. Dynamic equivalent translations, and especially common language translations, are generally used in the second way; but both these and other translations are used in the first way also. The references to other translations and the use of TEV as a running text should be understood as suggestions, not as models to be followed in every case. The responsibility for finding the closest natural equivalent of the original text always rests upon the translator; no translation made in another language, no commentary, and no Handbook can remove this responsibility.

In dealing with expository discourse such as the letters of Paul, it is difficult to strike a balance between giving the translator the necessary information on different ways of understanding the text and overburdening him with unnecessary details. Wherever there exists the possibility of understanding the text in different ways, we have tried to give, not only our own preference, but the reasons for our choice. However, no translator should regard this Handbook as all he needs for dealing with the many exegetical and linguistic problems found in Paul's letters to the Thessalonians. Good commentaries and other helps should be consulted. The Bibliography lists a number of standard commentaries, some of which are of particular value to the translator.*

As in the earlier Handbooks in this series, the traditional chapter divisions of the text are adhered to, with a single exception. Verse 17 of chapter 2 of 1 Thessalonians so clearly begins a new major division of the letter that we have considered it necessary to treat the closing verses of this chapter and all of chapter 3 as a single unit. It is a well-known fact that none of the Scriptures as originally written had chapter and verse divisions. These were gradually introduced by scholars—and to some extent by printers—at a later date. Generally the chapter divisions are acceptable, but occasionally they are unfortunate, or even misleading, as in the present case. This Handbook follows the arrangement found in in the UBS Greek New Testament and in most modern translations and commentaries.

The authors wish to express their gratitude to Professor Ernest Best of Glasgow for his valuable comments on draft material on 1 Thessalonians, and to Dr. Elizabeth G. Edwards for her careful review of the entire manuscript and her many helpful suggestions; also to Miss Lucy Rowe of the Translations Department staff of American Bible Society for her patient labor in typing and retyping the manuscript, and to Mr. Paul C. Clarke of the same staff for attending to the many details of style and format in preparing this volume for the press. However, the authors alone remain responsible for all judgments made and for any errors which may appear in this Handbook.

Paul Ellingworth
Eugene A. Nida

August 1975

---

*Attention is also called to an article by Robert and Carolyn Lee, "An Analysis of the Larger Semantic Units of I Thessalonians," appearing in Notes on Translation, No. 56, June 1975, pp. 28-42 (published by Summer Institute of Linguistics, Huntington Beach, CA 92648, U.S.A.).

CONTENTS

ABBREVIATIONS OF VERSIONS CITED

(for details see Bibliography, page 213)

BJ	Bible de Jérusalem (French)
Brc	Barclay
DuCL	Dutch common language translation
FrCL	French common language translation
GeCL	German common language translation
JB	Jerusalem Bible (English)
KJV	King James Version
Lu	Luther
Mft	Moffatt
NAB	New American Bible
NEB	New English Bible
Phps	Phillips
RSV	Revised Standard Version
RV	Revised Version
Seg	Segond
SpCL	Spanish common language translation
Syn	Synodale
TEV	Today's English Version
TNT	Translator's New Testament
TOB	Traduction Oecuménique de la Bible
Zur	Zürcher Bibel

1 THESSALONIANS

INTRODUCTION

Commentators are generally agreed that apart from greetings at the beginning of this letter, and the conclusion, the letter is divided into two main parts. The first three chapters consist mainly of teaching based on the relationship between Paul and his fellow evangelists on the one hand, and the Christians in Thessalonica on the other hand. The second part consists mainly of exhortation or calls to action. More detailed subdivisions, and the translations from one subsection to another, are discussed in the text of the Handbook. The general plan is understood to be the following:

Greeting (1.1-2)

A. The evangelists and the Thessalonians
   1. The life and faith of the Thessalonians (1.2-10)
   2. Paul's work in Thessalonica (2.1-12)
   3. After Paul left Thessalonica (2.13-16)
   4. Paul's desire to visit Thessalonica again (2.17—3.13)

B. Calls to action
   1. Introduction (4.1-2)
   2. Sex (4.3-8)
   3. Brotherly love (4.9-12)
   4. The Lord's coming (4.13-17)
   5. Be ready for the Lord's coming (5.1-11)
   6. Life in the community (5.12-22)
   7. Final instructions and greetings (5.23-28)

1 THESSALONIANS

CHAPTER 1

The dates at which Paul wrote his various letters are usually uncertain, and they are not very important for the translator. There is, however, good reason to believe that 1 and 2 Thessalonians, in that order, are the first two of Paul's letters to survive. It is also fairly certain that 1 Thessalonians was written about fifteen years after Paul's conversion, that is, early in the year 51 or late in the previous year. Paul was writing to young Christians, but he himself was already an experienced evangelist.

TEV	RSV
1 From Paul, Silas, and Timothy-- To the people of the church in Thessalonica, who belong to God the Father and the Lord Jesus Christ: May grace and peace be yours. (1.1)	1 Paul, Silvanus, and Timothy. To the church of the Thessalonians in God the Father and the Lord Jesus Christ: Grace to you and peace. (1.1)

All of Paul's letters follow the normal Greek pattern of stating at the beginning the name of the sender(s), the name of the person(s) to whom the letter is addressed, and a greeting. Paul, however, fills this conventional form with a new and Christian content. The introduction to this letter is the shortest we have in any of Paul's letters to a church. Some early copyists, followed by the older translations, apparently found the ending of verse 1 too abrupt and so added "... from God our Father and the Lord Jesus Christ" or a similar phrase (cf. 2 Thess. 1.1), but these words are probably not original here.

Three people are mentioned as senders of the letter: Paul, Silas, and Timothy. They had visited Thessalonica together, and they were together in Corinth while the letter was being written (see Acts 17.1—18.5). The repeated use of "we" in this letter, more frequently than in any other of Paul's letters, shows that the message comes essentially from all three senders. Especially in the first three chapters, they refer continually to experiences they have lived through together. But there is no reason to think that either Silas or Timothy had much share in the actual writing of the letter. The sentence structure, vocabulary, and style are similar to those of Paul's other letters, and in a few places (2.18; 3.5; 5.27) he speaks in his own name, using the first person singular.

In translating this opening salutation, it is necessary in many languages to introduce a verb indicating that the three are writing or sending the letter. Thus it may be necessary to translate "We who are Paul, Silas, and Timothy write to you people in the church at Thessalonica." Since Paul is essentially the author of the letter, one may find it preferable in some languages to translate "I, Paul, together with Silas and Timothy, write to you people...." If a language requires the identification of Paul as "I" and of Paul together with his companions as "we," it is almost inevitable that the people of the church at Thessalonica be addressed as "you." This will fit quite readily with what is said in verse 2.

Here and in other places (for example, 2 Corinthians 1.19), Paul calls one of his companions "Silvanus," but there is no doubt that this is the same person who is called "Silas" in Acts. TEV and FrCL rightly recognize this by using the form Silas everywhere; most older translations (also some modern ones, including NEB GeCL NAB TNT) do not.

The repeated conjunction "and" ("Paul and Silas and Timothy") of the Greek text is reproduced in older translations (for example KJV Lu Seg), but not in RSV NEB Syn FrCL GeCL DuCL. The repetition should not be made in translation unless it is natural to the receptor language.

At the time this letter was written, Thessalonica (now Salonika) was the most important city in Macedonia; but Paul writes, not to the population in general, but to the Christians in the city. The Greek word translated "church" does not refer to a special building (Christians met for worship in one another's homes) but to the coming together of people, in this case of Christians. Best accordingly translates "the Christian community of the Thessalonians"; Knox "the church assembled at Thessalonika"; TEV the people of the church in Thessalonica; FrCL "the members of the Church of Thessalonica." In some languages the only satisfactory equivalent of "church" in this context is "believers in Jesus Christ" or "followers of Christ" or "those who trust in Jesus Christ." Such a rendering may be particularly important in situations where the common word for "church" identifies a building. Furthermore, the Greek word translated "church" indicates a group which recognizes itself as a group, and not just a collection of individuals. If possible, this fact should be reflected in translation.

The context shows clearly that Paul is not writing to the church universal but to the local gathering of Christians. In some languages, though not in Greek, this distinction is reflected in a difference of spelling, between "Church" (capital C) and "church" (small c) respectively. Since this distinction disappears when the passage is read aloud, it is better not to rely on it to make the meaning clear.

The Thessalonians are here mentioned for the first time. The Greek text marks this as new information by omitting the article (literally "the church of Thessalonians"). In Thessalonica may need to be translated in some languages with a classifier, for example, "in the city of Thessalonica."

Grammatically it would be possible, but it would almost certainly be wrong, to link who belong to God the Father and the Lord Jesus Christ with what follows, giving the translation: "May grace and peace be yours in God the Father and the Lord Jesus Christ." Paul often does speak of Christian individuals or groups as being "in Christ" or (less often) "in God," and sometimes he uses both expressions. What does he mean? Clearly his use of "in" is figurative. For Paul Christ is a person, not a kind of gas physically diffused through the atmosphere. In some passages, it is possible to think that Paul is speaking of the mystical identification of two individuals; but that is not possible here, since he is referring to the whole Christian community. Who belong to God (TEV cf. FrCL GeCL) is the essential meaning of this phrase. This may be rendered in some languages as "who are God's possession," "whom God possesses," or even "who are God's."

In some languages the phrase God the Father poses a difficulty, especially if the term for "Father" must indicate whose father. In such cases it may be necessary to say "who belong to God our Father" or "to God who is our Father." In languages which make a distinction between exclusive and inclusive first person plural, the inclusive form should be used, since Paul clearly includes the Thessalonian Christians with himself and his companions among those to whom God is Father.

Christ was originally not a proper name but a title, corresponding to "Messiah" and meaning "the Anointed (One)." For Paul, however, as for us, it is usually a proper name. In this and most other Pauline passages, Christ should therefore be transliterated and not translated.

For some languages the term Lord is not a title which can readily be added to the name of Jesus Christ, because it expresses a relation between men and Christ. Therefore, it may be rendered as "Jesus Christ who controls us" or "...who commands us," equivalent in some languages to "Jesus Christ our chief."

Paul wishes his readers grace and peace, as he does in all his letters. The context does not narrow the meaning of these words, which should therefore be taken in their widest sense. There is a considerable overlap of meaning between them. Grace here means, not physical gracefulness and not a specific favor, but God's willingness to look upon Christians as his people, and to give them good gifts, such as forgiveness. In secular Greek peace meant the cessation or absence of war, just as it usually does in modern English. Paul, however, uses the term to mean a right and harmonious relationship among men or between men and God, a total well-being which God himself gives. TEV FrCL GeCL NEB, like older translations, retain the traditional nouns, grace and peace.

Some scholars view the phrase grace and peace in this type of salutation as being a combination of a Greek and a Semitic greeting. At any rate, it is certainly a distinctive expression, and no doubt it had wide usage among the members of the early church. In view of the distinctive value of the expression, it is not easy to do justice to all the meaning which may be involved. In some languages an appropriate equivalent may be "May God be good to you and show you his peace" or "May God show goodness to you and cause you to have peace." Since "peace" in this context suggests general well-being, it is expressed in some languages in a figurative way, for example, "May you be able to sit down in your heart" or "May you rest in happiness."

In some languages it is difficult to express a wish or prayer such as may grace and peace be yours without indicating clearly the relation between the one who desires such a blessing for others and the agent, who is God. Therefore one may need to translate this clause as "I pray to God that he will be good to you and make you to have peace."

TEV

The Life and Faith of the Thessalonians

2 We always thank God for you
all and always mention you in our
prayers. 3 For we remember before
our God and Father how you put your
faith into practice, how your love
made you work so hard, and how your
hope in our Lord Jesus Christ is
firm. 4 Our brothers, we know that
God loves you and has chosen you to
be his own. 5 For we brought the
Good News to you, not with words
only, but also with power and the
Holy Spirit, and with complete conviction of its truth. You know how
we lived when we were with you; it
was for your own good. 6 You imitated us and the Lord; and even
though you suffered much, you received the message with the joy
that comes from the Holy Spirit.
7 So you became an example to all
believers in Macedonia and Achaia.
8 For not only did the message
about the Lord go out from you
throughout Macedonia and Achaia,
but the news about your faith in
God has gone everywhere. There is
nothing, then, that we need to say.
9 All those people speak about how
you received us when we visited
you, and how you turned away from
idols to God, to serve the true and
living God 10 and to wait for his
Son to come from heaven--his Son
Jesus, whom he raised from death
and who rescues us from God's anger
that is coming. (1.2-10)

RSV

2 We give thanks to God always
for you all, constantly mentioning you in our prayers, 3 remembering before our God and Father
your work of faith and labor of
love and steadfastness of hope in
our Lord Jesus Christ. 4 For we
know, brethren beloved by God,
that he has chosen you; 5 for our
gospel came to you not only in
word, but also in power and in the
Holy Spirit and with full conviction. You know what kind of men
we proved to be among you for your
sake. 6 And you became imitators
of us and of the Lord, for you received the word in much affliction, with joy inspired by the
Holy Spirit; 7 so that you became
an example to all the believers in
Macedonia and in Achaia. 8 For
not only has the word of the Lord
sounded forth from you in Macedonia and Achaia, but your faith in
God has gone forth everywhere, so
that we need not say anything.
9 For they themselves report concerning us what a welcome we had
among you, and how you turned to
God from idols, to serve a living
and true God, 10 and to wait for
his Son from heaven, whom he
raised from the dead, Jesus who
delivers us from the wrath to
come. (1.2-10)

The section heading The Life and Faith of the Thessalonians may be difficult to translate in some languages, since both life and faith may need to be expressed as verbs. One can sometimes translate "How the Thessalonian Christians believed in Jesus." It may be advisable to add "and how they lived as Christians" or "and how they lived as believers," but the resultant heading would probably be too long. If one wishes to include the idea of the Thessalonian Christians being an "example," it may be necessary to employ a rather extensive phrase, for example, "How the Thessalonian Christians showed others how to live as believers." Such an expansion is due to the fact that concepts expressed in English by nouns like "life," "faith," and "example" must be expressed as verbs in other languages. It may be necessary, therefore, not to attempt to comprehend all the aspects of the section which follows, but to use a section heading which will emphasize a single important element.

This first principal section of 1 Thessalonians (vv. 2-10) is a skillfully organized statement in the form of a prayer of thanksgiving which brings together two themes: (1) the manner in which Paul and his colleagues shared their faith with the Thessalonians (vv. 2-5) and (2) the response of the Thessalonians (vv. 6-9). The statement of these themes not only serves to remind the Thessalonians of their experiences in the past and their relation to Paul and his colleagues, but it also leads to Paul's mention in verse 10 of one of his reasons for writing to the Thessalonians, namely, their concern about the return of the Lord, a subject dealt with more fully in chapters 4 and 5, and with additional detail in his second letter to them.

Because of the shift of emphasis, it may be useful in some languages to make a paragraph break at the end of verse 5.

Verses 2-5 form a single sentence in Greek, but even KJV divides it into two. This sentence illustrates two important points: first, a typical way in which Paul develops his thought; and second, the difference between the grammatical structure of a sentence and its semantic structure, that is, the structure of its meaning.

First, Paul begins with a general statement, we always thank God for you all, and follows it with three parallel dependent clauses, each beginning with a Greek participle, and each longer and more detailed than the one preceding it: literally "mentioning..." (v. 2b), "remembering..." (v. 3), and "knowing..." (v. 4). Paul emphasizes how thankful he is by repetition, with more and more details added.

Secondly, however, the meaning is not exactly parallel to the form of this long sentence. The sentences which in TEV begin for we remember (v. 3) and our brothers, we know (v. 4) express the reasons for Paul's thankfulness, but the same cannot be said for the grammatically parallel words translated "mention you in our prayers," which are virtually a repetition of "thank God for you."

In this sentence, Paul introduces the message of the first three chapters, which remind the readers of the visit of himself and his two companions, and of the events resulting from that visit. The unity of this long passage is reinforced by repeated references to thankfulness (see 2.13; 3.9). Secular Greek letters sometimes included in their introduction a prayer to some god, but not often a prayer of thankfulness. Paul regularly does so (Galatians is an exception), but the theme of gratitude in this letter goes far beyond the introduction.

1.2 We always thank God for you all and always mention you in our prayers.

Here and in most of the letter, Paul is thinking of Silas and Timothy as joint senders of the message. We, therefore, is not merely the so-called "epistolary we," which Paul sometimes uses and which is really the equivalent of "I."

The last word in the Greek text of verse 2 is translated always in TEV. The oldest Greek manuscripts had neither punctuation nor verse numbers. This second "always" may therefore be taken with what precedes (as in TEV RSV NEB FrCL Lu BJ) or with what follows (as in KJV NAB TNT BJ [1st ed.] Seg Syn GeCL). In other words, Paul may be saying that he and his friends "continually mention" the Thessalonians in their prayers, or that they "continually remember" them. If the first alternative is chosen, it confirms the impression that verse 2b repeats the message of verse 2a.

The two words translated always are not to be understood in an absolute sense, as if Paul meant that he and his companions prayed without a moment's interruption. GeCL translates "Every time we pray, we think of you" (cf. DuCL "We thank God always, when we think of you in our prayers"), but there is the strong implication that their prayers were frequent.

A literal translation of We always thank God for you all may be understood in some languages to imply that Paul and his companions were especially thanking God because he had given the Thessalonians to them. In a sense this may be true, but a more natural equivalent in some languages is "We are always telling God how thankful we are for you all," or "We constantly tell God how thankful we are that you remain Christians." In rendering always mention you in our prayers, one may translate as "whenever we pray to God, we pray to him for you." More is implied here than merely mentioning the Christians in Thessalonica.

1.3 For we remember before our God and Father how you put your faith into practice, how your love made you work so hard, and how your hope in our Lord Jesus Christ is firm.

This verse explains a little more fully the reasons for Paul's thankfulness. The Christians at Thessalonica have the three great Christian virtues of faith, love, and hope (see 1 Corinthians 13.13; Galatians 5.5-6; Colossians 1.4-5; 1 Thessalonians 5.8; etc.), and each of these virtues has expressed and proved itself in action. The Greek contains three pairs of nouns, and these are reflected in the RSV translation: "your (1) work of faith and (2) labor of love and (3) steadfastness of hope." Within each pair, the first item is probably best regarded as the result of the second. Because the Thessalonians trusted Christ, they worked—for Christ? for one another? Paul does not specify here, but see 5.11. Because they loved Christ, they worked hard. Because their hopes were centered on him, they were able to stand firm under attack. All six nouns refer to what the Thessalonians had done or experienced.

Before we look in more detail at the meaning of these terms, there are two more questions about the meaning of the verse as a whole.

First, do the words in our Lord Jesus Christ refer only to hope, or to faith, love, and hope together? Most traditional translations follow the order of the Greek so closely that the question is left open. TEV Phps Knox FrCL GeCL DuCL TNT link these words exclusively with "hope," but the wider reference is not impossible. Lu identifies hope with Christ and translates "your patience in hope, which is our Lord Jesus Christ." This interpretation seems strained, and it is certainly unusual; even Colossians 1.27 and 1 Timothy 1.1 are not strict parallels to what Paul is saying here.

Secondly, how are the words before our God and Father related to the rest of the sentence? Knox (cf. Phps) thinks that they are linked with "hope," and so he translates "...hope...which gives you endurance, in the sight of him who is our God and Father." Most modern translations restructure the verse to bring together we remember and before our God and Father, although these phrases are widely separated in the Greek. This brings out more clearly the parallel between verses 2 and 3, which GeCL emphasizes still more by combining the two verses: "Every time we pray, we think of you and thank God, our Father, for you all. We continually remember...."

The Greek word translated before has a spatial meaning and calls to mind the picture of a subject facing his king. BJ and TNT remove the metaphor and translate "in the presence of." It may be very difficult to translate this figure of speech meaningfully, especially since the phrase before our God and Father must refer in some way to the event of praying. Accordingly, one must translate in some languages as "for whenever we pray to our God and Father, we remember how...." To indicate that what is remembered is also brought to the attention of God in prayer, it may be necessary to translate "Whenever we pray to our God and Father, we remember and mention how you put your faith into practice."

Faith here, as so often elsewhere in Paul's writings, is trust in or reliance on Christ, not simply a general belief in God or an acceptance of a body of doctrine. Faith is what defines somone as a Christian; he is a "believer" (see v. 7). Faith, love, and hope, especially when they are mentioned together, constitute the total human response to what God has done, is doing, and will do; that is why they are mentioned in this order. When the word for love stands alone, it more often refers to God's or Christ's love for men, but that is almost certainly not the meaning here.

Both faith and love result in work. Paul uses two different words for work. The first includes the idea of producing something, and the second includes an element of discomfort or hardship.

As for the third pair of words in this verse, the traditional translation "patience of hope" (KJV) misleadingly suggests to the present-day reader a totally passive attitude. The real meaning, however, is rather that of resisting or holding out against an enemy, especially over an extended period of time. RSV's rather old-fashioned "steadfastness," NEB's literary "fortitude," and Bests' "endurance" (cf. TNT) are better. DuCL uses a negative form, "unshakable hope." Phps' "sheer dogged endurance" (cf. Knox) gives the right idea but with perhaps exaggerated emphasis. TEV perhaps errs slightly in the other direction.

It is not always easy to indicate in translation the specific relations between faith, love, and hope and their respective results in practice, labor, and steadfastness. One may find it necessary to alter the order in which each pair of terms is mentioned. How you put your faith into practice may need to be translated as "what you did because you trusted in Jesus" or "how you worked because you trusted Jesus." Similarly, how your love made you work so hard may be rendered "how you worked so hard because you loved Jesus Christ." How your hope in our Lord Jesus Christ is firm may require even more restructuring, since firm qualifies hope, and hope in many instances must be translated as a verb. Therefore, one may need to translate as "how you hope (or hoped) so firmly in our Lord Jesus Christ."

Part of the difficulty in translating the term hope is that it is a rather complex concept, involving both the expectation of a future event and a confident waiting for that event. In some languages one may translate as "how you looked forward with complete confidence to our Lord Jesus Christ," and in other languages the firmness of hope may be indicated by a negative, "how not once did you in any way stop looking forward confidently to our Lord Jesus Christ."

1.4 Our brothers, we know that God loves you and has chosen you to be his own.

Paul seems to have been writing to a mixed group which included both Jews and former pagans (compare verse 9 and Acts 17.1-3). This makes it all the more remarkable that he should call them all brothers, as he does repeatedly in this letter and elsewhere. In the ancient world, it was almost unheard-of for anyone to call a foreigner "brother," but in the Christian family it was common from the beginning. It makes no difference to Paul that not long before this some of his readers had been fellow Jews and others had been pagans; now, without any distinction, they are all brothers. Though in many languages the Christian community refers to all its members by a word which more or less literally means "brothers" or even "brothers and sisters," in some instances a term for broader kinship is employed, for example, "relatives" or "clansmen," since this would be the only appropriate way in which one could address a larger group with which one is intimately associated.

We still includes, of course, Silas and Timothy, but not the Thessalonians. This is the case in the entire section until verse 10, where the first person plural becomes inclusive; that is, the expression us there includes the Thessalonian Christians as well as Paul and his companions.

TEV rightly makes explicit two things which are only implicit in the Greek: (1) the connection between we know and God loves you (literally, "we know, brothers beloved by God") and (2) the component of meaning expressed by to be his own. TEV, like RSV NEB etc., avoids the traditional word "election," which now has political associations, and translates this noun by a verb, since it clearly refers to something God does. But it is not enough to translate simply "we know ... that he has chosen you" (RSV cf. NEB SpCL DuCL TNT), because the word Paul uses has clear associations in the minds of his readers with God's choice of Israel to be his special people and to fulfill a special mission. God's choice of the Thessalonian believers must be brought out by some such phrase as to be his own, "to belong to him" (FrCL), "to belong to his people" (GeCL), or "for a special purpose" (Phps).

Has chosen you to be his own may be translated more or less literally as "has selected you out so that you could belong to him," but it is sometimes better expressed in more figurative language, for example, "has chosen you and put his mark upon you," "has labeled you as his possession," or "has selected you and marked you as his."

Expressions corresponding to God loves you frequently reflect terms which denote the love of parents for children, but in some languages figurative expressions are used, for example, "God holds you in his heart," "God's heart goes out to you," or "God treasures you very much."

1.5 For we brought the Good News to you, not with words only, but also with power and the Holy Spirit, and with complete conviction of its truth. You know how we lived when we were with you; it was for your own good.

Paul goes on to mention some of the things which convince him that God has chosen the Thessalonian Christians. There is no question of logical proof, so TEV's link-word for is perhaps better than "because" (JB Phps). However, since for in verse 5 introduces a rather general reason and primarily marks a transition, it may be preferable in some languages to omit this word and allow the relation between the preceding verses and verse 5 to remain implicit.

We brought the Good News to you is translated more literally by Zur as "our proclamation of the gospel happened among you not merely in word," but to introduce a word like "proclamation" or "preaching," as Lu does, appears to limit the Good News to words, and so produces an unnecessary clash with the last part of the sentence. On the contrary, the preaching of Paul and his companions, like that of Jesus, was linked with acts which showed God's power. In translating we brought the Good News to you, it is important to avoid the implication that the Good News is a kind of substance which can be carried. The equivalent of this expression in some languages is "we were the first to announce to you the Good News."

The word translated Good News is also the word for "gospel." Here it is not yet, of course, the title of a book, but among Christians it has already become almost a technical term for the message about Jesus. That is why Paul uses the definite article the and why TEV uses capital letters: Good News. Paul can safely assume that his readers already know to which "good news" he refers. Likewise, any reader of the New Testament, by the time he gets to Paul's First Letter to the Thessalonians, will almost certainly understand Good News in a more or less technical sense. However, it may be useful at this first occurrence to introduce a fuller phrase, "the Good News about Jesus Christ."

This verse describes an act of communication from Paul and his friends to the Thessalonians: we...to you. The question therefore arises whether the phrases with power and the Holy Spirit and with complete conviction of its truth refer to the evangelists or to their hearers; that is, to the way in which the message was proclaimed or to the way in which it was received. One could assume that in theory both are referred to, but it is more likely that either the one or the other aspect of the act of communication was in the forefront of Paul's mind. The immediate context suggests that here (though not in verses 3-4 and 6) Paul's main concern is with the giving of the message; that is, with the way in which the message was brought rather than the way in which it was received. That is how TEV (cf. FrCL) understands it. Other translations make the same meaning more explicit (Mft "with ample conviction on our part" [cf. TNT text]; SpCL "with complete certainty that this message is the truth"; DuCL "based on a firm conviction"). A few translations suggest that at least the conviction is in the hearers of the message (GeCL "his Holy Spirit...gave us...power to convince"; Brc "carrying complete conviction"; Phps "the convincing power of the Holy Spirit"), but this is less likely. Translations which attempt to avoid a decision concerning this question are unclear and often unnatural.

Not with words only may be rendered as "we did not use just words" or "we did not just speak words" or even "we did not just talk."

Power and the Holy Spirit are often associated, and can be translated together as "the dynamic power of the Holy Spirit" (Brc). The contrast between words and power and the Holy Spirit may be indicated clearly by "we did not just talk, but we also showed the power of the Holy Spirit." Power is best understood as referring to "miracles." Therefore the contrast may read "not just with words, but with miracles done by the Holy Spirit."

The phrase with complete conviction of its truth may be translated in some languages as "we showed how completely we believed the truth of the Good News," or "we showed how much we believed that the Good News is certainly true."

The last sentence of verse 5 in TEV is very general: You know how we lived when we were with you: it was for your own good. We should like to know what it was in the evangelists' way of life which impressed their hearers so deeply. The following verse suggests that it may have been their shared experience of persecution (cf. Acts 17.5-13), but the text does not tell us that, and we should not read it into our translation. JB's "for your instruction" is too specific. The fact that one does not want to be too specific and thus rule out the broader meaning, makes this sentence difficult to translate. When a language has a verb with the general sense of "to behave," "to carry on," "to do," etc., it may be employed here. But in some languages it is necessary to use other types of expression for such general activity, for example, "you know what we did when we were with you." The final clause, it was for your own good, is likewise difficult to render in a satisfactory way, but one can sometimes employ an expression such as "all of this was to help you," "this was good for you," or "this benefited you."

1.6 You imitated us and the Lord: and even though you suffered much, you received the message with the joy that comes from the Holy Spirit.

From this point until the end of the chapter, the focus changes. Paul's attention is concentrated, not on himself and his companions, but on the way in which their message was received. The change of focus is marked by an emphatic pronoun: "as for you, you became imitators."

Imitated and, still more, "imitators" (JB), and "imitation" tend to include a negative component of not being real or authentic. That is not the case here.

The Greek suggests an adult pupil's relationship with his teacher, in a cultural situation in which education was not limited to formal instruction during fixed hours, but involved the sharing of a way of life. We are in the same area of meaning as example in verse 7, "come after" in Mark 1.17, and "follow" in Luke 5.11. (See also 1 Thess. 2.14; 1 Corinthians 4.16; and, more distantly, Matthew 5.48.) NEB has "example" here (cf. Brc Best) and "model" in verse 7.

It may be necessary to expand the expression you imitated us and the Lord, for example, "you learned to live just as we lived and as the Lord lived," "you followed us and the Lord in the way you lived," or "you were like us and the Lord in the way in which you behaved."

The Lord always means "Christ" in Paul's writings, unless the context clearly indicates otherwise. The meanings of the Greek word range from "sir" to the name of God, "Yahweh." Here it indicates the relationship of a servant to the one whom he serves and to whom he belongs, but the negative implications of "slaveholder" should be avoided. At the same time, it may be necessary to employ a pronoun to show the relationship of Lord to the believers, for example, "our Lord" or "our chief." However, Paul always uses Lord in speaking of the risen Christ, and the translator should avoid titles which suggest merely the earthly life of Jesus.

Suffered translates a noun whose meaning, like that of the English "pressure," extended from physical pressure to more general suffering or hardship. To understand suffered in the broader sense probably implied here, it may be useful to employ a phrase such as "you endured many troubles" (cf. TNT "the message brought you great trouble"), "you underwent much persecution," or "you suffered many times because people were troublesome to you." Introducing the agents of the suffering may be necessary in order to indicate that the suffering was not the result of illness, for example, "people caused you to suffer much," or "... to have troubles many times." The word here translated received (translated accepted in 2.13) may have the meaning of receiving willingly or welcoming; but it is also the ordinary word for receiving a letter. In this type of context, it is essentially equivalent to "believed."

The Thessalonians to whom Paul writes have received the message. This is literally "the word," but now in a different sense from that in verse 5, where it was a question of "mere words." Here it is a synonym for "the Good News"; it is the Christian message, called the message about the Lord in verse 8 and God's message in 2.13. It is clearly, in this context, a spoken rather than a written message. In translating the message, it may be important to specify what it is about, for example, "the message about Jesus Christ."

The joy that comes from the Holy Spirit specifies more clearly the point of comparison between Jesus, the evangelists, and their hearers. It is not simply that they suffered, but that the Holy Spirit (GeCL "God's Spirit") gave them the power to do so with joy. Thus their joy is the effect of what the Holy Spirit has done. This is not entirely clear in JB ("the joy of the Holy Spirit") or NEB ("rejoiced in the Holy Spirit"). The joy that comes from the Holy Spirit or "the joy which the Holy Spirit gives" (Brc TNT cf. FrCL GeCL SpCL) is to be preferred.

It may be somewhat difficult to express clearly the relation between received the message and the phrase with the joy, since joy is not the means of receiving, but the manner in which the people of Thessalonica came to believe, and in which they endured suffering. In some languages this is best expressed as a kind of accompanying experience, for example, "you believed the message about Jesus Christ, and you were joyful," but it is important to indicate clearly the relation between the Holy Spirit and the joy. Since the relation is one of cause, it is perhaps best to translate, as in some languages, "you believed the message, and the Holy Spirit caused you to have joy," or "...caused you to be exceedingly happy."

It is possible that the joy experienced by the Thessalonians is better related to their experience of suffering, rather than to their reception of the good news. Accordingly, it may be possible to say "You received the good news, and because of this you experienced many kinds of hardships. Yet, in spite of these hardships, the Holy Spirit continues to make you joyful."

1.7 So you became an example to all believers in Macedonia and Achaia.

This verse expresses the result of which the reason has just been given. Believers is here a synonym for "Christians," a rare term in the New Testament (see Acts 11.26). Paul does not mean that the Thessalonian Christians set out to evangelize the rest of Macedonia and areas beyond, but that the Christians in those places were strengthened when they heard what had happened in Thessalonica.

The term example takes up the concept of imitation. The word is in the singular ("example," not "examples"). It does not refer to the lives of certain outstanding individuals, but to the life of the whole Christian community which has influenced others. One may translate as "So you became the kind of people that all the believers in Macedonia and Greece could imitate," or "...that all the believers in Macedonia and Greece should be like." In a more extended form, this sentence may be translated as "So you lived in such a way that all the nonbelievers in Macedonia and Greece could see and could live as you live."

Achaia is "Greece" in some translations (e.g. FrCL) and was so rendered in earlier editions of the TEV. There had been times when the name Achaia was applied to the whole of Greece, but at the time Paul wrote, Macedonia and Achaia were two Roman provinces whose boundaries corresponded to those of no modern state. Together, they covered almost the whole area of modern Greece and Albania, and also the southern part of Yugoslavia, which is still called Macedonia.

Verses 8-10 form a single sentence in the Greek text. This sentence illustrates two tendencies of Paul's style. The first is his movement from the general to the specific, which we have already noticed in verses 2-5. There is nothing totally new in verse 9a. This verse simply amplifies three earlier statements: there is nothing...that we need to say (v. 8), we brought the Good News to you (v. 5), and your faith in God (v. 8). Secondly, verses 8b-9a illustrate Paul's tendency to make a negative statement (there is nothing...that we need to say), and then to repeat the substance of it in positive terms (all those people speak...). Paul has already used the same device twice, in verses 5 and 8.

1.8 For not only did the message about the Lord go out from you throughout Macedonia and Achaia, but the news about your faith in God has gone everywhere. There is nothing, then, that we need to say.

This verse and verse 9 describe in more detail how the Thessalonians' example has influenced Christians in other areas.

The word translated go out is uncommon. It combines the metaphor of a gong, trumpet, or similar instrument with the idea of moving outwards: "a sound is made and it is used spreading out from a center over an area" (Best). NEB has "rang out"; Brc "has sounded out"; Knox "has echoed out."

The phrase "the word of the Lord" (JB NEB and most older translations) does not make it clear that in this context Paul is not thinking of a word which came from the Lord, but rather of a word or message about the Lord Jesus Christ. The message about the Lord indicates this fact more clearly. The sense is thus quite different from that of places in the Old Testament where "the word of the Lord" is used to introduce prophetic oracles.

From you in Greek comes at the beginning of the verse and is thus emphatic.

In some languages it is difficult (perhaps even impossible) to speak about a message "going out from" a person, because messages do not literally move. But a report about a message may be heard by more, and yet more, persons. Therefore the first clause of this verse may be recast as "more and more people, not only in Macedonia and Achaia, heard the message about the Lord because of what you have done," "...because of what you are doing," or "...because of how you live." As in the previous verses, the emphasis here is upon the behavior of the Thessalonians, and therefore the extent to which the message about the Good News spread as the result of their example.

But the news about your faith in God may be treated in a similar manner. One may need to indicate, not only the places, but the persons who heard the news about the faith of the Thessalonians, for example, "but people everywhere have been hearing the news about how you have trusted in God."

Everywhere (literally, "in every place") is, of course, an exaggeration. "Everywhere we have been since we visited you" is surely implied though it should not be specified in translation. In this passage Paul is approaching a climax in which, as in poetry, the emotive meaning is as important as the information he gives. This is not to say that the referential meaning is unimportant; indeed, some commentators see in verses 9b-10 a summary of the first Christian preaching.

There is nothing, then, that we need to say. Many translations (including Brc BJ FrCL GeCL Phps Seg Syn) add "about it" (that is, "about your faith"), and Best adds "about you" in brackets. This meaning is quite possible, and it is strongly suggested by the corresponding positive statement in verse 9. It would certainly be reading too much into the verse to emphasize a more general reference such as "there is nothing left for us to preach about." However, the word translated "say" normally refers to the act of speaking, rather than to the content of what is said. TEV's translation is therefore preferable, unless the receptor language requires that the content of to say be specified. One way of rendering this sentence is "We do not have to say anything, for people have already heard." In this way the content of what would be said is linked closely with what has already been indicated, namely, the message about the Lord which has already gone out because of the outstanding example of the Thessalonians. Note also how this closing sentence of verse 8 is closely linked with the beginning of verse 9.

1.9 All those people speak about how you received us when we visited you, and how you turned away from idols to God, to serve the true and living God

This verse reminds us that Paul is not writing to the whole population of Thessalonica, but to the church in that city (cf. v. 1). Those who are now members of the Christian community made Paul and his companions welcome, but others created an uproar (see Acts 17.5-9).

All those people are the people in the various places loosely referred to as everywhere, perhaps mainly the people in the towns and villages visited by Paul, Silas, and (especially) Timothy in their travels between Thessalonica and Corinth. All is not explicit in the Greek, which means literally "themselves" (emphatic).

Those people, whoever they are, are talking about (1) the visit of Paul and his companions to Thessalonica and (2) how the Christian community in Thessalonica was born and grew. Paul's main concern at the moment is with the second point. He will return in chapter 2 to the subject of his visit.

How you received us when we visited you is literally "what kind of an entry we had to(wards) you." The word for "entry," in Greek as in English, can mean either (1) a place through which one enters or (2) the act of entering. The first meaning is impossible here. The second can be extended to include "visit," and this seems to be the meaning of the same word in 2.1; that meaning is also possible here (cf. NEB TNT SpCL). Some authorities claim that the word can mean "reception" or "welcome," and this sense is chosen by Brc RSV (cf. Syn) FrCL GeCL. However, this third meaning of the Greek word is not certain in any text in the New Testament or the Septuagint (Greek Old Testament). The word for "entry" itself seems to refer to the evangelists' entering the city of Thessalonica (cf. RV JB Lu Zur) rather than to the way in which the Thessalonians received them. However, the word for "what kind of," together with the rest of verses 9-10, suggests that Paul's deepest concern is neither with the fact of their entering Thessalonica, nor with anything special about the way in which they entered, nor even with the personal friendliness with which some of the Thessalonians welcomed them, but with the results of their visit, that is, with what happened as a consequence of their entering. This is specified by NEB ("our visit to you and its effect"), and it is confirmed by what follows in chapter 2.

In some languages how you received us when we visited you may be appropriately rendered as "how kind you were to us when we came to you," or "how friendly you were when we came to your city." In translating the word visited, it is important to avoid a term which would imply that Paul and his companions had already established friendly relations with the Thessalonians and so were on "visiting terms" with them. In other words, Paul was not making a "return visit" but an initial proclamation of the Good News.

The second how, before you turned away from idols to God, may mean simply "that." If so, Paul would be speaking, not of the manner, but simply of the fact of the Thessalonians' conversion. This makes good sense, since Paul says nothing more in this context about the manner of their conversion.

Acts 17.1-4 mentions Jews and Greek adherents to Judaism among the people Paul met in Thessalonica, but Paul here lays more stress on those who had been converted to Christianity from paganism and who had thus come to faith in God for the first time. The language of this verse recalls the speech of Paul and Barnabas at Lystra (Acts 14.15) and certain Old Testament passages (e.g. Jeremiah 10.10 and context). In the Septuagint, the word for idols refers not only to images, but to the pagan gods themselves—like the German Götzen (Lu Zur GeCL). Idols may be translated as "images of God" or "likenesses of God." Sometimes idols are simply called "wooden gods" or "stone deities."

You turned away from idols to God must often be made more explicit, since two different directions of movement, or types of behavior, are indicated. Moreover, it is often impossible to use an expression such as "turned away from," which indicates physical motion, when what is meant is really a change of allegiance. Hence, in some languages one must translate "how you refused to worship idols any longer and began to worship God."

The contrast which Paul makes here between idols and the true and living God shows that he is thinking primarily of the pagan gods themselves. To serve ... God indicates a total state of belonging to God, as a slave belongs to his master, but with the added element of willingness, so that the relationship includes not only obedience but worship. True does not mean only that what God says is true, or that he is "a God who really exists" (Knox), but that he is the only being who is really God (cf. Brc "real and living God"). Paul never (not even in 1 Corinthians 8.4-5) clearly states that other deities do not exist; what he is concerned to deny is their right to men's obedience and worship.

To serve the true and living God expands the preceding expression you turned ... to God. Many languages have appropriate terms for "serve" which are approximately equivalent to "worship" or "acknowledge as God," but in some languages it may be better to identify both aspects of "serve," which would then be rendered as "to obey and to worship." The true ... God is often equivalent to "the only one who really is God." The ... living God not merely expresses the fact that God is alive, but serves to reinforce the concept of "true." In other words, true and living God may be rendered in some instances as "the God who really exists." The focus of meaning in living is on existing and giving life, not merely on being alive.

1.10 and to wait for his Son to come from heaven—his Son Jesus, whom he raised from death and who rescues us from God's anger that is coming.

Paul introduces here, at the end of the first section, a theme which he will discuss in greater detail in 4.13—5.11, and which will be one of the two main subjects of his Second Letter to the Thessalonians. Paul is always anxious that the Thessalonian Christians should maintain a balance between the present and future dimensions of Christian experience. The link between the two is Jesus, whose name here (as in Hebrews 12.2) is in an emphatic position at the climax of a long sentence. TEV reproduces the emphasis by repeating his Son (cf. FrCL).

Son is one of the most important titles of Jesus in the New Testament. It expresses his uniquely close but dependent relationship with God, whom he was probably the first to address in prayer as "Abba." Like most, if not all, human language about God and most titles of Christ, it involves a figurative extension of the central meaning of the word "son." Because of its theological importance, the metaphor should, if possible, be maintained in translation. And since the concept of sonship is common to all cultures, it usually can be retained. However, connotations of youth and physical generation should be avoided.

In rendering to come from heaven, it is important to use a word which clearly indicates "the abode of God" rather than merely "sky." In this context an appropriate equivalent in some languages is "to come from where God is."

From death is literally "from the dead." In Greek, as in English, raised is a common word used here with an uncommon meaning. In some languages, this meaning is normally translated by a different and more literary word. FrCL maintains a common language level by translating "whom he has brought back from death to life" (cf. Brc). It is important to be specific and clear in rendering whom he raised from death. It is "God" who "raised Jesus from death," but only rarely can one render the phrase "raised from death" literally. An expression such as "caused to live again" may be necessary.

Rescues is a synonym of "saves," but one which places greater emphasis on the negative aspect of liberation from some danger. There is no contradiction between the present rescues and the future reference of that is coming. In Greek rescues is a present participle which implies a process having duration, something which has begun but is still incomplete. In many languages rescues is best translated as "causes us to escape," "releases us from," or "causes us not to suffer because of."

For the first time in this letter, us includes both senders and readers, as the context shows (see comments on v. 4).

It is important to note that it is his Son Jesus who is raised from death (that is, he is the object of God's activity), but it is this same one who rescues us from God's anger. The shift in agent must be clearly indicated in the receptor language.

God's anger that is coming rightly expands a Greek phrase which literally means "the anger (or wrath) which is coming." Jews reading Hebrew aloud refrained from pronouncing the name of God, and although Paul is writing Greek, he seems to be influenced here by Jewish usage. The use of the article "the" shows that Paul assumes his readers know to whose anger he is referring.

The problem in translating anger is that of expressing the idea of God's permanent, total, and personal opposition to evil, without suggesting an outburst of bad temper. It is a particularly acute example of the difficulty of using human language about God (technically called "anthropomorphism"). The Greek word which TEV translates anger is a common word, and it is also used to refer to human anger (for example in Ephesians 4.31). It corresponds to the even more "human" Old Testament metaphor of someone's nose being inflamed against someone else—an expression which is used freely in speaking both of God (Exodus 4.14) and of men (Genesis 30.2). The addition of that is coming shows that Paul is thinking of a final manifestation of God's opposition to evil which is very close to the meaning of "judgment," the term used here by NEB GeCL Phps. Other, less satisfactory, translations are "vengeance" (Knox) and "punishment" (SpCL). The Greek word for anger does not in isolation have a future reference, but NEB interestingly takes the whole phrase closely together and translates "the terrors of judgment to come."

It is difficult in some languages to find adequate terms to translate the expression God's anger. The focus of meaning in this context is judgment, but it would be wrong simply to translate "rescues us from God's judgment that is coming," even though the Greek term does imply a measure of God's opposition to sin and his anger because of it. In some languages the best equivalent seems to be "angry judgment." Some persons would prefer a translation such as "who rescues us from God's stern judgment." Some recasting of this last clause may result in "who rescues us from the judgment that is going to come because God is so angry because of men's sins," or "...because God is so angrily opposed to men's sins." Yet there are other languages in which it is impossible to speak about a "judgment that is going to come," because "judgment" is not thought of as something that can "come." One can, however, speak about "judgment which is going to take place," or "a will-be judging." This fact may require a recasting of the last clause to read "who will rescue us when God is about to judge people, for he is angry because of their sins."

CHAPTER 2.1-16

TEV

Paul's Work in Thessalonica

1 Our brothers, you yourselves
know that our visit to you was not
a failure. 2 You know how we had
already been mistreated and insulted in Philippi before we came
to you in Thessalonica. And even
though there was much opposition
our God gave us courage to tell you
the Good News that comes from him.
3 Our appeal to you is not based on
error or impure motives, nor do we
try to trick anyone. 4 Instead, we
always speak as God wants us to,
because he has judged us worthy to
be entrusted with the Good News. We
do not try to please men, but to
please God, who tests our motives.
5 You know very well that we did
not come to you with flattering
talk, nor did we use words to cover
up greed--God is our witness! 6 We
did not try to get praise from anyone, either from you or from others, 7 even though, as apostles of
Christ, we could have made demands
on you. But we were gentle when we
were with you, like a mother[a] taking care of her children. 8 Because of our love for you we were
ready to share with you not only
the Good News from God but even our
own lives. You were so dear to us!
9 Surely you remember, our brothers, how we worked and toiled! We
worked day and night so that we
would not be any trouble to you as
we preached to you the Good News
from God.

[a]we were gentle when we were with you, like a mother; *some manuscripts have* we were like children when we were with you; we were like a mother. (2.1-9)

RSV

1 For you yourselves know,
brethren, that our visit to you
was not in vain; 2 but though we
had already suffered and been
shamefully treated at Philippi, as
you know, we had courage in our God
to declare to you the gospel of God
in the face of great opposition.
3 For our appeal does not spring
from error or uncleanness, nor is
it made with guile; 4 but just as
we have been approved by God to be
entrusted with the gospel, so we
speak, not to please men, but to
please God who tests our hearts.
5 For we never used either words of
flattery, as you know, or a cloak
for greed, as God is witness;
6 nor did we seek glory from men,
whether from you or from others,
though we might have made demands
as apostles of Christ. 7 But we
were gentle[a] among you, like a
nurse taking care of her children.
8 So, being affectionately desirous
of you, we were ready to share with
you not only the gospel of God but
also our own selves, because you
had become very dear to us.

9 For you remember our labor and
toil, brethren; we worked night and
day, that we might not burden any
of you, while we preached to you
the gospel of God.

[a]Other ancient authorities read *babes* (2.1-9)

Care must be taken to avoid any implication that the section heading Paul's Work in Thessalonica refers to his manual labor to support himself and thus not to burden the Thessalonians. Terms that indicate a broader scope of activity should be chosen, for example, "What Paul did in Thessalonica," or "Paul's activities in Thessalonica."

In this chapter, as in chapter 1, Paul's thoughts move back and forth between himself and his companions on the one hand, and his readers on the other. In verses 1-12 (as in 1.3-5), the evangelists are in focus; in verses 13-16 (as in 1.6-10), Paul is thinking mainly of his readers. The distinction must not, however, be pressed too far. Even in the first part of this chapter, Paul is constantly aware of his readers and their situation, and he repeatedly uses words like you know (vv. 1, 2, 5, 11, cf. 1.5) and you remember (v. 9). Conversely, towards the end of the section (v. 16), Paul's thoughts begin to return to himself and his fellow evangelists. This to-and-fro movement shows a keen desire on Paul's part to communicate with the Thessalonians, a desire which should be reflected in the style of the translation. Paul was forcibly thrown out of Thessalonica, and (as 2.17 ff. shows) he found it frustrating not to have news of the Christians there. Even now his letter is his main link with his readers.

TEV divides this principal section of chapter 2 into three paragraphs. Verses 1-9 describe briefly Paul's activity and motivation, and verses 10-12 summarize and emphasize what has just been said in verses 1-9. (Verses 1-12 form a single paragraph in the UBS Greek text.) The last paragraph, verses 13-16, reintroduces the theme of thanksgiving (see 1.2) and then proceeds to emphasize one of the special problems of the Thessalonians, namely, the opposition of the Jews.

2.1 Our brothers, you yourselves know that our visit to you was not a failure.

The vocative brothers (cf. v. 17; 4.1, 13; 5.12, 14; 2 Thessalonians 3.1, 13) tends to mark the beginning of a new section, or at least, as in 1.4, the introduction of an important new idea. Here the beginning of a new section is indicated also by a change of grammatical subject, marked by the emphatic yourselves. On the other hand, this new section is carefully linked with what precedes. Paul does this by repeating the rather unusual word visit (cf. 1.9), and by using a link word translated "for" in KJV RSV (cf. Lu Zur SpCL) but omitted in TEV. This word usually has the function of linking one clause with the immediately preceding one, but a glance at 1.10 shows that this is not the case here. Paul's thought has jumped back to the beginning of the previous long sentence. He is saying, in effect, "Not only do other people talk about the results of our visit, but you yourselves know that it was not a failure." Because the conjunction is used in such a loose and unemphatic manner, and because the connection with chapter 1 is established in other ways, most modern translations (including NEB Phps JB Brc Seg GeCL DuCL TNT) omit it.

The word translated a failure literally means "empty." It is often used in speaking of work which is either futile and useless in itself (1 Corinthians 15.58, where TEV has "without value"), receives no reward (Mark 12.3; Luke 20.10 f.), or produces no result (1 Corinthians 15.10, TEV "without effect"). NEB and Best take the present text in the last of these senses and translate "fruitless" (cf. NAB "without effect"). A similar expression is used in 3.5 (TEV "for nothing") and Philippians 2.16 (TEV "wasted"), also in contexts which speak of work. It is therefore no coincidence that the word is used here at the beginning of a section which presumably mentions not only Paul's tent-making activities (v. 9), but also the labor and effort of his whole evangelistic work (vv. 2, 8).

Was (preceding not a failure) is in the perfect tense in Greek, indicating an event which continues, or whose effects continue, into the present. It is not always necessary or even desirable to bring this out in translation, but JB (cf. Best) does so here: "our visit to you has not proved ineffectual."

For the translator, probably the most serious difficulty involved in this verse is the double negative which tends to occur in rendering was not a failure. More often than not, failure must be expressed by a negative, namely, "not to succeed," "not to produce results," "not to be effective." When this is preceded by another negative, the resulting expression is usually awkward and may be quite incomprehensible to the average reader. The closest equivalent, therefore, in some languages is simply "our coming to you was successful" or "our coming to you accomplished its purpose." Note that (as also in v. 9) visit should not be translated in terms of a friendly get-together.

2.2 You know how we had already been mistreated and insulted in Philippi before we came to you in Thessalonica. And even though there was much opposition our God gave us courage to tell you the Good News that comes from him.

Again, Paul follows the negative statement of verse 1 with a positive one, marking the contrast with an emphatic "but." In this case, however, the form of the sentence does not correspond to its content. The reader may expect some statement about the success of Paul's visit to Thessalonica, and Paul may have intended to say something of this kind when he began dictating the sentence; but a new idea now occurs to him, and he abruptly changes the subject. Not until verse 13 does Paul come back to the theme of his visit and its results. In these circumstances, TEV rightly leaves the misleading "but" untranslated. Phps JB BJ Brc GeCL FrCL Knox Mft TNT do the same, NEB (cf. DuCL) emphasizes the misleading conjunction by rendering it as "far from it," and so gives the impression that Paul is illogical (since he could have preached "frankly and fearlessly" and still have had a "fruitless" visit). BJ and JB, on the other hand, somewhat overemphasize the change of theme by beginning a new paragraph at verse 2.

The repetition of you know, so soon after you yourselves know in verse 1, shows that Paul is conscious of the change of theme; his readers know both that the visit to Thessalonica was not a failure and that the previous visit to Philippi had not been easy.

Two statements are included in this verse: (1) "we were illtreated and insulted in Philippi"; and (2) "God gave us courage to tell you the Good News."

The relation between these statements is not explicit in the Greek, and the RV translates the sentence with such slavish faithfulness to the form that the content could easily be misunderstood: "having suffered before...at Philippi, we waxed bold...." The reader is likely to misunderstand the first statement as a reason and the second as a result (that is, "we had suffered so much in Philippi that nothing could frighten us in Thessalonica"), but that is not what Paul means. The courage of the evangelists did not come from their previous experience but from a new strengthening by God. Virtually all commentators and translators, therefore, take the first statement as meaning "although we suffered before in Philippi." TEV divides the sentence.

What happened to the evangelists in Philippi is described in Acts 16.12-40. Mistreated in Greek is the normal word for "suffer," with a prefix meaning "before." A pluperfect is clearly needed in English, since there is a double backward reference from Paul's present situation in Corinth to his visit to Thessalonica, and then further back to Philippi. Before we came to you in Thessalonica (cf. FrCL GeCL DuCL etc., but not SpCL) is implicit. Paul is mainly thinking, no doubt, of the attack by the crowds (Acts 16.22), the official whipping, and the discomfort of being fastened in the stocks. Insulted includes also the nonphysical aspect of the bad treatment Paul and Silas had received, something which, according to Acts 16.37, Paul had resented as deeply as the physical mistreatment.

There is, however, considerable overlap between the two terms. The Greek word which TEV translates insulted in this verse is translated mistreat in Acts 14.5. It refers generally to insolent and outrageous behavior. In many languages mistreated can be translated as "caused us to suffer" or "caused us pain," while insulted may be rendered as "spoke to us with bad words" or "spoke to humiliate us." In some languages it may be necessary to indicate the agents of the mistreatment and insults, and therefore one can say "how the authorities had mistreated us and insulted us." "The authorities" would be "the government officials" or "the local rulers."

It is always possible to identify Philippi in this context by a classifier, for example, "in the city of Philippi."

Opposition represents a Greek word which can refer either to the effort of one individual or (more often) to a struggle between two or more people, as, for example, in an athletic contest. RSV Phps FrCL etc., like TEV, take the latter meaning, and this seems to fit the context better. Mft comes down firmly for the first meaning and translates "in spite of all the strain." Even if this interpretation is correct, Paul would still be thinking of his need for courage. TEV's translation links verse 2b with 2a and verses 8-9. The idea of opposition may be expressed as a verb, for example, "even though many people were opposed to us, yet our God gave us courage to tell you the Good News that comes from him." The opposition may be stated even more specifically, for example, "even though many people tried to make us stop talking," or "...tried to prevent us from telling the Good News."

There is some overlap of meaning between the verbs translated gave us courage and tell, since each of them refers to speaking. The first word, with its related noun, refers in nonbiblical Greek to democratic freedom of speech and to the openness of close friends in speaking to one another. In the Greek Old Testament, this verb describes the frankness of Job's protests to God. In the New Testament, it indicates both the Christians' confidence in approaching God and the confident and outspoken way in which the apostles preached (cf. Ephesians 6.19 f.; Philippians 1.20; and often in Acts). The second edition of BJ changes "confidence" to the stronger term "boldness." Brc translates here "freely and fearlessly," NEB "frankly and fearlessly." The context suggests that our God probably still means the God of Paul, Silas, and Timothy, though a wider reference is not impossible.

The concept of courage is frequently rendered by an idiomatic expression, for example, "to have a strong heart," "to be brave in our insides," "to not fear anyone." In some instances, our God gave us courage may thus be rendered as "our God took fear out of our hearts."

The Good News that comes from him is literally "the gospel of God." The form is similar to "word of the Lord" (RSV) in 1.8, but the meaning is different (see the comments on that verse). The message is about the Lord Jesus Christ, but it comes from God. Taking the two expressions together, Christ is the content of the Christian message, but God the Father is its source. The latter should be specified in translation, as TEV and FrCL do here and also in verses 8 and 9 (cf. Romans 15.16). "From God" should certainly not be omitted, as Phps does here and in verse 9, and as Mft and JB do in verse 8. (On the Good News, see the comments on 1.5.)

While it is most important to indicate the source of the Good News, it may not be possible in some languages to speak of it as "coming," since only agents that are able to move about may be said to come. Accordingly, that God is the source may be indicated by such an expression as "the Good News that God caused us to hear," or "...caused us to know."

Verses 3-7a pose two general problems:

1. It is clear that in this passage Paul is concerned with the motives behind his preaching and that of his friends, the manner in which they went about their work, and to some extent their methods. It is also clear in verse 2, and again in the second part of verse 7, that Paul is speaking specifically about their work in Thessalonica. The question is whether, in the verses in between, Paul is still focusing on the Thessalonian situation, or whether he is stating the general principles which he claims to have followed everywhere. The answer to this question may vary from verse to verse, and we cannot make a definite answer before examining all the verses in detail. However, an answer to this question will vitally affect the translation at many points. For example, in verses 3, 5, and 7, TEV assumes that Paul is thinking specifically of the Thessalonians, and therefore it inserts certain words which are not in the Greek text: to you in verses 3 and 5, and on you in verse 7. In verse 4, on the other hand, TEV assumes that the reference is general, and accordingly it inserts always. If, in verse 5, the translator thinks that the reference is specific, you know will confirm this; but if he thinks it is general, he will understand it as

meaning "This is how we behave everywhere, and you can confirm that we did so when we were with you." Again, in verse 6, if the reference is specific, either from you or from others will mean "either from you Christians in Thessalonica or from your fellow-citizens there" ; but if the reference is general, the words will mean "either from you Thessalonians or from people in other places."

One thing at least is clear: verse 4 contains Paul's most general statement so far about his apostolic commission—he has not even used the title of apostle in the introduction, as he does in all of his letters except 1 and 2 Thessalonians, Philippians, and Philemon.

Someone has said that Paul "uses a sledge hammer to crack a nut." In 1 Corinthians 12—14, he builds up a whole doctrine of the church, and writes a whole hymn about Christian love, in order to settle a local problem which is threatening to divide the Christian community. In the same way, though on a smaller scale, Paul's thought in this passage moves from the local situation in verse 2 to a general statement in verse 4, and then back to the local situation from verse 7 onwards.

2. A distinct but related question is whether, in these verses, Paul has in mind some slanderous rumors which may have been spreading around in Thessalonica since his departure. We do not know—and for the purpose of translation we do not need to know—what such slanders may have been. What the translator cannot help noticing is how Paul's negative-positive contrasts follow one another almost without interruption, each marked by an emphatic "but," as indicated in the following diagram.

NEGATIVE	POSITIVE
3 Our appeal does not spring from error... nor is it made with guile;	4 but...as we have been approved...so we speak,
4 not to please men,	4 but to please God....
5 We never used...words of flattery... or a cloak for greed... 6 nor do we seek glory...	7 but we were gentle... (RSV text used)

DIAGRAM 1

All of this strongly suggests that Paul is contrasting himself and his companions with a specific group. The cities of the ancient world were full of traveling philosophers and preachers, many of them fakes seeking only applause and profit. Paul's concern is to show why he and his friends are not just another group of people like these.

2.3 Our appeal to you is not based on error or impure motives, nor do we try to trick anyone.

The Greek here has the same link word "for" which we noted in verse 1. Here it may indicate a logical link between verses 1 and 2. It may mean "our stay in Thessalonica was a hard and costly time for us, and this proves that we had not come to win cheap popularity or to make easy money"; or it may mean "we spoke openly and fearlessly because we had no unworthy motive to hide." But either of these interpretations makes rather too much of an unemphatic conjunction, and it is probably best to omit it in translation, as is done in various translations (TEV Phps Brc JB Knox GeCL DuCL).

Some translations understand appeal as a synonym of Good News in verse 2 and so translate as "preaching" (Lu Syn) or "what we preach" (SpCL) or simply refer back to verse 2 with an adverb "thereby" (GeCL). Appeal in this sense, however, refers not to the whole content of the message as such, but to its application to a particular group of hearers, that is, to the preachers' appeal to them to accept the message. (In Acts 2, for example, the appeal would be, not Peter's entire sermon, but the application of his message in verses 38-40; the related verb meaning "made his appeal" is, in fact, used in verse 40.) TEV FrCL RSV NEB Knox Mft Brc Best all translate by appeal.

TEV's addition of to you is justified, partly by the nearness of verse 2, which refers explicitly to Thessalonica, and partly by the likelihood that Paul is here thinking of criticisms made against himself and his friends (see general note on 2.3-7a).

Neither the Greek text nor TEV uses a verb such as "make" with appeal ("the appeal which we make"), but in many languages a verb must be supplied. Should it be in the past or in the present tense? If the reference is general, the present tense must be used in English. If, as seems more likely, the reference is specifically to the Thessalonians, the verb should probably be in the past tense, since Paul does not begin making any appeal to his readers until chapter 4 of the present letter. Among English translations, Mft RSV NEB take the reference as specific, and therefore they use the present tense; Knox takes it as specific and uses the past tense; Brc and TNT take it as general but use the present tense.

The noun appeal must frequently be rendered as a verb, for example, "when we were appealing to you," but sometimes appeal must be translated as "try to convince." When one translates appeal as a temporal clause beginning with "when," it is necessary to restructure the latter part of the clause, for example, "when we were trying to convince you about the Good News, we did not use lies," or "...we did not speak lies." In this type of context, the closest equivalent of error is often "lies" or "untruths," and "lies" is usually the more effective term.

Paul is fond of grouping three similar expressions (cf. 1.3), but the three nouns represented by error, impure motives, and nor do we try to trick anyone do not seem to be arranged in any particular order. Error is more than an innocent mistake. It means a wandering from the path of truth, a voluntary (and therefore sinful) giving in to influences which lead one astray (see 2 Thess. 2.11; Ephesians 4.14). "Impurity" (motives is implied) can mean literal or ritual uncleanness, but it is often associated with sexual immorality (e.g. in Romans 1.24; Galatians 5.19; Ephesians 5.3; Colossians 3.5). Paul may be referring to the sexual immorality which, in the Greek world as well as in the world of the Old Testament, often accompanied pagan worship. However, the word for "impurity" has a wider meaning in Romans 6.19 and perhaps in Ephesians 4.19; 5.3, and Paul does not refer to sex in 1 Thessalonians until chapter 4; so a more general meaning such as "impurity" is more likely here. If error is the state of having been led away from truth, deceit is the attempt to trick other people. Paul is indeed describing a vicious circle.

The phrase not based on...impure motives is often rendered in a figurative manner, for example, "our heart was true," "our hearts had no shadows in them," "there was no darkness in us," or "we had no twisted thoughts." Nor do we try to trick anyone may simply be rendered as "and we do not try to deceive anyone," or, idiomatically, "we do not try to make people think that bad is good."

2.4 Instead, we always speak as God wants us to, because he has judged us worthy to be entrusted with the Good News. We do not try to please men, but to please God, who tests our motives.

Paul now makes his most general statement thus far concerning the commission he has received from God, and he associates his companions with this commission, even giving Silas and Timothy the title of apostles (v. 7).

Has judged...worthy means "approved after having been tested," and the term is often applied to people being chosen after examination for a particular piece of work (cf. 1 Corinthians 16.3). The Greek tense indicates that this did not happen once and for all, but that both the testing and the approval continue. Both the judging worthy and the entrusting of the Good News are acts performed by God. TEV therefore rightly turns the Greek passive verb of the former into an active verb which has God as its subject. The tense of to be entrusted, which is left in the passive voice, indicates that it happened once, at a particular point of time; but having once received the Good News, the evangelists must go on speaking (present tense) to pass it on (cf. TNT "God decided that he could trust us with the Good News, and we speak with his approval"). The first part of this verse contains a comparison (literally "as we have been approved...so we speak"), the point of which is probably "we speak as men (speak) whom God has found fit to have the Good News entrusted to them" (cf. JB GeCL DuCL). TEV's as God wants us to is implied.

As God wants us to can be misunderstood as referring merely to the manner of speaking rather than to the content, but Paul is referring here to the nature of the message he was commissioned to proclaim. Accordingly, if one wishes to make explicit the expression as God wants us to, it may be necessary to render it as "say what God wants us to say."

It is altogether appropriate in some languages to render has judged... worthy as involving two aspects of God's activity: (1) the testing and (2) the statement of approval. This may be expressed in some languages as "because having tested us, he knew we could be trusted, and hence he gave to us the work of telling the Good News." To be entrusted with the Good News does not mean that God gave the Good News to Paul and his associates, but that he gave to them the responsibility of proclaiming the Good News. This relation must be made clear.

To please translates a verb sometimes used in speaking of prominent citizens who, by their public service, have earned the good opinion and respect of the city or the state. The idea of service is therefore included. Try to is not in the Greek text, the form of which makes it clear that Paul is speaking not only of intentions but of facts : "we do not speak in such a way as to please men, but God...."

In this context it is not always easy to find an appropriate term to translate please men. An appropriate equivalent is sometimes found in "we do not try to make men like us," or "we do not try to just do what people want us to do." The latter expression provides a good contrast for the phrase which follows, but to please God, for example, "but to do what God wants us to do."

The verb translated tests is the same as that translated has judged... worthy earlier in this verse, but now it is in the present tense, emphasizing the continuing aspect of God's testing. The implication is still that Paul and his companions come through the test successfully, and so retain God's approval.

Motives is literally "hearts" (SpCL NEB as well as older translations). In Hebrew thought, the heart is not, as in English, primarily the center of the emotions, but of the whole of the inner life, especially the thoughts and the will. TEV rightly avoids a metaphor which could be misleading in English, but motives is perhaps too narrow. FrCL has "the intentions of our hearts" and GeCL "our most secret thoughts." The context suggests that, linguistically, our still refers to the evangelists, even though theologically the statement could, of course, be applied to the readers as well. Who tests our motives is often rendered idiomatically "who sees into our hearts," "who knows our insides," or "who listens to our inner voice."

2.5 You know very well that we did not come to you with flattering talk, nor did we use words to cover up greed—God is our witness!

In Greek this verse begins a new sentence which continues at least into verse 7 (see the notes on that verse). Paul continues his self-defense with a series of three parallel negative statements which expand what he has said in verses 3-4, particularly his claim that we do not try to trick anyone, and prepare the way for the positive statement which begins at verse 7b. Into these negative statements are set two brief parenthetical expressions which complement one another and which Mft translates "(you know that)" and "(God is witness to that)."

A brief look at the items in this verse may help us decide whether Paul is thinking specifically of the Thessalonians or (as in the previous verse) of general principles.

a. This sentence, like verses 1 and 3, contains an introductory "for," which TEV omits. If Paul is thinking of the Thessalonians, this word would relate the general statement in verse 4b to the more specific statements in verses 5-7. If he is thinking in more general terms, "for" would indicate an unfolding in verses 5-7 of the content of verse 4. The conjunction itself does not help us decide one way or the other.

b. The expression translated "never" in RSV etc., used by Paul here and in a slightly variant form in Ephesians 5.29, is also omitted by TEV. It tends to indicate a general reference, but it could mean "at no time during our stay with you."

c. The tense of the verb translated did come normally indicates a specific event, but here it probably indicates the act of entering into a state in which, it is understood, one then remains. One might paraphrase: "At no time did we take up flattery as part of our normal practice."

d. On "as you know," see the general note on verses 3-7a. By themselves these words tend to indicate a specific reference, but they are less emphatic in the Greek than in TEV.

The evidence is thus inconclusive. The wider context does not settle the matter either, since verse 4 is clearly general and verse 7 clearly specific. The translator has to weigh the points at issue, make up his mind, and produce a translation which is clear-cut and consistent. TEV is an admirable example of a translation based on the decision that Paul is here thinking specifically of the Thessalonian situation. Most commentators agree, and most translators either agree (as do Brc SpCL GeCL) or leave the matter unclear. NEB (cf. Phps? FrCL) is a good example of a translation based on the more general interpretation: "Our words have never been flattering words, as you have cause to know; nor, as God is our witness, have they ever been a cloak for greed." Best (97) thinks that Paul speaks in verses 3-4 of his mission in general, and in verses 5-12 of his mission to Thessalonica. This may, on balance, be the best solution of the problem.

Flattering talk (literally "[a] word of flattery") can mean either "talk which consists in flattery" or "talk which flatters"; it makes little practical difference. "Flattery" combines the ideas of insincere talk and the desire to use someone else for one's own ends. Most languages have excellent equivalents for flattering talk, since flattery is a universal phenomenon. In some languages flattery is described in a very direct manner, for example, "telling you that you are very good," "telling you how great you are," or "saying beautiful words about you."

Greed (also NEB) means the desire to possess something one does not have. It is the sin condemned in the Tenth Commandment (Exodus 20.17), except that greed does not make explicit the idea of wanting what belongs to someone else. It is a more general term than "the love of money" (1 Timothy 6.10), though Paul may already have this in mind (cf. FrCL SpCL) and may be preparing to mention it specifically in verse 9. There is no sexual connotation in the word itself, though (as in the Tenth Commandment) greed can have a sexual object. It is better here to use a general word like greed, "self-seeking" (Mft), or "(our) own advantage" (GeCL); cf. Best "with a veiled desire to exploit."

TEV's words (in the phrase words to cover up greed) is not absolutely necessary. The essential idea is that of covering up one's true motive, which is greed. There is an implied contrast: "You know that we did not flatter people by anything we said, and God knows that greed was not our hidden motive." On calling God to witness something, see Romans 1.9; 2 Corinthians 1.23; cf. Genesis 31.50 and other Old Testament passages.

If one follows the TEV rendering, words to cover up greed, some misunderstanding may arise. If one translates "We did not use words to cover up our taking advantage of you," a reader might assume that Paul and his colleagues used another technique to cover up their greed. A more satisfactory equivalent in some languages is "and in nothing that we said to you were we trying to take advantage of you," "we did not speak to you in order to serve our selfish desires," or "we did not proclaim the Good News in order to profit from you."

God is our witness may be rendered in some instances as "God knows very well what we did," or "God knows our hearts."

2.6 We did not try to get praise from anyone, either from you or from others,

The third negative statement, following the denial of flattery and greed, amplifies the last part of verse 4. Paul does not feel the need to repeat anything like "it is from God alone that we seek praise" (cf. Romans 2.29; John 5.41, 44). TEV Knox TNT (cf. FrCL) rightly prefer praise to "glory," a term which is passing out of use, except in church language. Paul is referring to someone's good opinion of a man, not to a man's real worth. Mft Phps JB NEB Best (cf. SpCL DuCL) have "honour"; Brc has "human reputation" (but a reputation is not necessarily good!); GeCL transforms the noun into a verb: "We do not want to be honored by men."

Paul did not try to get (literally "seek") praise, but he uses the same word in 2.20 to express the idea that, in another sense, the Thessalonians were a source of "pride" or "glory" to him. The expression to get praise from anyone is essentially a causative, and it may therefore be necessary to change the order of participants, for example, "we did not try to cause anyone to praise us," or "we did not do things just so that people would praise us."

On the two possible meanings of either from you or from others, see the general note on verses 3-7a. It is not necessary to specify either meaning in translation. Either from you or from others is an emphatic indication of the range of agents which might be involved in the praise. Hence, this entire verse 6 may be rendered as "We did not try to get anyone to praise us" or "...to cause anyone to praise us," or "We did not try to get you to praise us, and we did not try to get anyone else to praise us."

2.7 even though, as apostles of Christ, we could have made demands on you. But we were gentle when we were with you, like a mother taking care of her children.

There is disagreement among the various editions of the Greek text and consequently among translations as to where verse 7 begins. Some include the words up to demands on you with verse 6 and begin verse 7 with but we were gentle.

There are two basic problems in the connectives employed in the first clause of verse 7. Even though may be rendered as "but," and as may be rendered here as "since," for example, "but, since we are apostles of Christ, we could have rightfully asked things of you."

DuCL makes explicit the contrast between 7a and 7b: "True, we could have asserted ourselves as apostles of Christ. But as a mother...."

There are differences of opinion about the punctuation of this verse. As we have seen (see notes on 1.2), the punctuation is not part of the original text. Most editions and translations end the sentence with demands on you, but it is possible to end it with when we were with you, or even, as Mft does, to include the whole of verses 5-8 in one long sentence. This may well reflect the way in which Paul dictated, but it does not make for clear and precise translation.

The problem of punctuation affects the translation in the following way. In the Greek text, the comparison "as a mother taking care of her children" can refer either backwards or forwards, or both. The third possibility can be discounted for the purposes of translation, since even if it were theoretically correct, it would produce an unnaturally heavy sentence in translation. If it refers backwards, TEV's translation is correct, comparing the apostles' way with a mother's gentle care. The other possibility would produce the translation: "On the contrary, we were gentle among you. As a mother takes care of her children, and gives them her own milk, so...we were ready to share with you not only the gospel of God but also our own selves..." (cf. Best).

The previous verse states the result of the clause even though, as apostles of Christ, we could have made demands on you.

This is the first time Paul describes himself and his companions as apostles, and the word is emphatic. Silas and Timothy are not described elsewhere as apostles, but it is clear that this title is not restricted to the original twelve disciples. It is given to Andronicus and Junias (Romans 16.7), Apollos (?) (1 Corinthians 4.9), and Epaphroditus (Philippians 2.25), as well as to Paul, Silas, and Timothy. What these men have in common is the fact of being sent by Christ to give a personal witness to the good news about him. The closeness with which Paul associates his companions with himself confirms that it is right, in most cases, to take his "we" as referring to the three evangelists.

Though many languages have a borrowed term for apostle (coming originally from Greek but often changed in form by intermediate languages), some languages employ a phrase meaning "those specially sent by" or "those commissioned by," so that in this context apostles would be equivalent to "ambassadors."

In this clause the Greek contains a metaphor of weight which is well brought out in SpCL: "We could have made you feel the weight of our authority" (cf. Mft Phps TNT "heavy demands," NEB FrCL BJ). Paul is referring in a general way to how people in authority sometimes make burdensome demands on their subordinates. He may already be thinking of his refusal to be a financial burden to the Thessalonians, but he does not say so explicitly until verse 9. Could have made demands on you can also be rendered as "would have been justified in making demands on you," or "it would have been right for us to have asked you for this."

In some languages the closest equivalent of gentle, especially for this type of context, would be "loving and kind," since gentle combines concepts of affection and of considerate treatment.

Many good manuscripts read "babies" instead of gentle. The Greek words nēpioi 'babies' and ēpioi 'gentle' are easily confused, especially since the previous word ends in n̄. One or two translations follow the reading "babies." Knox (cf. BJ text) combines translation and exegesis in his "innocent as babes." It is true that Paul does not always handle figures of speech very skillfully, but it is difficult to believe that, immediately after comparing himself and his companions with babies, he would proceed to compare them with a mother looking after children. For this reason, and also because the manuscript evidence is fairly evenly divided, the UBS Greek text and the vast majority of translations follow the reading "gentle."

Like a mother taking care of her children. The word translated mother means any woman who breast-feeds (in American English "nurses") a baby. It could therefore refer also to what used to be called a "wet nurse." In classical Greek, the words translated her children would have meant "her own children," but this was not always so in New Testament times. Even so, since it was more normal for babies to be fed by their own mothers, it is best to translate the word here by "mother" (JB; cf. Lu Zur Syn FrCL GeCL DuCL) or "nursing mother" (Mft Knox NAB Best) rather than by "nurse" (KJV RSV NEB Phps Brc TNT, cf. Seg). Perhaps the best solution of all is that of SpCL, which restructures the whole expression to read "as a mother suckles and looks after her children."

2.8 Because of our love for you we were ready to share with you not only the Good News from God but even our own lives. You were so dear to us!

The phrase because of our love for you must be rendered in some languages as a clause, "because we love you so much." The term used for love should include all the activities which express friendship and fellowship.

To share...the Good News is often rendered as "to let you also know about the Good News."

It is difficult in some languages to speak of "sharing our own lives with you." Some interpret it as "willingness to die for you," and others as "doing everything that we possibly could to help you."

You were so dear to us may be equivalent to "we loved you very much indeed" or "we loved you so much."

2.9 Surely you remember, our brothers, how we worked and toiled! We worked day and night so that we would not be any trouble to you as we preached to you the Good News from God.

You remember could, grammatically, mean "remember!" (cf. TNT), but Paul's repeated use of the similar expression "as you know" makes this unlikely.

Again we have the conjunction "for" (compare verses 1, 3, 5), indicating simply that Paul has not passed on to a completely different subject. TEV rightly leaves this for the reader to infer, since it was more natural in ancient Greek than it is in current English to make explicit the relations between sentences. The translator will need to decide whether it is necessary to express in his language the relation between this sentence and the preceding one. If it is necessary, he will also, of course, need to decide how it should be done.

Brothers does not here (see notes on 2.1) mark the beginning of a new section, but it is an intensification of emotive meaning. Worked and toiled are two close synonyms which are often used together (see 2 Thess. 3.8; 2 Corinthians 11.27). They both mean work which is "hard," the first in the sense of tiring and the second in the sense of difficult. Paul used the first word in 1.3 in describing how the Thessalonians' love made them work so hard. In some languages it may not be possible to distinguish between "work" and "toil," but the terms can be combined in a single expression including an emphatic qualifier, for example, "we worked very, very hard" or "we worked so very much."

Day and night is literally "night and day." The word order does not come from the Jewish method of counting nightfall as the beginning of the day; it was normal Greek usage too. The order should be modified, if necessary, to conform with what is more natural in the receptor language (as in TEV Phps SpCL FrCL NAB DuCL).

Be any trouble comes from the same root as made demands in verse 7. Here the context shows clearly that Paul is thinking of the financial burden which would have been thrown on the Thessalonians if he had not earned his own living. Paul implies that Silas and Timothy also worked. In a Jewish setting, there would have been nothing unusual about this, since every rabbi had a trade. In Thessalonica it would have been more remarkable, since non-Jewish traveling lecturers were often less scrupulous, and the Greeks generally despised manual labor. The Greek means literally "lay a burden on any one of you" (cf. Phps "be a burden to any of you" and TNT).

So that we would not be any trouble to you may be translated in some languages as a direct reference to financial costs, for example, "so that our being with you would not cost you anything," or "so that you would not have to pay anything for our being with you."

Preached translates a common secular word used of an official herald making a public proclamation. It is used throughout the New Testament to refer to the communication of the Christian message. In current English, preached (unless otherwise specified in a phrase like "open-air preaching") tends to refer to a part of formal worship in a church building. SpCL and FrCL have "announced"; NEB uses the more literary word "proclaimed." The important component to introduce in a verb designed to translate preached is the urgency with which the proclamation is made. In some languages the most appropriate equivalent is "we spoke earnestly to you about the Good News from God," or "we spoke urgently to you about the Good News we received from God."

TEV

10 You are our witnesses, and so
is God, that our conduct toward you
who believe was pure, right, and
without fault. 11 You know that we
treated each one of you just as a
father treats his own children.
12 We encouraged you, we comforted
you, and we kept urging you to live
the kind of life that pleases God,
who calls you to share in his own
Kingdom and glory. (2.10-12)

RSV

10 You are witnesses, and God also,
how holy and righteous and blameless was our behavior to you believers; 11 for you know how, like
a father with his children, we ex-
horted each one of you and encouraged you and charged you 12 to
lead a life worthy of God, who
calls you into his own kingdom and
glory. (2.10-12)

Verses 10-12 form a single sentence in Greek. Paul has called separately on his readers and on God to confirm the truth of what he says (v. 5). Now he does so again, more emphatically, joining the two "witnesses" more closely together. As already noted, verses 10-12 constitute an emphatic summary of the preceding paragraph (vv. 1-9). The first statement in verse 10 refers to verse 5, while the final clause of verse 10 summarizes the contents of verses 3, 4, and 6. Verse 11 takes up the theme in verse 7, but instead of a reference to a nurse or mother, the reference is to a father and his relation to his own children. Verse 12 serves as a summary for various aspects of the preceding paragraph and in a sense amplifies the theme of the Good News from God mentioned in verses 2, 8, and 9.

2.10 You are our witnesses, and so is God, that our conduct toward you who believe was pure, right, and without fault.

The noun witnesses is better rendered as a verb in some languages, for example, "you yourselves know just what we did," or "you yourselves can tell just what we did," or "...how we behaved." A parallel expression may then be used to render and so is God, for example, "and God himself knows just what we did," or "...saw the way we behaved." In general, the Greek term for "witness" involves two aspects: (1) personal knowledge, and (2) the ability to speak about this personal experience. In some languages one needs to be explicit in indicating both these aspects. However, if both "the people" and "God" are combined as joint witnesses, it will probably be necessary to restrict the focus of attention to either "knowing" or "seeing," for example, "both you and God know exactly how we behaved."

Our conduct may be translated as "just what we did," "how we acted towards you," or "how we carried on when we were with you."

You who believe is a common synonym for "you Christians" (cf. 1.7). This expression may need to be expanded in some cases, for example, "you who believe the Good News," or "you who accept our message." However, in other instances "you Christians" may express the meaning adequately.

Pure, right, and without fault represent another of the series of three terms which, as we have seen (1.3; 2.3 cf. 2.12), are a feature of Paul's discourse style.

There is a considerable overlap of meaning between these terms, and it is more important in translation to convey the total meaning of the three words together than to look for three precise equivalents. In some contexts, pure refers to conduct in relation to God ("pious" without the negative connotation of this word), and right refers to behavior towards other people. However, this is not always so, and the present context (toward you who believe) makes it clear that Paul is speaking of human relationships. There is no suggestion that Paul behaved less well towards nonbelievers, but here he is appealing to what his (Christian) readers know from their own experience.

It may be difficult in some languages to find adequate terms to translate pure, right, and without fault, since the first two terms are positive and the third is negative. In many languages the closest equivalent of pure is itself a negative expression, for example, "without anything wrong." The translation of right normally focuses on "the way things should be"; and without fault may often be translated as "there is nothing for which we could be blamed in what we did." All three expressions may be combined with an expression for "conduct," for example, "The way in which we behaved towards you who believe was without anything wrong. It was just the way we should have acted, and there was nothing that we should be blamed for." Three complete clauses to translate three words in Greek may seem to be rather heavy, but in some languages this expansion may be the closest natural equivalent.

2.11 You know that we treated each one of you just as a father treats his own children.

All editions of the Greek New Testament do not mark the division between verses 11 and 12 at the same point in the text. Some editions, followed by some versions (e.g. KJV RV RSV NEB), include We encouraged you, we comforted you in verse 11. TEV, here as elsewhere, follows the verse division of the UBS Greek New Testament.

Again, Paul appeals to what the Thessalonians themselves know. In verse 9 he has said that he did not want to be a burden to "any one" of them. Here, he reinforces this personal reference by the emphatic each one of you (NEB has "we dealt with you one by one"; DuCL "each [one] personally"). Paul has already called his readers "brothers" and compared himself and his companions to a nursing mother (v.7). Now he compares the Christian family relationship with the relationship between a father and his children. In verse 7 Paul was thinking of the intimacy of a shared life; here he chooses the relationship between a father and his children, because the teaching and preaching function of the evangelists is in focus. This sentence has no main verb in Greek. We treated is supplied by TEV TNT (NEB "we dealt with"). In some languages it may be difficult to supply an appropriate corresponding expression. One may, in some cases, employ a phrase such as "you know that our relation to each one of you was...." In other instances it may be necessary to use a more specific expression, for example, "you know that we helped each one of you just as a father helps his own children."

2.12 We encouraged you, we comforted you, and we kept urging you to live the kind of life that pleases God, who calls you to share in his own Kingdom and glory.

Here, as in verse 10, there is a considerable overlap of meaning between three terms, and again the translator must aim to convey as fully as possible the total meaning of the three terms together. Encouraged is related to the noun translated appeal in verse 3. There Paul is thinking of his first appeal to non-Christians. Here he is thinking of his approach to those who are already believers, so encouraged is more appropriate. Comforted is a close synonym of encouraged; indeed both Greek words can have the meaning of either English word. All three verbs ("encourage," "comfort," "urge") imply continuous action in Greek, but this force is brought out in TEV only in connection with the third verb: kept urging. It would be stylistically clumsy to say "kept encouraging, kept comforting, and kept urging." It is sometimes possible to combine a rendering of encouraged and comforted, since they are closely related concepts and may, in fact, be rendered by idiomatic expressions, for example, "we strengthened your hearts," "we made your liver warm," or "we gave strength to you." The expression kept urging may be rendered as "we said to you strongly that you should," "we continued saying to you most clearly," or even, idiomatically, "we kept on speaking to you with our hearts exposed."

Live is literally "walk," a Hebrew metaphor which cannot be literally transferred to current English. It refers to a person's behavior or way of life, particularly from the moral point of view.

That pleases God is literally "worthily of God." Paul does not mean that his readers should behave so well as to become worthy of God's love or his gifts. It is rather that their behavior should be such as is appropriate in the relationship to God in which they now live. One might translate "behave like people who belong to God" (cf. SpCL and the notes on 1.4). That pleases God may be rendered in some languages as "that causes God to have a happy heart." Often it is "God" who must become the subject of an expression for a pleased response, for example, "a life that God loves," or "a life about which God says, This is how it should be."

Instead of who calls you (present), some manuscripts have "who called you" (past). The latter is more common in Paul's writings (cf. Galatians 1.6; 1 Thess. 4.7; 1 Corinthians 1.9). There is no contradiction between God's initial call and his insistent renewal of that call, but Paul is thinking of the latter in this verse. In translating who calls you, it is important to avoid the implication that God is shouting to someone. The proper equivalent in some languages is "who invites you" or "who asks you," in the sense of an urgent request.

God is calling the Thessalonians to share in his own Kingdom and glory. Paul does not speak very often about the kingdom of God, but it is a central theme in the Gospels, especially in the Synoptics. The expression does not mean a territory over which God rules (like "the Kingdom of the Netherlands"), but the kingship of God, his act of ruling over men and the world. In all the Gospels, Jesus speaks about "entering the kingdom" (e.g. Mark 10.25; John 3.5).

This means "entering the community of those who acknowledge God as king." The kingship of God is a dynamic concept having several aspects. In one sense, God was always king, and he was so worshiped in Old Testament times. Yet Jesus preached that the kingdom of God had come near (Mark 1.15), that is, that God's kingship was about to become effective in a new way. However, the complete fulfillment of God's reign is still to come (cf. Matthew 16.28), and it is this future aspect of the kingdom which is uppermost in Paul's thought (see 1 Corinthians 15.24, 50; Ephesians 5.5; cf. 2 Thess. 1.5; 2 Timothy 4.1).

To share in may be most readily translated in many languages as "to have a part in" or "to be a part of," though, in the Greek, the clause is literally "God, who calls you into his kingdom and glory." One should avoid an expression which would imply that the kingdom of God is divided among various individuals. Rather, the biblical writers think in terms of a group of people sharing together in the rule of God.

It is difficult, in translation, to find a term flexible enough to include all the aspects of New Testament teaching about the kingdom of God at the same time and to exclude geographical associations. TEV retains the traditional word "Kingdom," indicating by a capital letter that it has a specialized meaning. TEV FrCL SpCL include the expression in their glossaries. GeCL normally translates "(God's) new world."* In this kind of context it is essential to employ a term for Kingdom which is the same as the one used in the Gospels, but it is most important that any term used for Kingdom focus upon the "rule of God"--especially his future rule--and not upon some territory over which God reigns. Hence, to share in his own Kingdom may be equivalent to "have a place in God's ruling," or possibly "be given by God a share in his ruling."

It is possible that the focus here is on being part of God's people. If Kingdom and glory are taken together, then the following possibilities are suggested: "to share in this wonderful experience of being part of God's people," or "to be part of God's wonderful people." If, on the other hand, Kingdom and glory are not taken together, it may be possible to render this expression as "to know God's greatness and to be part of his own people."

Against the protests of some scholars, Phps translates Kingdom and glory together as "the splendor of his own kingdom." Brc and TNT have "glorious kingdom," JB (but not BJ) "the glory of his kingdom," and GeCL "share his glory with him in the new world." There are four arguments in favor of a translation along these lines. First, in Hebrew one may express with two nouns a single idea which includes them both, and Paul's style often shows the influence of Hebrew. Second, Paul links Kingdom and glory together with a single pronoun his (not "his kingdom and his glory"). Third, there is so much in common between the meanings of the two nouns that where Mark 10.37 reads "in your glory," the parallel in Matthew 20.21 has "in your kingdom." Fourth, the semantic overlap of the two

---

*See R. Kassühlke, "An attempt at a dynamic equivalent translation of *basileia tou theou*" in *Practical Papers for the Bible Translator*, Vol. 25, No. 2, April 1974, pages 236-238.

terms is increased if we are right in thinking that Paul sees the kingdom of God as mainly a future event, since "glory" also had future connotations for him.

Glory is the word translated *praise* in verse 6. There it refers to human relationships, but here it refers to the visible splendor of God as it will be revealed in the "last days."

If one combines *Kingdom and glory* into a single phrase, in which *glory* modifies *Kingdom* as "glorious ruling" (and in many respects this is a preferable rendering), it may be possible to translate as "have a share in God's wonderful rule," or "have a part in God's ruling; it will be wonderful." If, however, one separates *Kingdom* and *glory* as two different aspects of the future promise, it may be necessary to employ expressions which would appear to distinguish these aspects even more than they should be, for example, "have a part in God's rule and in his wonderfulness." In many languages it is not possible to speak of *glory* as "something shining" or "something brilliant." More satisfactory equivalents are found in the area of "wonderful," "majestic," or "that which causes great admiration."

TEV

13 And there is another reason
why we always give thanks to God.
When we brought you God's message,
you heard it and accepted it, not
as man's message but as God's message, which indeed it is. For God
is at work in you who believe.
14 Our brothers, the same things
happened to you that happened to
the churches of God in Judea, to
the people there who belong to
Christ Jesus. You suffered the
same persecutions from your own
countrymen that they suffered from
the Jews, 15 who killed the Lord
Jesus and the prophets, and persecuted us. How displeasing they are
to God! How hostile they are to
everyone! 16 They even tried to
stop us from preaching to the Gentiles the message that would bring
them salvation. In this way they
have completed the full total of
the sins they have always committed. And now God's anger has at
last come down on them! (2.13-16)

RSV

13 And we also thank God constantly for this, that when you received the word of God which you
heard from us, you accepted it not
as the word of men but as what it
really is, the word of God, which
is at work in you believers. 14 For
you, brethren, became imitators of
the churches of God in Christ Jesus
which are in Judea; for you suffered the same things from your own
countrymen as they did from the
Jews, 15 who killed both the Lord
Jesus and the prophets, and drove
us out, and displease God and oppose all men 16 by hindering us
from speaking to the Gentiles that
they may be saved--so as always to
fill up the measure of their sins.
But God's wrath has come upon them
at last![b]

[b]Or *completely*, or *for ever*
(2.13-16)

This third paragraph of chapter 2 introduces a new theme, but it very effectively relates to what has already been said before by the emphasis upon thanks to God (see 1.2) and upon the bringing of God's message (discussed in both chapter 1 and chapter 2). Even the theme of suffering relates to what Paul has already mentioned about what he and his companions suffered in bringing the Good News to the Thessalonians (v. 2). Now Paul elaborates specifically concerning the source of the oppositions to the gospel, namely, the attitude of certain Jews.

2.13 And there is another reason why we always give thanks to God. When we brought you God's message, you heard it and accepted it, not as man's message but as God's message, which indeed it is. For God is at work in you who believe.

A literal translation of the first part of this verse would be "and for this (reason) also we give thanks to God unceasingly." "And" and "also" represent the same Greek word, here used twice. Most translations omit the first "and," but RSV and TEV retain it. Some New Testament writers, under Hebrew influence, begin sentences frequently with "and." Mark is an extreme example of this tendency. Paul begins with "and" less frequently, but he does it more often than modern writers of English do. When Paul uses "and," it is likely to have more significance than when Mark uses it, and therefore a greater impact on his original readers. Where he does begin sentences with "and," his purpose is often to indicate a division of medium importance, to introduce a new development, but one which is nevertheless related to what has gone before. He is saying, in effect, "Don't forget what I have just told you, but bear it in mind while I tell you something more." Compare Romans 13.11; 1 Corinthians 2.1; 3.1; also 1 Corinthians 12.31b (though here there is an implied contrast with what precedes, and FrCL and GeCL translate "but"). In modern English, "and" sometimes has a similar function of marking a transition within the treatment of a given theme, and that is how TEV uses the word here.

A related question is whether the words "for this (reason)" refer back to a reason for thankfulness which Paul has already mentioned, or forward to a fresh reason he is about to state. It is curious to note that the French BJ takes the phrase as backward-looking ("that is why, on our side, we never stop thanking God that..."), and the parallel English JB takes it as forward-looking ("another reason why we constantly thank God for you is that..."). The context does not provide an easy answer to the problem. It would be difficult to relate Paul's thanksgiving to what he has been discussing immediately before, since 2.1-12 has been concerned with Paul's own activity, and not with the Thessalonians' response. It would be quite possible, on the other hand, for Paul to be recalling and summing up the reasons for thankfulness which he has mentioned in 1.2-10. There are certainly points of contact between 2.13-16 and earlier passages; the references to the effectiveness of the Thessalonians' faith (1.3, cf. 2.13b), to the warmth of their response (1.6, cf. 2.13), to the theme of imitation (1.6, cf. 2.14), to the power of the Christian message (1.5, cf. 2.13), and to the persecution experienced by the Thessalonians (1.6, cf. 2.14) and by Paul himself (2.2, cf. 2.15).

Together with these similarities, however, there are differences of both content and emphasis. The passage beginning when we brought you God's message is more than a summing up of what has gone before. Paul has not said earlier that the Thessalonians received the Christian message as the word of God (God's message), nor has he drawn the parallel with the sufferings of Christians in Judea (v.14). It is therefore probably better to understand "for this (reason)" as pointing ahead to the words which follow.

The problem then becomes one of making it clear to the reader of the translation that the reference is forward-looking. The English pronoun "this" is frequently backward-looking. TEV (cf. TNT FrCL DuCL) tries to override this tendency by replacing "this" with there is and by adding another (there is another reason), at the cost of perhaps over-emphasizing the differences between verses 13-16 and the preceding passage. GeCL makes the forward reference unambiguously clear by reversing the order of 13a and 13b: "When we brought you God's message, you received it...as God's word.... For this we thank God unceasingly." Because of the difficulty in indicating the direction of reference in the phrase "for this (reason)," the solution adopted in the German translation GeCL is highly recommended, that is, "When we brought you God's message...you heard and accepted it.... Therefore, we thank God...," or "...because of this we thank God," or "...because of what you did we thank God." Many languages lack a noun such as "reason" (as used in the present context), but they can always express a causal relation by some type of conjunction or arrangement of clauses.

The second "and" of verse 13 has been understood in at least three ways. The first interpretation, suggested by the order of the Greek words, is to take we and "and" ("also") closely together, suggesting "we, like other people, give thanks," but the context does not support this interpretation. Many translations (including KJV Lu FrCL) render the second "and" as "also," but relate it to "for this reason." This rendering fits well with taking "for this reason" as forward-looking and with emphasizing the distinction between the present passage and what has gone before. However, Moule (167) gives reasons for suggesting the translation "that is in fact why we give thanks," linking the Greek "and" with "we give thanks." NEB follows this interpretation with its "this is why we give thanks." It is probably the most satisfactory of the three solutions.

When we brought you God's message, you heard it and accepted it. The text expresses very concisely the following basic structures: (1) you received the word, (2) you heard the word, (3) we brought the word, (4) the word came from God, (5) you accepted the word. The logical order would appear to be (4), (3), (2), (1), (5). The structure of the Greek emphasizes (5), which is technically "new information," while (1), expressed in a subordinate participle, is assumed or old information. But what precisely is the distinction in meaning between (2), (1), and (5), and what is the relation between them? The relation is not contrastive (the contrast is expressed later in the verse) but unfolding: each statement in the series is defined more clearly by the one which logically follows it. To hear the word (2) does not imply any response, positive or negative: (1) and (5) make it clear that the response was active and positive. (1) in Paul's vocabulary is a technical term for receiving something that is handed on, in this case the Christian message. Among the first Christians, as in Judaism, a close personal relationship was set up between the teacher or rabbi and his pupils, as living links through which a tradition was handed on. Much more is involved than the passive receiving of information. The use of a word evoking this relationship is a point of contact with 2.7b-12. Between (1) and (5) there is considerable overlap of meaning, but in (5) the implied setting is that of a host welcoming a guest, rather than that of a pupil receiving wisdom from a teacher. The two verbs reinforce each other. TEV (cf. FrCL GeCL) combines them in the one word accepted.

Not as man's message but as God's message, which indeed it is. So far, the different elements in the transmission of the Christian message have been closely intertwined in Paul's thought. Now Paul makes two closely related statements, the first of which includes a subordinate contrast:

(1) you received it (a) as a message from God,
(b) not as a (mere) message from men:

(2) it really is a message from God.

In (1) the emphasis is on the Thessalonians' welcoming response to the message. Paul is not here concerned to deny what he has just affirmed, that the message did in one sense come from or through human messengers. There is no corresponding negative statement in (2), such as "it really is not a message from men." Nor does (2) mean merely "what I am telling you is true: it is a word of God," but "it is in reality a word of God." Indeed, as most translations make clear, refers to the truth of the Christian message itself, and not to Paul's statement about it.

A more literal translation, "you received not a word of men but...a word of God," would be misleading, as even KJV realizes ("ye received it not as the word of men"), since Paul is here speaking of the Thessalonians' response.

It is extremely difficult in some languages to render this second sentence of verse 13 in such a way as to do justice to the intricate interrelations. The problems are made more complex by some of the lexical difficulties which may be encountered. For example, in some languages one cannot speak of "bringing a message." Rather, it is necessary to say "to come and speak a message"; obviously, "to bring a message" involves both coming and speaking. Furthermore, it is often difficult to speak of "a message from God," since it must be more clearly indicated that God is the original source of the message. Therefore, when we brought you God's message must be rendered in some languages as "when we came and told you what God had told us to say." At the same time one should avoid a translation which would imply that Paul and his colleagues were simply repeating verbally what God had dictated to them.

You heard it and accepted it. In many languages to "accept a message" is equivalent to "believe a message." Hence, "you heard what we said and believed it."

In order to make clear that this message was "not man's message," it may be necessary to be more specific, since a literal translation of this expression may seem to be a denial of Paul and his colleagues as human messengers. It may be necessary to introduce the positive statement about the message being God's message, before introducing the negative statement, not as man's message.

Hence, one may be required to translate "you believed it as a message which God spoke, and not as words which just came from people."

Which indeed it is may be added directly to God's message (as in TEV), or it may be made a separate sentence, for example, "Indeed these words do come from God."

For God is at work in you who believe can also mean "for it (the message) is at work in you who believe." Most translations follow this second interpretation, though NEB mentions the first in a footnote. The idea of a word having an active power of its own is common in both Old and New Testaments (e.g. Jeremiah 23.29; Isaiah 49.2; Ephesians 6.17; Hebrews 4.12; Revelation 1.16). The difference of meaning between the two interpretations is slight, since Paul has just said emphatically that the message comes from God. However, if the second interpretation is chosen, this will have consequences for the translation of "word" or message. The idea of a "word" acting or working is strange in English outside of church circles. The reference is (1) to a spoken, not to a written message; (2) to a complete message, not to an individual word; (3) to a message which produces effects (SpCL "gives its results"). DuCL links the last part of this verse closely with what precedes, making explicit a logical relation which is implicit in the Greek: "That it [the word] is indeed [from God] is proved by the effect it has on you believers."

The verb translated is at work regularly refers to the activity of God or a supernatural power. The TEV translation is almost certainly correct. The BJ note "is made active" (explained as God acting by his word in the believers) and Mft "proves effective" follow a less natural understanding of the Greek,* and it is significant that the translators who follow this line either feel the need to add an explanation (like the note in BJ) or to phrase their translation in such a way that it becomes almost indistinguishable from the first interpretation (like Mft).

If one adopts the interpretation "the message which is working in you who believe," it may be rendered as "the message is producing results in you who believe," or "...has an effect...," or "...is influencing you...."

However, the interpretation which makes God the agent of the activity within the believer is usually easier to translate, since God as an agent "who works in people" is far more understandable than "the message working in people." Because of the indefiniteness of this activity, it may be necessary to say "for God is doing something in you who believe," or "for God is changing you who believe." It may be impossible to use here a word meaning literally "to work," since this might imply physical labor. It is God's activity to change and modify people's thoughts and behavior that is referred to.

---

*The question is whether to take the voice of the Greek verb as middle, as TEV and most other translations do, or as passive.

2.14 Our brothers, the same things happened to you that happened to the churches of God in Judea, to the people there who belong to Christ Jesus. You suffered the same persecutions from your own countrymen that they suffered from the Jews,

Verses 14-15 and most of verse 16 (down to always committed) form a single sentence in Greek. Such long sentences in Paul's letters often indicate high emotive content. Different but equivalent ways of doing this should be found in translating. Other formal indications of emotive content in this sentence include (1) the emphatic you which begins the sentence and is repeated later in verse 14; (2) the use of the word brothers; (3) the rhetorical repetition of and in verse 15 (more prominent in the Greek than in TEV); (4) the piling-up of participles in verses 15-16a; (5) the abruptly contrasting short sentence in 16b. It is also significant, though not a formal feature, that Paul refers here to the Jews as if he were not a Jew. Formal features in TEV which go some way toward conveying the emotive content include (1) the exclamation How displeasing...! and (2) the insertion of even before tried to stop us.

The first words of verse 14 are literally "for you became imitators" (RSV). There are two objections, however, to the English word "imitators" in this context. First, it carries the suggestion, foreign to the text, of something not genuine or authentic (see the notes on 1.6). Second, it suggests that the Thessalonians took the initiative, "began to copy" (Mft) the churches in Judea. The context makes this meaning most unlikely. The idea is rather that, just as the Thessalonians have listened eagerly to Paul's message (v. 13), so (RSV's "for" makes the connection with v. 13 clear) the churches in Thessalonica have become like those in Judea. The point of comparison is not subjective: the courage or faith of Judeans and Thessalonians under pressure, but objective: the fact of undergoing persecution from their fellow countrymen. Their situation is similar: the same things happened to them, as TEV (cf. NEB) puts it; they became "companions-in-distress" (DuCL). The kind of suffering they have endured has given them the honorable status of disciples, close followers of the mother churches in Judea.

The order of the expressions the same things happened to you and happened to the churches...in Judea will need to be inverted in many languages so that the prior happening will be mentioned first and the latter happening afterwards, for example, "what happened to the churches of God in Judea also happened to you," or "what the churches of God in Judea already experienced, you yourselves have also experienced." In both cases, that of the churches in Judea and the Christians of Thessalonica, these persons were the objects of the persecution. Therefore it may be necessary, in some cases, to place the reference to them in the predicate of a verbal expression, for example, "The way people persecuted the churches of God in Judea is the same way in which people have persecuted you" ("people" referring to an indefinite subject). It is possible, however, to make the churches in Judea and the people in Thessalonica the subject if one uses a verb such as "suffer," for example, "In the same way that people in the churches of God in Judea suffered, so you have also suffered."

"The churches of God in Judea which are in Christ Jesus" (RSV; cf. Galatians 1.22) illustrates the fact that at this early date the word translated "church" had not yet narrowed its meaning to the local Christian community (still less to the meaning of the whole body of Christians, which is not in question here). The word still has many of its secular associations, like the ordinary English word "assembly." Paul feels the need to specify, first that these communities belong to God, and secondly that, in contrast to Jewish synagogues, they belong to Christ Jesus. Since churches is sometimes translated as "groups of believers" or even "groups of believers in Christ," churches of God may be rendered as "groups of believers in Christ who belong to God."

Despite the order Christ Jesus, it is probable that Paul is here, as usual, thinking of Christ as a name rather than a title. The translation "the Messiah Jesus" should be avoided.

The phrase in Judea is often related directly to an expression for "groups of believers," for example, "groups in Judea who believe in Christ and belong to God." The name Judea commonly included the neighboring areas of Galilee and Samaria.

A complication is involved in translating churches of God and the people there who belong to Christ Jesus, since churches of God would indicate some kind of possessive relation and the believers would be spoken of as people who... belong to Christ Jesus. Both possessive relations are true, but stylistically it would be important to express them in different ways, even as is done in TEV.

Countrymen means primarily those belonging to the same ethnic group, rather than those living in the same area. At Thessalonica (cf. Acts 17.5, 13) the Jews had been the first to stir up trouble for the Christians, many if not most of whom were no doubt of Jewish origin themselves. Your own countrymen reflects an accidental similarity in form between Greek and English. In New Testament Greek, own is not emphatic. Some French translations, for example, have simply "your compatriots" (BJ FrCL), while others have "your own compatriots" (Seg Syn), which is too emphatic. In English, expressions like your own countrymen tend to become set phrases in which own loses much of its usual emphasis. (The reason for this is probably the need to distinguish between "countrymen" in the sense of "compatriots," and "countrymen" in the sense of "inhabitants of rural areas.") Perhaps for that reason, NEB's "your countrymen" seems too weak.

Since the countrymen are really agents who cause the suffering, it is often necessary to shift the relation, for example, "your own countrymen have caused you to suffer in the same way that the Jews caused those in Judea to suffer." The equivalent of countrymen in many areas of the world is "fellow tribesmen," "people who are one with you," or even "people who talk as you do."

2.15 who killed the Lord Jesus and the prophets, and persecuted us. How displeasing they are to God! How hostile they are to everyone!

The emotive tone becomes stronger in verse 15. The reading the prophets is certainly better than "their own prophets" (mentioned in NEB in a note). The punctuation of the UBS Greek New Testament: "killing Jesus and the prophets, and persecuting us" is generally accepted, though one or two commentators have argued for a punctuation which would give the meaning: "killing Jesus, and persecuting the prophets and us." Hostile translates a word usually applied to such objects as the wind blowing against someone.

The participles translated killed and persecuted refer to actions at a specific point in time. Displeasing, on the other hand, refers to a permanent or at least a long-lasting state.

Note that Paul here uses the word killed rather than "crucified" to show that the Jews were as much responsible for the death of Jesus as were the Romans, even though it was the latter who directly condemned and crucified him. Since the killing of the prophets preceded the killing of Jesus, it may be necessary to introduce a temporal distinction, for example, "and had earlier killed the prophets." The persecution of Paul and his colleagues represents still a different period of time, and a temporal distinction may be required here also, for example, "and more recently they have been causing us to suffer," or "...have been persecuting us."

Since the historical order of the events mentioned in the first clause of this verse differs from the linguistic order, it may be necessary in some languages to rearrange the linguistic order, for example, "who long ago killed the prophets, and then caused the Lord Jesus to be killed, and recently have been persecuting us." It may not be possible, in some languages, to use the one pronoun "they" to refer to those who killed the prophets, caused the Lord Jesus to be killed, and persecuted the apostle and his companions, because different groups of people performed these various acts. It may be necessary to mention three distinct groups, for example, "long ago some of them killed the prophets, and then others caused the Lord Jesus to be killed, and now some of them have been persecuting us."

The exclamation How displeasing they are to God! may need to be made an emphatic statement such as "They displease God very much!", "They cause God to be very angry!", or "God is surely very angry with them!"

It is not easy to find a term which can readily translate hostile. The closest equivalent is normally an expression such as "enemy," for example, "they are very much enemies of everyone," or "they are very much against everyone."

2.16 They even tried to stop us from preaching to the Gentiles the message that would bring them salvation. In this way they have completed the full total of the sins they have always committed. And now God's anger has at last come down on them!

In tried to stop us, "tried to" is implied. The verb Paul uses means to prevent or hinder, either by words (cf. the English "forbid") or by actions. Phps' "refused to allow" limits the reference to verbal pressure, but more is probably included here. In English, "prevent," like its more common equivalent "stop," includes the idea that the pressure is effective. This suggestion should be avoided here, since the Jews clearly did not succeed in preventing Paul from preaching to the Gentiles. That is why TEV inserts tried to. RSV and NEB (cf.

Modern Greek) have "hindering." The Greek implies continual pressure over a period of time.

In some languages an attempt which does not succeed must be clearly marked as such, for example, "they tried to stop us from preaching...but they could not."

Gentile is a technical word which the TEV word list defines as "a person who is not a Jew." (The Greek word can sometimes mean "peoples," but here there is an explicit contrast with Jews.) "Pagans" (cf. Lu Seg Syn) emphasizes the religious aspect of the distinction between Jews and non-Jews, to the exclusion of the racial aspect. It also has bad overtones which were far from Paul's mind. SpCL (cf. Phps) avoids the need for an explanatory note by translating "those who are not Jews," while FrCL has "non-Jews" and GeCL "the other peoples."

Preaching to the Gentiles the message that would bring them salvation. The more literal RSV (cf. NEB) "speaking to the Gentiles that they may be saved" fails to express an implied but quite specific reference to the communication of the Christian message. TEV accordingly inserts message (cf. FrCL), GeCL "the Good News"; Mft has "words of salvation" and Phps "the message by which they could be saved." "Speak" (TEV preaching) does not, however, suggest a formal discourse within the setting of public worship, usually in a church building. Phps avoids this misunderstanding by translating "tell"; TNT, similarly, has "telling the Gentiles how they may be saved"; FrCL and GeCL have "announce" (cf. DuCL "make known to the Gentiles how they can be saved.")

In many languages it is impossible to talk about "bringing people salvation." This would be especially true of the activity of a "message," since the real agent of salvation is always God. Accordingly, the last part of this first sentence in verse 16 may be recast as "the message by which God would save them," or "the words that told them how God would save them." In some languages "save" is translated "to be given a new liver by God," or "God has given them new hearts." Another possibility is "to receive new life from God."

In this way they have completed the full total of the sins they have always committed. The difficulties here are cultural as well as linguistic, so that even the clearest translation will not solve all the problems of understanding. In speaking of a full total, Paul may have in mind the rabbinical idea of God's keeping a record of a person's good and bad deeds and judging the total. Genesis 15.16 suggests a similar idea, but BJ and JB seem to go too far in labeling Paul's words as a direct quotation of this passage. The expression total is not explicit, and some translations remove or change it. FrCL has "sum," BJ "culmination," Phps "finishing touch."

It is difficult to decide whether the "filling up" or "completing" refers to the whole series of the Jews' misdeeds, or only to the last sin mentioned, that of trying to keep the gospel from reaching non-Jews. The form of the Greek verb suggests action(s) at one or more specific points in time, and the idea of repeated action is emphasized by the word always. TEV's image of a total amount being filled or completed again and again makes sense of this text, but it does not seem to have any parallel. NEB's "have been filling up the full measure of their guilt" is ambiguous, since "have been filling" could (in this context wrongly) suggest a process rather than repeated action. JB's "they never stop trying to finish off the sins they have begun" conveys well the idea of repeated action, but unfortunately implies that their sinning was interrupted! Paul's thought, here as in many other places, is compressed and therefore not entirely clear, but the main elements are: (1) the Jews have sinned repeatedly in the past, and (2) now the total of their sins has been completed. In (2) Paul is probably referring to the last sin in his list, as being the last sin, or at least the last type of sin, for which there will be time before the End. As the last part of the verse will show and many other passages in 1 and 2 Thessalonians confirm, Paul's mind is full of the nearness of Christ's coming and the judgment which will accompany it.

The translation of in this way they have completed the full total of the sins they have always committed is perhaps even more difficult than the interpretation, especially if the translation must be done in a language which employs only a verb for sins. One can sometimes say "this is only the last of all the sins that they have always been committing." The use of "all" is one way of reproducing the concept of "full total." If a language requires a verb for "sins," one may translate such as "and this finally is how they have sinned, just like all the other times that they have been sinning."

The last sentence in verse 16, and now God's anger has at last come down on them, is abrupt. The abruptness is reinforced by the verb has come down, which suggests a sudden event. Best translates "has caught up with them." For the meaning of anger, see the notes on 1.10. God's is implied by the use of the definite article (KJV cf. Lu "the anger"). In using this expression, Paul, like a good Jew, commonly omits the name of God. For the reader of today, "the anger" would be at best too general, and at worst unclear. Accordingly, RSV FrCL SpCL GeCL DuCL Brc (cf. Phps) like TEV add "God's." BJ has "the wrath" with an explanatory note, and Mft has "the Wrath" (capital W), but neither solution is appropriate for a translation intended to be read aloud. JB and NEB have "retribution."

In some languages God's anger must be translated as "God is judging them harshly" or "God is angry with them and judging them." As already noted in 1.10, anger includes the concept of judging.

The translations of at last vary. Moule (70) suggests "completely," under Hebrew influence. Most translations, on the other hand, see some kind of a reference to time, which would fit in well with the preceding always. Two kinds of time reference are possible: (1) backward: at last (TEV cf. JB FrCL; Phps "finally," cf. BJ Seg Syn DuCL), contrasting a single recent event with a preceding period: ——→——↓ and (2) forward: "to the end" (cf. Lu Mft; NEB "for good and all"; GeCL "God's irrevocable anger"), linking a decisive event with its future consequences: ↓——→—— The backward reference seems to suit better both the immediate context and Paul's general view of time.

CHAPTER 2.17-20 and CHAPTER 3

Paul's attack on the Jews in 2.14-16 has been a diversion from the main theme of his relationship with the Thessalonians, to which he now returns. Once again, as he has done twice already, he begins by speaking about himself and his companions (2.17—3.5, cf. 1.2-5; 2.1-12), and then he goes on to speak about the Thessalonians (3.6-13, cf. 1.6-10; 2.13-16).

In 2.17—3.5, however, Paul's thought takes a step forward. Until now, he has been concerned with his previous visit to Thessalonica and its immediate results for his readers. Now he turns to his own situation, to his attempts to renew contact with Thessalonica, either personally or through Timothy. This transition is marked by a word commonly translated "but" (so RSV), and by an emphatic "we." However, no contrast is involved. TEV (cf. FrCL) correctly marks the transition by as for us.

The emotive content of the entire passage remains high, though now the emotion is one of affection and no longer of righteous anger. Indications of high emotion in verses 17-20 include (1) rough and broken sentence structure; (2) the use, once again, of the address brothers; (3) the rare word translated separated; (4) a number of expressions with overlapping meaning, indicating longing or effort; (5) the piling up in verse 19 of nouns linked by "or" (see RSV); (6) the references in verses 19-20 to joy, boasting, and pride; and (7) rhetorical questions in verse 19. The emotion is not just subjective and personal; it is part of what is often spoken of as a cosmic struggle of good and evil. On the one hand is Satan, the tempter (2.18; 3.5); on the other, God and Christ who is soon to come. We shall discuss below the different but equivalent means by which TEV and some other translations seek to communicate the tension of the original.

TEV

Paul's Desire to Visit Them Again

17 As for us, brothers, when we were separated from you for a little while--not in our thoughts, of course, but only in body--how we missed you and how hard we tried to see you again! 18 We wanted to return to you. I myself tried to go back more than once, but Satan would not let us. 19 After all, it is you--you, no less than others!--who are our hope, our joy, and our reason for boasting of our victory in the presence of our Lord Jesus when he comes. 20 Indeed, you are our pride and our joy! (2.17-20)

RSV

17 But since we were bereft of you, brethren, for a short time, in person not in heart, we endeavored the more eagerly and with great desire to see you face to face; 18 because we wanted to come to you --I, Paul, again and again--but Satan hindered us. 19 For what is our hope or joy or crown of boasting before our Lord Jesus at his coming? Is it not you? 20 For you are our glory and joy. (2.17-20)

The section heading Paul's Desire to Visit Them Again may need to be translated as a sentence, either "Paul desires to visit them again," or "Paul desired [past tense] to visit them again." The choice of tense is based entirely upon the usage in a receptor language. In a title the use of a pronoun such as "them" may be misleading, so one may be justified in introducing a noun such as "the Thessalonians." In some languages a different verb must be used for "visit" in this context, since Paul would be going back to people who had already become his friends. This would require a different verb from what is often used in speaking of a first visit, as for example in 2.1.

This short paragraph serves to reintroduce the main concern which Paul has in this letter, namely, his desire to learn more about how the Thessalonians are making out. He must, therefore, explain why he himself could not visit them, but he also wishes to emphasize why he wants so much to do so. He no longer needs to remind the Thessalonians about how much they have been able to do in witnessing to their faith; he only needs to indicate how much they mean to him personally, a theme which is mentioned in verses 19 and 20.

2.17 As for us, brothers, when we were separated from you for a little while—not in our thoughts, of course, but only in body—how we missed you and how hard we tried to see you again!

The phrase as for us is a very convenient device in English for shifting focus, but some languages do not have any such mechanism. The closest equivalent may be an expression of "speaking" or "thinking," for example, "now I want to speak about us," or "and now think about us."

Separated translates a strong and unusual word which literally means "orphaned," but it can also be used to mean the separation of parents from children and a lover from his beloved. "Bereft" (RSV Mft) gives the right meaning by the use of a somewhat archaic word. NEB's "you were lost to us" reverses the focus, and Brc's "you and I were lost to each other" steers a middle course. Paul is referring to the moment of being torn away from his friends, not to the period of separation which followed. It may be difficult in some languages to employ a passive expression such as were separated without indicating the agents. Moreover, this separation was not a physical act of removing Paul from the people, but the persecution which forced Paul and Silas to leave (Acts 17.10). Accordingly, it may be necessary to translate "we were forced to leave you," or "some people there made us leave you."

For a little while does not mean that Paul had already been reunited with the Thessalonian Christians, as he makes clear in the following verses, but it indicates that he is confident that the separation will not be long. It may be difficult to translate for a little while, since we do not know specifically how much time had actually lapsed. One must certainly not give the impression that the lapsed time was merely a matter of a few days or weeks, and though Paul wishes to emphasize the relative shortness of the time, a literal translation could be quite misleading. In order to emphasize that the separation is still continuing but should not be permanent, some languages may employ a perfect tense, for example, "we have been forced to be away from you for a while."

Not in our thoughts, of course, but only in body is (as of course indicates) an aside which is literally translated "in face, not in heart." Mft appropriately uses the idiom "(out of sight, not out of mind)". TEV (cf. FrCL), by its use of thoughts, reminds us that in Hebrew thinking the heart was considered to be the seat of the intellect and the center of the whole personality, not primarily the seat of the emotions.

As in many instances, it may be necessary to introduce the positive statement before the negative one and to make more explicit what "body" and "thought" mean, for example, "we were only away from you as far as our bodies were concerned, but we never stopped thinking about you," or "we ourselves were not with you, but we were always thinking about you."

How we missed you and how hard we tried to see you again! TEV effectively turns a statement into an exclamation and reverses the Greek sentence so that the longing is mentioned before the effort to which it gave rise. How hard is comparative in form ("more," "more abundantly"), but the context shows that there is no real comparison; "more than if we had not been separated" would be nonsense. The comparative form is an idiomatic equivalent of "very" (cf. NEB "exceedingly anxious"). Formal equivalents such as KJV "the more abundantly" and RSV "the more eagerly" are misleading.

There are two problems involved in translating how we missed you. First, many languages do not use an exclamation, but prefer a type of emphatic statement, as in the Greek text. Second, this concept of "missing" must often be expressed in an idiomatic way, for example, "our heart was pained because of you," "we hurt within ourselves because of you," "our love for you grabbed us," or "our insides went out to you."

How hard we tried to see you again may likewise be changed into an emphatic statement, either of frequency, "we tried many times to see you again," or of intensity, "we tried very much to see you again." To see you is literally "to see your face." TEV and NEB eliminate the redundancy, while RSV and TNT "to see you face to face" somewhat overemphasize it. In this context "see" must often be translated as "to visit," since it is not simply sight, but more particularly fellowship, which is involved.

2.18 We wanted to return to you. I myself tried to go back more than once, but Satan would not let us.

We wanted implies, not longing over a period of time (cf. Phps), but specific action. TEV is therefore right, when the subject changes abruptly to the singular, I myself, to supply a verb tried (cf. Best "we resolved"). This is one of the few passages in this letter in which Paul expressly distinguishes himself from Silas and Timothy. The reason is clearly that Timothy has returned to Thessalonica, and Paul has not. More than once rightly translates the idiom "once and twice," since Paul is not really specifying the number of occasions on which he tried to get back to Thessalonica. Nor do we know what, in human terms, prevented him from doing so. Like most biblical writers, Paul sees beyond purely human reasons and attributes his failure to Satan.

Again it may be necessary to translate return to you as "to visit you again," since Paul does not imply that he wishes to go back to be with the Thessalonians permanently.

The Greek text has "I, Paul" as the subject of tried to go back. In some languages it would be awkward to say "I, Paul"—especially if the introduction to the letter makes it clear that Paul is the principal writer and Silas and Timothy are simply associated with him. For this reason TEV translates I myself.

More than once may be rendered as "repeatedly" or "again and again." Since the number of times is indefinite, the translation should employ an indefinite term, but not one that would indicate a large number of times. The word order in TEV is slightly ambiguous; "tried more than once to go back" would be clearer.

In translating Satan would not let us, it is important to avoid giving the impression that Paul and his colleagues required permission from Satan to do anything. It may be better to translate "but Satan prevented us from doing so," "Satan made it impossible for us," or "Satan stopped us."

Verses 17 and 18 are linked by a conjunction meaning "because" or "for." Here, however, it does not express a relation of reason and result, and TNT's "for that reason alone we wanted to come to you" is much too strong. The function of the conjunction is to indicate a transition from verse 17, in which Paul speaks of his longing, to verse 18, which unfolds the meaning of verse 17 by speaking of the efforts by which the desire was expressed.

2.19 After all, it is you—you, no less than others!—who are our hope, our joy, and our reason for boasting of our victory in the presence of our Lord Jesus when he comes.

The translation of the transition after all may be difficult, since a rendering implying a cause or reason might refer back immediately to Satan's preventing Paul from visiting the Thessalonians. The real connection is not with Satan's activity but with Paul's desire. It may be necessary to repeat this fact at the beginning of verse 19, for example, "I wanted to visit you because you are the ones who are...."

Verse 19 consists of a rhetorical question within a rhetorical question, literally: "For who is our hope and joy and crown of boasting (is it not also you?) before our Lord Jesus at his coming?" Paul is dictating, and his feelings are running high. Underneath the questions, he is giving the reason for his desire to see the Thessalonian Christians again. Our hope, as the parallel with our joy shows, means "a reason for hope" or "a source of hope," not "an object of hope" or "something for which we hope." The "crown" Paul mentions is not a sign of kingship, but of victory, as in an athletic competition. In removing the metaphor, TEV makes this clear by using the words of our victory (cf. FrCL and GeCL). The word translated reason for boasting means the basis for being justly proud (cf. Romans 4.2: TEV "something to boast about"; TNT "evidence of proud achievement"), as distinct from the act of speaking boastfully (cf. Romans 3.27).

In rendering our hope and our joy, it is important to indicate clearly the implied causative relation. The Thessalonians were the ones who caused Paul and his colleagues to hope and to have joy. In some languages an equivalent translation may be "you are the ones who caused us to have hope, and you are the ones who caused us to be joyful." Similarly, our reason for boasting is a causative relation, for example, "you are the ones who have caused us to boast." But "boast" must be carefully translated, since it can easily imply a wrong kind of verbal self-praise. An appropriate equivalent in some languages may be "you were the ones who caused us to speak so confidently about our victory."

The translation of our victory is often difficult, since any term which seems to suggest victory implies fighting and war. This is obviously not what Paul means. It may be even more difficult to suggest victory in some kind of competition or game, since this might introduce unacceptable connotations such as of gambling. It may be necessary to shift this figure of speech to the concept of success, for example, "you are the ones who caused us to speak so confidently about our success," or "...about what we have accomplished."

The second rhetorical question, like the first, became an emphatic statement in the third edition of TEV: you, no less than others! This was a great improvement on the earlier editions, which had "you, and no one else!"—a statement which was not only emphatic, but also apparently exclusive. Paul's "also," omitted by most modern as well as traditional translations, is given its full value in GeCL's "you certainly belong to those who are our hope and our joy." The church at Thessalonica was not the only one of which Paul was proud.

In rendering no less than others, one might be tempted to introduce a negative comparison, for example, "you do not surpass others in this," but that would produce the wrong emphasis. The focus here is upon the Thessalonians' being fully equal to all others in causing Paul's hope and joy. Therefore an equivalent may be an emphatic statement such as "you are completely equal to others in this," or "no one surpasses you in this." This statement may very well be placed at the end of verse 19 so as to refer to all the various aspects of what the Thessalonians contributed to Paul's hope, joy, and confidence. Such an arrangement would also provide a good transition to verse 20.

When he comes represents a noun which is a key word in Paul's vocabulary. In nonbiblical texts, it can mean either (a) "presence" (cf. TNT) or (b) "coming," "arrival" (not "return"). It can be used to speak of the presence of a (pagan) god in a temple or a sacred meal, or to his appearance in a vision. It is also used to refer to the ceremonial arrival of a king. Here, as usual in Paul's writings, the word means the appearing or coming of Jesus at the end of time. The eager waiting for this coming is a recurring theme in both 1 and 2 Thessalonians. Though English may use a present tense in a clause such as when he comes, even though it refers to an indefinite future, many languages require a specific future tense, for example, "when he will come."

Though the focus of meaning in the Greek term is upon "presence" or "coming," in some receptor languages it is necessary to employ a term which means "return." Otherwise the implication would be that Jesus had not been on earth before.

2.20 Indeed, you are our pride and our joy!

Verse 20 adds no new idea. Pride means practically the same as reason for boasting (v. 19), which NEB translates "pride"; and joy is repeated from the previous verse. The function of this sentence is simply to sum up and reemphasize, and this is indicated by indeed (also Phps NEB; FrCL GeCL have "Yes"). The word translated pride means "glory" in other contexts. The causative relation implied in our pride and our joy may be expressed in some languages as "It certainly is true that you are the ones who cause us to be proud and to have joy." It is important to employ a rendering of pride which will not suggest a haughty or boastful attitude. Paul's pride is not in himself but in the Thessalonians. It may be possible to render our pride as "you are the ones who cause us to be so proud of you."

TEV

1 Finally, we could not bear it
any longer. So we decided to stay
on alone in Athens 2 while we sent
Timothy, our brother who works with
us for God in preaching the Good
News about Christ. We sent him to
strengthen you and help your faith,
3 so that none of you should turn
back because of these persecutions.
You yourselves know that such persecutions are part of God's will
for us. 4 For while we were still
with you, we told you ahead of time
that we were going to be persecuted; and, as you well know, that is
exactly what happened. 5 That is
why I had to send Timothy. I could
not bear it any longer, so I sent
him to find out about your faith.
Surely it could not be that the
Devil had tempted you, and all our
work had been for nothing! (3.1-5)

RSV

1 Therefore when we could bear
it no longer, we were willing to
be left behind at Athens alone,
2 and we sent Timothy, our brother
and God's servant in the gospel of
Christ, to establish you in your
faith and to exhort you, 3 that
no one be moved by these afflictions. You yourselves know that
this is to be our lot. 4 For when
we were with you, we told you beforehand that we were to suffer
affliction; just as it has come to
pass, and as you know. 5 For this
reason, when I could bear it no
longer, I sent that I might know
your faith, for fear that somehow
the tempter had tempted you and
that our labor would be in vain.
(3.1-5)

These verses form a unit; they are concerned with the sending back of Timothy to Thessalonica. The directness of this unit is marked by verse 5, which sums up and partly repeats verses 1-4. On the other hand, the unit is linked with what precedes by a conjunction which RSV (cf. KJV Zur Lu Syn) translates "therefore," and Mft and NEB (cf. Brc Seg BJ TOB) translate "so." The relation of this unit with 2.17-20 is one of reason and result: Paul sends Timothy back because of the affectionate anxiety he has just described.

How is the translator to make clear both the unity of 3.1-5 and the relation of this unit to what has gone before? The answer to this question will naturally vary from one receptor language to another. In English and many other European languages, the current tendency towards shorter sentences is accompanied by a tendency (except in formal language) for transitional expressions to be used less frequently than in the past. But the TEV shows the transition by the adverb finally and translates the Greek dependent clause "when we could bear it no longer" as a separate sentence: Finally, we could not bear it any longer (cf. GeCL FrCL). A different but equivalent backward reference is provided by the word it (cf. GeCL and many other translations). FrCL specifies here and in verse 5 what it was that could not be borne: it was "this waiting" (for v. 5, cf. JB Syn).

Once more the question arises whether Paul is speaking only of himself, or is including one or both of his companions, Silas and Timothy. Generally, as we have seen, Paul's use of "we" in this letter is to be taken literally and not as equivalent to "I." Because of the very meaning of the Greek word for alone, Moule (119) thinks that Paul must be referring exclusively to himself. This interpretation is followed by GeCL and Mft. However, it seems perfectly possible for the first "we" in verse 1 to mean Paul, Silas, and Timothy, and for the "we" in the following references to mean Paul and Silas alone. This is the view of most translators. When in verse 5 (as in 2.18) Paul wants to distinguish himself from his companions, he does so in the normal way, that is, by changing to the first person singular. The pattern here (3.1 and 3.5) and in 2.17 and 18 is the same: first Paul associates himself with his colleagues (we could not bear it), and then he emphasizes his personal involvement (I could not bear it).

3.1 Finally, we could not bear it any longer. So we decided to stay on alone in Athens

We could not bear it any longer must refer to the intense emotion which Paul and his colleagues felt in missing the Thessalonians. It may be necessary to make this reference more specific, for example, "we could not endure any longer not seeing you," or, stated idiomatically, "our being away from you was crushing us."

The word so is important because it introduces clearly the reason for the decision. In some languages this reason may need to be made explicit, for example, "because of how we felt." Or the preceding sentence may be combined with this statement about the decision, for example, "At last, because we could not endure any longer being away from you, we decided...."

We decided is the same verb which in 2.8 is translated we were ready, but here the tense shows that Paul is not thinking of a state of being ready and willing, but of a specific decision. This is not brought out by RSV ("we were willing"), Syn ("we preferred"), or TOB ("we thought it best," cf. Zur). Decided is rightly chosen, not only by common language translations, but by Knox Brc TNT (cf. Lu JB). Mft has the equivalent "made up my mind" (cf. Seg BJ).

In translating we in verses 1 and 2, it is important to make the proper transitions and to indicate clearly who is involved. This will mean that in many languages the first "we" in verse 1 will be the exclusive first person plural to include Paul, Silas, and Timothy. The second "we" will be the same ("we decided"), but the implied third "we" must refer merely to Paul and Silas, for the two of them were the ones who stayed on alone in Athens. Therefore it may be necessary to translate "so we three decided that we two would stay on alone in Athens." The we of we sent would then refer to Paul and Silas, but our in the phrase our brother would be inclusive first person plural (for languages having the inclusive-exclusive distinction), since Timothy would be a fellow believer, not only of Paul and Silas, but of the Thessalonians as well. Us in the phrase who works with us would again refer simply to Paul and Silas. Only a careful sorting out of precise references in the use of we, our, and us can prevent serious misunderstanding.

To stay on is passive in form, literally "to be left behind" (RSV), but the context shows that Paul is writing from his own point of view, not that of Timothy. TEV and most other translations make this clear by the use of "remain" or the more common equivalents "stay on" or "stay behind" (TNT).

3.2 while we sent Timothy, our brother who works with us for God in preaching the Good News about Christ. We sent him to strengthen you and help your faith,

The first separate reference to Timothy is followed by an accumulation of titles which serve both to describe and recommend him. GeCL lightens the construction by including these titles in a separate sentence beginning "he is God's co-worker."

The best Greek text, followed by a majority of modern translations (including Phps NAB NEB Zur JB Seg BJ FrCL TOB DuCL), describes Timothy as, literally, "our brother and co-worker of God in the gospel of Christ." Many copyists seemingly were shocked that Paul should call Timothy "God's co-worker," though a similar idea is expressed in 1 Corinthians 6.1. Some manuscripts (followed by Mft RSV Knox Lu Syn JB SpCL) replace "co-worker" by "servant." Others omit "God" or place "of God" after "gospel."

TEV adopts the reading "co-worker" but links it with "our" rather than with "of God," making it necessary to understand "of God" as "for God": our brother who works with us for God (cf. TNT FrCL). It seems on the whole better to keep the two phrases "our brother" and "God's co-worker" distinct in translation. Timothy, like any Christian, is Paul's brother, but he also has the more specific calling to work with God in preaching the Good News about Christ. Preaching is implied; see the notes on 2.16.

Paul has used the expression "Good News of God" in 2.2, 8, 9, always with the meaning "Good News from God," "Good News of which God is the author," or "Good News sent by God." Here it would be possible to understand "Good News of Christ" in the same way, but TEV's Good News about Christ fits the context better.

If one combines the concept of "co-worker" with Timothy's colleagues Paul and Silas, it may be necessary to make clear the relation involved in the phrase for God. This is done in some languages as "who works with us in serving God." On the other hand, if one combines "co-worker" directly with "God," one must translate "he works with God" or "he works together with God," something which must be expressed in some languages as "he and God work together." But this may be awkward, since it may shift the focus of attention from Timothy as a collaborator to joint operations conducted by Timothy and God. Under such circumstances it may be better to adopt the construction employed in TEV.

We sent him to strengthen you, in Greek as in TEV, is slightly ambiguous. Does Paul mean (1) "we sent him so that he might strengthen you," or (2) "we sent him so that (through him) we might strengthen you"? Those translations which specify (including Zur GeCL SpCL DuCL) choose the first alternative, which is simpler and more probable, though the difference in meaning is minimal. In translating to strengthen, it is important to avoid the implication that Timothy was to make the Thessalonians physically strong or to increase their health. The strengthening obviously refers to their faith and confidence as Christian believers. It may even be useful to combine this meaning with the phrase help your faith, for example, "to cause your faith to become strong."

Help translates a verb whose literal meaning is that of calling someone to one's side, but the literal meaning clearly does not fit the present context. Extensions of this meaning include two which are relevant here, and which partly overlap: (1) "appeal to, urge, exhort," in which the act of speaking is dominant, and (2) "encourage, cheer up," which emphasize the strengthening effect of what is said, rather than the act itself. The close link with strengthen (cf. 2 Thess. 2.17) makes the second meaning much more likely. Most translations have "encourage" or something similar. TEV's help is a more common equivalent, and KJV's "comfort" is no longer used in this sense.

Help your faith is more literally "encourage you concerning your faith," or possibly "on behalf of your faith," though the latter meaning is awkward and unlikely. Two questions arise: (1) What is the relation between "encourage" and "your faith"? and (2) What is the relation between this entire phrase and the preceding strengthen? TNT makes both relations explicit by translating "encourage you to stand fast in your faith" (NEB "...to stand firm for the faith," cf. Brc). It is clear that the Thessalonians' faith is affected inseparably by the strengthening and by the encouragement which Timothy brings. This is one of the few passages in which GeCL uses the noun "faith." It usually prefers to translate the "event" of faith by a verb, "to trust" or "to believe."

In those languages which normally employ a verb to translate faith, one may render to strengthen you and help your faith as "to cause you to believe more firmly," or "to cause you to have more confidence in your trusting in Christ."

3.3 so that none of you should turn back because of these persecutions. You yourselves know that such persecutions are part of God's will for us.

The word translated turn back is not used anywhere else in the New Testament. Of its possible meanings in New Testament or later times, the most appropriate here is "disturbed" (Best), "shaken" (TNT Brc), "unsettled" (JB). GeCL interestingly transfers "your faith" from verse 2: "He was to strengthen and encourage you, so that no one should let himself be turned aside from the faith."

In some languages there may be no meaningful connection between "turning back" and "faith" or "trusting." Therefore it may be necessary to say "so that none of you would give up believing," or "...would cease trusting Christ."

These persecutions (already mentioned in 1.6 and 2.14) must often be rendered as "the way in which you have suffered persecution," or "the ways in which people have caused you to suffer."

You yourselves know. TEV follows the Greek closely here in emphasizing you by the addition of yourselves; but the emphasis really attaches to the whole phrase; there is no contrast with any other group of people. Mft transfers the emphasis to know: "You know that well" (cf. Knox GeCL). Brc (cf. TNT) emphasizes both elements: "You yourselves well know." DuCL, like Mft, emphasizes the whole phrase by transferring it to the end of the sentence: "that you know."

Such persecutions are part of God's will for us. TEV and FrCL make explicit a reference to God which is implicit in the text, which could be translated almost literally "that is why we have been put here." Here, as in many places, the passive implies an activity of God. References to "our appointed lot" (NEB, cf. RSV), like the use of the verb "destined," wrongly suggest an impersonal fate, which is far from Paul's way of thinking. The context shows that here "we" includes Paul, his companions, and the Thessalonians. In the next verse, however, the Thessalonians are excluded from "we."

The rendering of such persecutions are part of God's will for us must be done with care. Otherwise the reader may think that God himself had purposely planned or even organized the persecutions against the Christians in Thessalonica. In some languages it may be necessary to say "God has permitted these persecutions to come to us," or "God has allowed these people to cause us to suffer." It is sometimes possible to speak of "God's will" as being "God's plan," for example, "God's plan for us includes our being caused to suffer."

3.4 For while we were still with you, we told you ahead of time that we were going to be persecuted; and, as you well know, that is exactly what happened.

This verse contains little that is new. It repeats and expands the content of verse 3, adding only "(you know) because we told you beforehand." In the original, this new statement is emphasized by "and," which Phps idiomatically translates "actually we did warn you."

Because verses 3 and 4 overlap so much, one of the stylistic problems in translation is to avoid excessive repetition of particular words. Even TEV has not avoided "persecutions...persecutions...persecuted."

Ahead of time in the original means simply "at a point of time earlier than another event"; in this context, earlier than the persecutions themselves. The same expression in English tends to mean "in advance of a fixed time," but this is not the meaning of the Greek. Ahead of time may be rendered simply as "before it happened to you," or "before you were caused to suffer."

We were going to be persecuted is one way of translating a phrase which sometimes, and probably here, refers not merely to something which is going to happen in the future, but to something which has to happen (with the implication, as in verse 3, that it is part of God's will). The same verb is used in Luke 9.31, where TEV translates "...he would soon fulfill God's purpose by dying in Jerusalem." TEV here reverses two phrases in the original, placing the semantically subordinate "as you know" before the new information "that is what happened" (exactly is implied).

The word we occurs three times in verse 4. In the first two instances Paul clearly refers to himself and his companions, but not to the Thessalonians. However, the Thessalonians are included in the third we, since they too are involved in the persecution. This distinction must be reflected in the translation in languages which distinguish between the inclusive and the exclusive first person plural.

That is exactly what happened may be rendered more specifically as "we did in fact suffer persecution."

3.5 That is why I had to send Timothy. I could not bear it any longer, so I sent him to find out about your faith. Surely it could not be that the Devil had tempted you, and all our work had been for nothing!

This verse summarizes and concludes the section which begins at 2.17. In the first part of the verse, Paul focuses on his own experience, but by the end of the verse he seems to be associating himself as usual with the other two men who have shared his work. (NEB translates otherwise.) Here, in contrast to verse 1, the transitional that is why points backwards to the reason Paul has just indicated. I had to send Timothy is implied. The Greek has simply "I sent (him)," but most translations supply "Timothy"; "had to" is less essential; DuCL restructures: "So I could hold out no longer, and therefore obtained information about your faith." The "know" of KJV and RSV fails to bring out a distinction between the words for "know" used here and in verses 3-4. Here it is a question of "getting to know" or "finding out" something.

The expression I had to send Timothy should not be translated in such a way as to imply that someone compelled Paul to send Timothy. The compulsion was born of Paul's own feelings and love for the Thessalonians. Therefore, one can often translate more effectively as "that is why I felt I must send Timothy."

I could not bear it any longer is a direct reflection of the first sentence in 3.1. Again, this is a reference to Paul's not being able to endure longer his absence from or lack of information about the Thessalonians. In this instance one may translate "I could not continue any longer not knowing about you."

About your faith is sufficiently clear in English, but GeCL makes the phrase rather more explicit: "how it stands" (that is, what the position is) "about your faith." Paul is here not so concerned about the specific content of the faith which the Thessalonians had, but about how they were continuing in their trust and confidence in Jesus Christ. This may be rendered as "to find out how you were progressing in your trusting Christ," or "to know how you were making out in your faith in Christ."

There is no serious doubt about the connection of 5b (surely it could not be . . . !) with what precedes, but Paul does not put it into words. Many translators supply a verb indicating anxiety: NEB "fearing that the tempter might have tempted you"; Brc "for I was worried in case the tempter had tempted you" (cf. Zur GeCL FrCL Seg JB TOB). TEV's exclamation conveys the implied emotion, but perhaps overstates Paul's confidence. Another possibility is to transform the original indirect question into a direct one: "What if the tempter . . . ?" or "Could it be that the tempter. . . ?"

"The tempter might have tempted" provokes the question: "What else would one expect the tempter to do?" How is the translator to avoid the flatness and redundancy of this expression? The question is not only stylistic; it is a question about what precisely Paul meant. One partial answer is that he was using "the Tempter" as a proper name or title of Satan (in the same way as "the Baptizer" became a title of John the Baptist). That is why TEV (cf. FrCL SpCL) has the Devil, and BJ and TOB have "the Tempter" with explanatory notes. A second factor is that the verb tempted, in the mood and tense used here, implies a real event at a specific point of time, not something like "lest perchance the devil might tempt you." This is brought out by TEV's pluperfect had tempted, and still more clearly by BJ's "already." GeCL's "the tempter could have brought you to (a) fall" makes explicit the fear that the Thessalonians had not only been tempted, but that they had given in to the temptation. This meaning is not normally included in the meaning of "tempt," but the last part of the verse virtually demands it here. One other possible rendering is: "What if the devil had tempted you in such a way as to make all our work useless?" The lack of explicit connections in this verse reflects the tension of the situation. Even the memory of his anxiety seems to start Paul's thought moving faster than he can dictate.

It is extremely difficult in some languages to render the type of exclamation occurring in the last sentence of verse 5, Surely it could not be that the Devil had tempted you, and all our work had been for nothing! This exclamation reflects his deep concern. Accordingly, it may be necessary to use a direct statement, as in the Greek text, introduced by a verb of "worry," "concern," or "constant thinking about," for example, "I could not keep from worrying that the Devil had tempted you and all our work had been for nothing," or "I kept asking myself whether perhaps the Devil had tempted you. . . ."

Work (cf. 1.3) is a word which implies costly effort (cf. Brc "hard work"); it should not be confused with the current usage in which "the work" becomes a mere synonym for church activities in general. For nothing (see the notes on 2.1) means here "unproductive," "fruitless," with the additional component of a change of situation, in which the evangelists' work is made useless or "reduced to nothing" (Seg). Phps' translation, "to make sure that the tempter's activities had not destroyed our work," is excellent and natural English, but it disguises the fact that the English word "work" can mean both labor, the act of working, and the product of that activity (cf. "handiwork"). In the first sense, work cannot be undone, yet this is the primary meaning of the Greek word Paul uses. In some languages, though not in English, it may be necessary to preserve the distinction by some such expression as "destroy the results of all our work."

The possible fruitlessness of Paul's activity in Thessalonica can be expressed in two different ways: (1) either as accomplishing nothing, for example, "all our work there had turned out to be nothing" or "all our work there really ended up with no result"; or (2) it can be an expression of destruction of what had been accomplished, for example, "that all our work there had been destroyed," or "that all we did there had been ruined."

TEV	RSV
6 Now Timothy has come back, and he has brought us the welcome news about your faith and love. He has told us that you always think well of us, and that you want to see us just as much as we want to see you. 7 So, in all our trouble and suffering we have been encouraged about you, brothers. It was your faith that encouraged us, 8 because now we really live if you stand firm in your life in union with the Lord. (3.6-8)	6 But now that Timothy has come to us from you, and has brought us the good news of your faith and love and reported that you always remember us kindly and long to see us, as we long to see you-- 7 for this reason, brethren, in all our distress and affliction we have been comforted about you through your faith; 8 for now we live, if you stand fast in the Lord. (3.6-8)

GeCL begins a new section here, under the section heading "Reassurance through Timothy." Though adequate in itself, this title gives little idea of the emotive content of the passage. This is marked by (1) a variety of words denoting thanksgiving, joy, and longing; (2) frequent repetition, sometimes to the point of redundancy (see notes on v. 6), of the personal pronouns "you" and "we"; (3) brothers, once more, in v. 7; (4) the use of strong expressions such as day and night and with all our heart (see notes on v. 10); (5) long sentences (6-8 and 9-10) with an element of repetition; (6) a rhetorical question in verses 9-10. The translator's most important decision in this passage will be his choice of means by which this emotive content can be transferred into the receptor language. Phps' use of parentheses, exclamation, and other features is a useful example of how this may be done in English, but Phps is not a common-language translation.

3.6 Now Timothy has come back, and he has brought us the welcome news about your faith and love. He has told us that you always think well of us, and that you want to see us just as much as we want to see you.

This passage is closely related to verses 1-5, but marks a new stage, introduced by a word which may indicate either a contrast or a transition. Those translations which take it as contrastive (KJV Mft RSV Phps NEB TNT Zur Lu Seg Syn FrCL SpCL) translate the word as "but" (cf. JB "however"); those which take it as a transitional (Knox Brc TEV GeCL BJ TOB DuCL) simply do not translate it. There is indeed an element of contrast: Paul sent Timothy to Thessalonica because he was anxious, but now that he has returned with good news, Paul is reassured.

A special problem for English translators is that now may indicate either a transition or a point in time. As a transition it usually occurs at the beginning of a sentence (e.g. Genesis 3.1 RSV: "Now the serpent was more subtle..."). In this verse, the Greek uses two different words to express (1) the contrast (or transition, see last paragraph) and (2) the now which indicates present time, and it may be necessary to use two different words in translation also.

In pre-New Testament Greek, the temporal now was used to refer to something which had just happened, and here, in an emphatic position at the beginning of the sentence, it may still have this meaning. Mft ("a moment ago"), Brc TNT ("has just returned"), GeCL Seg Syn BJ TOB translate it in this way. By New Testament times, however, the word more often meant simply "at the present time," and this is the translation chosen by Knox TEV Zur Lu FrCL DuCL SpCL.

Though the Greek text specifies that Timothy has returned "to us from you," it is strictly redundant to add these words in translation. They are one of the emotive elements in the original, but a literal translation may have the effect of making the sentence heavier. SpCL translates more simply "Timothy has come back from Thessalonica"; GeCL "has come back from you"; DuCL "is back with us." If either "to us" or "from you" is omitted, it fits in better with the context to omit "to us," since Paul's main concern is not with his reunion with Timothy, but with the news Timothy brought back about the situation in Thessalonica. TEV omits both phrases.

He has brought us the welcome news. Paul uses here the verb which generally refers to the communication of the Christian message, the announcement of the Good News. Here it has the meaning which is usual in secular writings: that of bringing any kind of good news. It is therefore essential to avoid any translation which might suggest the specifically Christian sense. It is probably for this reason that TEV has welcome news instead of the more common "good news" (RSV and NEB), which when read aloud could be misunderstood as "the Good News."

In some languages one does not say "to bring news." Rather, "one comes and speaks news." The translation of welcome refers to the emotive response of those who heard the news, for example, "news which made us happy" or, idiomatically, "news which soothed our ears."

About your faith and love. Commentators discuss whether Paul is thinking mainly of the Thessalonians' love for God or for one another. This becomes a problem for the translator only if the nouns are replaced by verbs requiring a direct object. In this case, it would be more natural to refer "love," like "faith," to the Thessalonians' relationship to God (see the notes on 1.3). This would give a translation something like "he has brought the welcome news that you still trust God and still love him." However, Paul rarely writes about men loving God (see notes on 2 Thess. 3.5), and it may be better to translate "he has brought the welcome news that you still trust God and still love one another."

He has told us that you always think well of us. He has told us is inserted in order to begin a new sentence. The components of meaning in the phrase translated think well of us include (1) remembrance and (2) either (a) affection or (b) respect or (c) both. In translating the first component, it should be borne in mind that the time between Paul's leaving Thessalonica and writing this letter was almost certainly counted in months rather than in years. TEV rightly avoids any suggestion that an effort of memory was needed. Within the second component of meaning, the Greek can convey both affection and respect, but the translator may have to choose which is more important in this context. The same expression is used in 2 Maccabees 7.20 in speaking of a heroic mother who "deserves to be remembered with special honour" (NEB). TEV's think well of us brings out this element of respect, while NEB's and Brc's "think kindly of us" emphasizes the element of affection (cf. Knox SpCL; also Phps "cherish happy memories of us," cf. DuCL; JB "remember us with pleasure"; cf. TNT BJ). On balance, the element of affection seems to fit in better with the warmth of the passage as a whole. An appropriate expression for affection in this context could be "you remember us with happiness," "you are happy when you think of us," or "your thinking about us causes you to have joy."

The center of gravity, so to speak, of this phrase is the Greek word often rendered as "good," and it is to this that always should be related: not "you are continually thinking of us" (unless possibly as an emotive exaggeration), but "your memories of us are all good ones," "whenever you remember us, it is in a good sense."

Some editions of the Greek text punctuate this sentence in such a way as to connect always with what follows (i.e. "wanting to see us"), but this is less natural than the punctuation followed by TEV and most other translations.

You want to see us. The word translated want conveys strong emotion, like the English verb "long" in "long to see us." As in verse 2.17, see must be rendered as implying "visiting" rather than merely looking at.

3.7 So, in all our trouble and suffering we have been encouraged about you, brothers. It was your faith that encouraged us,

So clearly refers back to what has preceded, implying "because Timothy has come back with such good news." This is what encouraged Paul and Silas. At the end of the verse, Paul indicates that Timothy's message is about the Thessalonians' faith. Since so must be related to the encouragement and not to an expression of trouble and suffering, it may be necessary to place the phrase in all our trouble and suffering at the end of the first sentence of this verse. This may be particularly important if the phrase in all our trouble and suffering must be turned into a clause.

In all our trouble and suffering. Paul uses here two nouns which are close to one another in meaning, and are both often used in passages about the last days. Trouble suggests the distress which comes from being under pressure, and having little or no freedom of action; suffering implies primarily, though not exclusively, bodily harm resulting from an enemy's attack. Since leaving Thessalonica, Paul has been rejected at Berea and Athens and has met with many difficulties at Corinth (see 1 Corinthians 4.11; 9.12; 2 Corinthians 11.6). In all our trouble and suffering is often translatable as a clause of what is sometimes called "attendant circumstance," for example, "while we have been undergoing so much trouble and have been suffering."

Faith, in this context, is seen as a continuing state of reliance on Christ, rather than an individual act of trust. Its meaning is amplified in the next verse by stand firm in your life in union with the Lord. It involves a relation of trust and dependence which, as Paul suggests in verse 10, can deepen and mature. It has a content which must increase and grow.

There is a direct causative relation between your faith and the encouragement which Paul and his colleagues received, but since in many languages faith must be expressed as a verb, the causative relation may be indicated by a conjunction such as "because" or "since," for example, "because of the way in which you trust Christ, we are encouraged." The focus here is not upon the fact that the Thessalonian Christians had believed in Christ, but upon the manner in which they were continuing in their faith. Phps changes the sentence into the active: "This has cheered us, my brothers."

3.8 because now we really live if you stand firm in your life in union with the Lord.

Now we really live. Really is implied, but most translators feel the need to add something to clarify the way in which Paul is using the word live. During the period in which he had no news from Thessalonica, his life in some sense went on; Paul is not denying this. Nor is he thinking of "eternal life," which remained a foretaste even after Timothy's return. Some commentators think that Paul meant "If I had gone any longer without news of you, the anxiety would have killed me," but this interpretation is rather farfetched. Some translators (Lu GeCL BJ FrCL TOB DuCL) add "again" or some equivalent after live, as if Paul had died during the period of his anxiety, but had now come to life again (cf. SpCL "It is like new life for us, to know that you stand firm"; JB, more weakly, "now we can breathe again"). The most likely explanation is that for Paul, as for Hebrew thought in general, life is not simply the opposite of death, just as peace is not simply the absence of war. There are degrees of being alive. Isolation from the community, like illness, can make a person less alive. In many languages, such an expression is not understood as mere figurative speech or interpreted as "spiritual truth," but as reality. Conversely, the renewal of a relationship, like the restoration of health, increases life and makes it full. So it was with the renewal, through Timothy, of Paul's relationship with the Thessalonians. Knox conveys this concept well: "it brings fresh life to us"; and so does Brc: "it makes life worth living for us." Paul's life is bound up with that of the Christian communities he has helped to found.

The ways in which live is qualified in this kind of context differ widely from language to language. In some instances one may simply say "now it is good to live if you stand firm," "now it means something for us to live if...," or "now we are happy to live if...."

If you stand firm. Paul makes here what, in classical Greek, would have been a grammatical error (which the pedantic copyists of a few manuscripts have "corrected") in order to express his confidence that the Thessalonians are in fact standing firm. The meaning is: "...if (as I know you are doing) you stand firm," but of course to put this in a normal translation would be to overemphasize the point. Some translations therefore replace "if" by "since" (BJ TOB) or "as" (JB). SpCL "to know that you stand firm" expresses Paul's confidence well, but loses the conditional relation. Paul's life (in the sense suggested in the last paragraph) depends on the stability of the Thessalonians' faith.

Stand firm seems so understandable that translators may not recognize how misleading a literal rendering might be. An expression such as this may have nothing to do with consistency of behavior. Far more frequently one must use an expression such as "continue strong," "remain hard," "walk the same path," or, negatively, "do not turn aside from" or "do not depart even a little from."

In your life is added in translation, to explain in union with the Lord (literally "in Lord"), an expression which Paul uses very often to show the Christian's relation of dependence on and belonging to Christ—the objective counterpart of the Christian's faith (cf. 1.1). In general, life must be modified in terms of some special quality, for example, "good," "real," or "meaningful."

"In the Lord" by itself has little impact in many languages, and may indeed be almost meaningless, at least to people outside church circles. There is no general solution to the problem of translating this expression, since its meaning varies somewhat according to the context. Brc has "if you remain unshakably true to your Lord." FrCL, in similarity with TEV, has "in your union with the Lord," reflecting the view that "in the Lord" involves a (mystical and/or moral) identification of the Christian with Christ. In some languages it is meaningless to employ a phrase such as "in the Lord," since there is simply no way in which one can conceive of a person's being "in Christ" or "in the Lord." However, one can speak about being "joined closely to the Lord" or even "living together with the Lord," thus being in union with the Lord, and in some languages the closest equivalent is "your life for the Lord."

TEV	RSV
9 Now we can give thanks to our God for you. We thank him for the joy we have in his presence because of you. 10 Day and night we ask him with all our heart to let us see you personally and supply what is needed in your faith. (3.9-10)	9 For what thanksgiving can we render to God for you, for all the joy which we feel for your sake before our God, 10 praying earnestly night and day that we may see you face to face and supply what is lacking in your faith? (3.9-10)

From this point onward Paul "takes off" into (1) a rhetorical question (vv. 9-10) which includes references to thanksgiving (v. 9) and petition (v. 10), and (2) a direct prayer for the Thessalonians (vv. 11-13). Together these form the climax and conclusion of the first half of the letter.

3.9 Now we can give thanks to our God for you. We thank him for the joy we have in his presence because of you.

Paul's question "For what thanksgiving can we render to God for you...?"

(RSV), is rhetorical, not only in the sense that it expresses frustration at there being no possible answer. The meaning is that no act of thanksgiving can possibly be enough to equal the joy which Paul has received from God in hearing about the Thessalonians' faith. Most translations keep this verse (but not verse 10 which in Greek is part of the same sentence) in the form of a question. Three translations (TEV GeCL Seg) change the form of the sentence. They adopt three different solutions. TEV turns the question into a statement, perhaps losing both some emotive impact, and also the idea that, although Paul and his companions do give thanks to God, their thanks will never bear any proportion to the joy they have received. Seg makes the sentence an exclamation: "What thanks we can give God for you... !" GeCL makes the verse a negative statement, and this is perhaps the most attractive solution: "We cannot thank our God enough for you." Several translations which keep the rhetorical question add "enough" or some equivalent after "thank God," and this is almost required by the context: Paul does thank God, but, he believes, not "adequately" (Brc). Give includes the meaning of giving in return for something one has received. It is often very difficult to translate "we cannot thank... enough." Rather than a negative expression, most languages seem to prefer one that is emphatic and positive, for example, "we do thank God very much." Another arrangement of the elements in this sentence may give a rendering which parallels TEV, for example, "the joy which we have when we pray to our God." For a language which uses inclusive and exclusive first person plural, "we" should be exclusive but "our" should be inclusive, since the latter reference must include the Thessalonians.

In translating we can give thanks to our God for you, it is important to understand for as indicating cause. It is not on behalf of the Thessalonians that Paul gives thanks; the Thessalonians are the ones who caused Paul to give thanks to God. Therefore, one can translate "now because of you we can give thanks to our God."

The Greek introduces the question with a conjunction which, in questions, is roughly equivalent to the English interjection "why!" (as in Matthew 27.23: "Why, what harm has he done?" NEB). Most translations omit this word here without appreciable loss of meaning.

The joy is literally "all the joy," like "all our trouble and suffering" in verse 7. In both verses, "all" intensifies the following noun(s), and does not mean "all" as opposed to a part. "All the joy" is therefore translated by GeCL as "the great joy."

KJV's "all the joy wherewith we joy" reflects a repetition in the text which goes back to a Hebrew idiom (e.g. Isaiah 35.2) which is strange in most other languages. It occurs also in John 3.29, where even KJV chose the idiomatic translation "rejoiceth greatly" instead of the literal "rejoices with joy." The combined effect of "all the joy with which we rejoice" is to intensify the expression of Paul's happiness.

For the joy is an expression of cause for thankfulness (compare for you in the previous sentence). Note, however, that in this instance the Thessalonians are the cause for the joy, and joy is the cause of thankfulness. In some languages this relation may be expressed as "because of you we have joy, and therefore we thank him."

In his presence translates the phrase "before our God." "Before" is often used in speaking about a relationship, especially of prayer. This can be brought out in translation, either as TEV does, with "presence" implying a relationship of prayer, for example, as GeCL translates the whole verse: "We cannot thank God enough for you and for the great joy which he causes us to have in you."

3.10 Day and night we ask him with all our heart to let us see you personally and supply what is needed in your faith.

Paul moves naturally from thanksgiving to speak of his prayers of petition. Most translations end the rhetorical question with verse 9, and begin a new, affirmative sentence. On day and night, see the notes on 2.9. This letter contains frequent, partly rhetorical expressions indicating continual action; for example, "unceasingly" 1.2; 2.13; 5.17; "always" 1.2; 3.6; 4.17; 5.15, 16.

With all our heart translates a rare but characteristic Pauline compound adverb, comparative in form, but in meaning conveying the greatest possible emphasis. It is simply an emphatic expression of desire, and it may be combined with ask as "we asked him very much indeed." In some languages the expression is rendered idiomatically as "we asked him with our hearts exposed," or "we asked him with a pain in our insides."

See you personally may be rendered either as "visit you" or "be with you." This is not merely physical sight, but association and fellowship.

Paul's anxiety about the Thessalonians has been removed, but his longing to see them personally (the Hebrew idiom "to see your face," which we have met in 2.17) is greater than ever. This is because neither the faith of the Thessalonian Christians, nor the evangelists' work among them, is yet complete.

What is needed in your faith means that their faith still lacks something which it is the task of Paul and his companions to supply. On faith, see the notes on 1.8. It is useless to speculate in detail on what Paul thinks the Thessalonians' faith still lacks, but the teaching of chapters 4 and 5 may be taken as a sample of the kind of instruction he would have wanted to give them in person. The Thessalonians have responded positively to the Christian message, but their faith needs to mature in particular acts of obedience. In translation, it is better to avoid any expression which suggests that Paul is blaming the Thessalonians for having a faith which is less than fully mature. JB's "shortcomings," Mft's "what is defective," and Best's "deficiencies" are unfortunate in this respect. Like the widow in Luke 21.4, with respect to whom the same word is used, the Thessalonians do not have everything they need (cf. Colossians 1.24). GeCL translates "For we would like to help you, so that nothing more is lacking to your faith." Similarly, TEV's supply is more appropriate here than Brc's "repair" ("any deficiencies"). The word Paul uses can indeed mean "repair" (as in Mark 1.19), but here it is less a question of repairing damage than of supplying a lack.

Supply what is needed may be rendered in some languages as "give you what still you do not have" or "give you what you should have," while in your faith may often be rendered as "for your faith." When a verb is required for "faith," one may translate as "give you what you still need if you are really to trust Christ as you should."

TEV

11 May our God and Father himself and our Lord Jesus prepare the way for us to come to you! 12 May the Lord make your love for one another and for all people grow more and more and become as great as our love for you. 13 In this way he will strengthen you, and you will be perfect and holy in the presence of our God and Father when our Lord Jesus comes with all who belong to him.[b]

[b]all who belong to him; *or* all his angels. (3.11-13)

RSV

11 Now may our God and Father himself, and our Lord Jesus, direct our way to you; 12 and may the Lord make you increase and abound in love to one another and to all men, as we do to you, 13 so that he may establish your hearts unblamable in holiness before our God and Father, at the coming of our Lord Jesus with all his saints. (3.11-13)

In these verses, which form a single sentence in Greek, Paul mentions three subjects of his prayer: (1) that the obstacles to a second visit to Thessalonica may be removed (v. 11); (2) that the Thessalonians' love may increase (v. 12); and (3) that they may be made completely holy (v. 13).

These verses are linked by (1) the reference to prayer in verse 10 and the direct prayers of verses 11-12; (2) the theme of "wanting to see" in 2.17; 3.6, 10 and in verse 11; and (3) the reference to supplying "what is needed" in their faith in verse 10 and to "growth" in verse 12.

The beginning of a new paragraph in verses 11-13 is marked, not, of course, by punctuation in the oldest manuscripts (see notes on 1.2), but by the introduction of a new grammatical subject, God...and...Jesus, and by a conjunction which here clearly indicates, not a contrast, but a transition (KJV RSV translate it by the English transitional "now").

There is a less important transition at the beginning of verse 12, marked by the same conjunction and by an emphatic "you." At this point, Paul moves from the first prayer, which is for himself and his companions, to the second and third prayers, which are for the Thessalonian Christians.

The form of the verbs (technically known as the optative mood) translated may...prepare (v. 11), may...make...grow more and more, and may...make ...become...great (v. 12) is rare in New Testament Greek. In Paul's letters, apart from one set phrase, this form is almost always used in the prayers which form the climax and conclusion of large sections of a letter (cf. 5.23; 2 Thessalonians 2.16 f.; 3.5, 16; Romans 15.5 f., 13). It does not involve so radical a break in the structure of the letter as would a prayer addressed to God in the second person (e.g. "O God, prepare our way..."). God and Christ are still referred to in the third person, but the form of the main verbs makes it clear that Paul is not merely telling the Thessalonians (as he does in verse 10) what he prays at other times, but that these verses are themselves an act of prayer. This is conveyed in most English translations, as in TEV, by the construction "May God...." However, a few modern translators, feeling perhaps that this or corresponding forms are no longer part of common language, use a normal indicative: "It is our prayer that our God...may open up the way..." (Brc); "We want God...to help us so that we can go and visit you" (SpCL); "We ask God...to smooth (our) path to you" (GeCL). In many languages it is impossible to use an indirect expression implying prayer. One must indicate clearly that verses 11-13 are the substance of a prayer by using some introductory phrase, such as "I pray to our God and Father himself." This is not a direct address, but it indicates clearly to the Thessalonians the content of Paul's prayer.

Another general feature of this passage, which it shares with verses 6-10, is the frequent repetition of nouns and (especially) pronouns referring to Paul and his companions, the Thessalonians, God, and Christ. The effect of this repetition is to emphasize the close relationship which exists between them. Yet it is not an exclusive or inward-looking relationship, for it includes an unrestricted love for all people (v. 12). This frequency of reference to personal relationships is illustrated in Diagram 2. The relations indicated by the arrows are of different kinds, and it is not suggested that the first all (item 8) refers to the same people as the second all (item 16). Details are discussed below. The purpose of the diagram is simply to illustrate the theme of personal relationships which underlies Paul's prayer. This is intensified by (1) the comparison expressed in items 6-8 and 9-10, (2) the reference to love, and (3) the repreated use of the title Father.

3.11 May our God and Father himself and our Lord Jesus prepare the way for us to come to you!

Paul's first prayer is that God and Jesus together may make possible another visit to Thessalonica. The word translated himself is commonly used by Paul at the beginning of his prayers (cf. 5.23; 2 Thess. 2.16; 3.16). By New Testament times, the word had lost some of its earlier emphatic force, and in this and similar contexts it may be something of a formula. If this is so, the word would be best omitted in translation, as in Mft GeCL DuCL. On the other hand, it is here in an emphatic position at the beginning of a sentence, and so may express a further link with the whole preceding passage 2.17—3.10. This would imply the following: "Satan has done everything possible (cf. 2.18; 3.5) to keep us apart, and has so far succeeded. We therefore pray that God himself and our Lord Jesus (the only higher power to whom we can appeal) may overrule Satan's efforts and bring us together again." In this case, the word himself, which is included in most translations, would be justified.

In many languages one cannot speak of Father without identifying the person(s) to whom he stands in that relation; that is, kinship terms such as "father" must always be possessed. In general, the possessive pronoun used with "Father" in this type of context would be the inclusive first person plural, if one must distinguish between first person inclusive and exclusive, for example, "I pray that

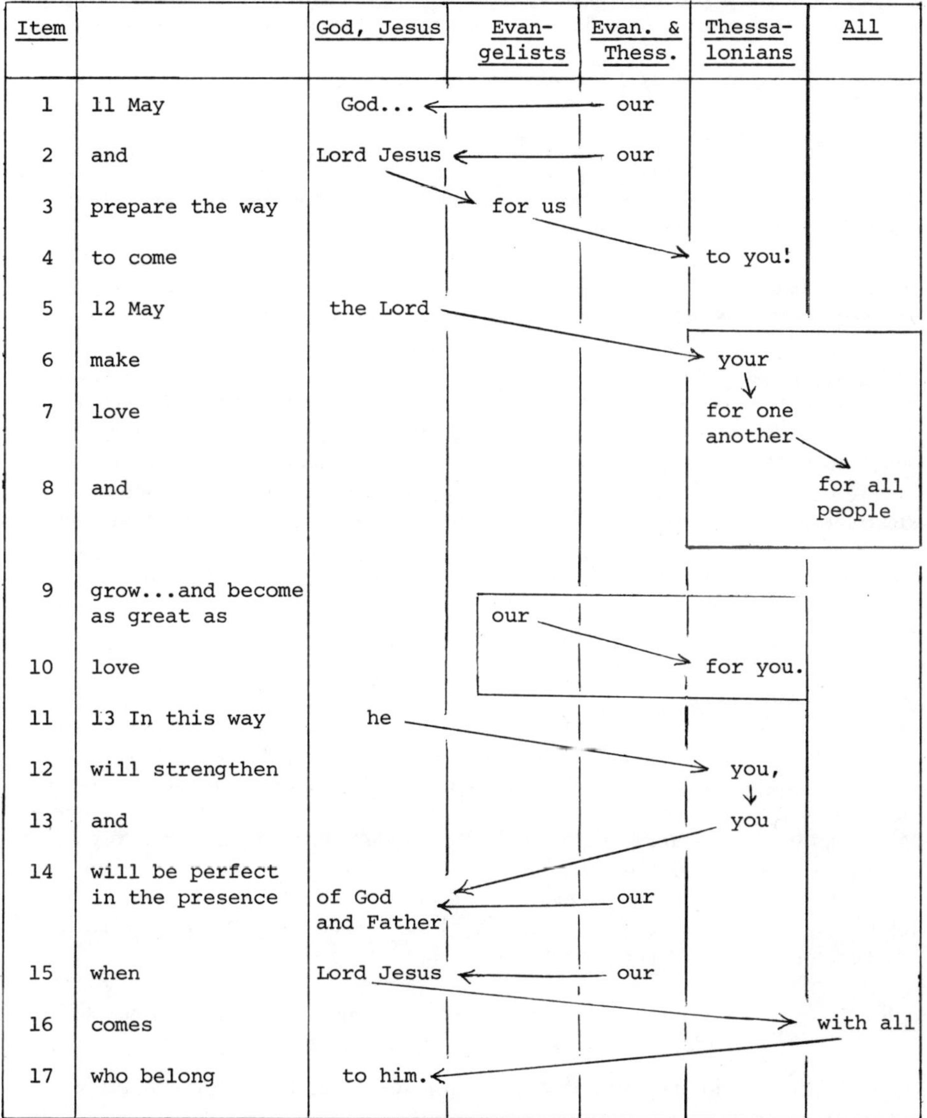
Item
God, Jesus
Evan-gelists
Evan. & Thess.
Thessa-lonians
All
1
11 May
God...
our
2
and
Lord Jesus
our
3
prepare the way
for us
4
to come
to you!
5
12 May
the Lord
6
make
your
7
love
for one another
8
and
for all people
9
grow...and become as great as
our
10
love
for you.
11
13 In this way
he
12
will strengthen
you,
13
and
you
14
will be perfect in the presence
of God and Father
our
15
when
Lord Jesus
our
16
comes
with all
17
who belong
to him.

DIAGRAM 2

our God and our Father himself." A connective such as "and" might give the impression that there are two deities. Accordingly, apposition or a relative clause may be necessary, for example, "our God, our Father" or "our God, who is our Father."

God and Jesus are so united in Paul's thought and prayer that he can link them as subjects of verbs (may...prepare, v. 11, may...make...grow more and more and may...make...become...great, v. 12) which in Greek are in the singular. This emphasizes the way in which Paul can speak first of God the Father and immediately after of Jesus in relation to the same activities. KJV's addition of "Christ" (after "Lord Jesus") is unlikely to be a part of the original text. Modern translations, with the exception of Knox and JB (but not BJ), have our Lord Jesus, which is almost certainly correct.

The exact meaning of the word translated prepare, and therefore of the metaphor prepare the way, is not certain in this context. The verb may mean either (1) "to make straight," or (2) "to guide or direct." If the second possibility is chosen, a human object must be supplied: "may God guide us along the path which leads to you." Phps, for example (cf. Knox NEB TNT Syn), translates "guide our steps to you." "To make straight" seems to fit the context better, since the problem is not that the evangelists may lose their way, but that outside obstacles need to be removed. Brc (cf. DuCL) accordingly translates "open up the way," and Zur GeCL Seg BJ have "smooth our path." The Greek word occurring here is related both in form and in meaning to that used in Mark 1.3b: "Make a straight path for him to travel."

In many languages prepare the way, particularly in the meaning which it has in this context, is rendered "make it possible for us to come," or "remove anything that keeps us from coming." In some languages an idiomatic expression, "to clear the path for us to come to you," may be employed.

In some languages it is often important to distinguish carefully the directional implications in terms such as "come" and "go." This means that some languages in this instance may require "go to you" rather than "come to you." It all depends upon the perspective used in a language. Is the point of reference the people to whom one is addressing a letter, or is it the place from which the letter is sent? Careful attention to such details are necessary if one is to avoid serious confusion (see notes on 4.14).

3.12 May the Lord make your love for one another and for all people grow more and more and become as great as our love for you.

Paul's second prayer, like the third in verse 13, is not for himself but for the Thessalonians. The transition is marked by an emphatic "you," almost "As for you, may the Lord..." (see general notes on 3.11-13). The first prayer was addressed jointly to God the Father and to Jesus; the second and third are addressed to the Lord, that is, to Jesus (see notes on 1.6) alone. A few manuscripts add "Jesus" after the Lord. This is not part of the original text, but it gives the correct meaning. God and Christ are so closely linked in this passage (see notes on v. 11) that the change of "addressee" should not be emphasized.

Make...grow more and more and make...become...great translate two Greek verbs. The first means usually "to become more, to increase," and in this sentence "to cause to increase, to make greater." The second is stronger; it means usually "to be more than enough, to be plentiful," and in this sentence "to make extremely rich." TEV's make...become as great as our love for you is the more likely meaning of a comparison which is slightly ambiguous in the original. It could mean either (1) "may the Lord increase your love...until it is as great as our love (already) is for you," or (2) "may the Lord increase (equally) your love...and also our love for you" (literally "as we to you"). TEV chooses the first alternative. As in 1.6 (cf. 2 Thess. 3.7-9), Paul is offering his experience and that of his companions as an example to younger Christians. The theme of growth recalls 3.10 and will be taken up again in 4.1.

The expression make your love...grow is a causative, in which grow refers to an increase of love, which is the central concept. One may need to change the relations in such a way as to say "I pray that the Lord may cause you to love one another and all people more and more."

Your love for one another and for all people. The word translated love is central to the vocabulary and experience of the first Christians (cf. 1.3; 1 Corinthians 13, and many other passages), and has a distinctively Christian meaning. However, one aspect of its distinctiveness was precisely the fact that this love was not limited in its objects to other Christians; it extended to people outside the church, and even, as probably in this verse, to enemies. This aspect distinguished it from the specific "brother-love," that is, love for other members of the Christian family, which Paul mentions in 4.9.

It is often difficult to find a satisfactory word for love, especially if it must include, not only persons of the "in-group," but also outsiders and even opponents. Frequently the term for Christian love is derived from an expression related primarily to affection within the family, but such a term may be so closely associated with in-group affection as to be unusable in a context such as this. In some languages an equivalent for Christian love may be "deep concern for." On the other hand, it is unwise to use one term for affection among Christians and another to indicate the attitude of Christians toward those outside the Christian community. It is also important to avoid terms which suggest mere sentimentality. What has actually happened in many receptor languages is that in the beginning a relatively inadequate term has been adopted, but it has grown in significance as the members of the Christian community have expressed their concern for one another and for others in new and dynamic ways. What began as an inadequate expression of Christian love becomes filled with meaning. That is essentially what happened in the case of the Greek terms which the Christians adopted to express their special love for one another and for God, as well as for God's love for them. As the term was used in the Christian community, the meaning of its content expanded.

It is difficult in some languages to talk about one kind of love being as great as another. This is particularly true if love must be translated as a verb. One may, however, be able to say "I pray that God will cause you to love one another and all people more, so that you will love others as much as we love you," or "...so that you will love others equally as we love you."

3.13 In this way he will strengthen you, and you will be perfect and holy in the presence of our God and Father when our Lord Jesus comes with all who belong to him.

This third petition is more closely linked with the second (v. 12) than the second is with the first (v. 11). The semantic relation between verses 12 and 13 is one of means and purpose (RSV "so that he may establish"), while the relation between verses 11 and 12 is additive (or possibly contrastive). TEV (cf. TNT FrCL) makes this relation one of means and result: In this way he will strengthen you. Many translations begin a new sentence here, either without (NEB Syn) or with (Knox JB TEV BJ) an indication of the link with verse 12. Some translators transfer the idea of purpose to a later point in the sentence, where it is indeed also implied and should be made explicit. RSV's literal translation "establish your hearts unblamable" lacks clarity and therefore impact. JB has "may the Lord so" (manner, "in such a way") "confirm your hearts...that you may" (purpose) "be blameless..." (cf. BJ TOB). Brc clarifies the meaning in another way, by emphasizing an element of time which is implied later in the word when: "It is our prayer that he may strengthen your hearts, until you can stand in blameless holiness."

The movement of thought, from the Lord (Jesus), who will strengthen you, to our God and Father, and back to the coming of our Lord Jesus, produces a rather awkward literary style, but it creates no great problems of understanding. Knox transfers "our Lord Jesus" to the first part of the verse: "So, when our Lord Jesus Christ comes..., may you stand boldly."

The phrase used for strengthen you in the receptor language must be carefully checked to make sure that the translation corresponds to the meaning of the original. Literally the phrase is "make your hearts strong," but it means not merely "strengthen your emotions, make your feelings warmer," but "strengthen your whole inner being," or strengthen you, with a special reference to the strengthening of the Thessalonians' understanding and courage, in preparation for the final test which lies ahead of them. See also the notes on "heart" in 2.4, 17. This interpretation is supported by the fact that everywhere else in the New Testament the word "blameless" (TEV perfect, see next paragraph) is applied to persons. Clearly "your hearts" is very close in meaning to "you yourselves."

The phrase in this way (an expression of means) may be regarded by some persons as ambiguous, because it could refer either to the increased love of the Thessalonian Christians for one another and for other people, or to the Lord's causing such love. If one assumes that the reference is primarily to the Lord's action, one may translate in this way as "by doing this,..." or "by causing you to love more and more, he will...."

The first Christians inherited from the Old Testament and from later Judaism a picture of the last days which they modified by putting Christ at its center. One element in this picture was a trial in which Satan would bring all kinds of accusations against people, and God would pass judgment. This may be in Paul's mind as he uses the word "blameless," which TEV (cf. FrCL GeCL) translates perfect. The implied picture of a court of law is strengthened by the word used for in the presence of, which is most commonly used of being in the presence of a superior, especially an accused before a judge or a subject before a king. The same word is used in a similar context in 2.19.

In many languages perfect must be rendered as a negative, even as the Greek term itself suggests; that is, "people who cannot be blamed," "those against whom there is no accusation," or "those who have no fault." A positive equivalent would be "people who will be acquitted," which suits the wider context well. In this particular context a translation such as "innocent" might suggest too much the idea of immaturity.

The two words translated perfect and holy, literally "unblamable in holiness" (RSV), complement and reinforce one another. The first word is negative in form, and the second positive. The central meaning of holy is that of being set apart from common use in order to be used only in God's service. The implications of the phrase may therefore be "No one (particularly Satan) will be able to blame you for anything, because you will belong so completely to God."

As in 2.19 and 4.15-17, Paul marks the end of a section by speaking of the coming of Christ. On the word for "coming" (when our Lord Jesus comes), see the notes on 2.19 and also below.

A few manuscripts (followed by KJV Knox JB but not by BJ) add "Christ" after Lord Jesus, but this is not likely a part of the original text.

The phrase with all who belong to him (cf. TNT), literally "with all his holy ones," presents two problems, one of text and one of meaning. Some manuscripts add "Amen," but it is not certain that this is part of the original text. The second edition of the UBS Greek New Testament puts "Amen" in a footnote; the third edition puts it in the text, but in square brackets.

The problem of meaning is easier to state than to solve. Who are the "holy ones" of whom Paul speaks? Are they Christians or angels or both? The coming of Jesus with angels is mentioned in 2 Thess. 1.7 (cf. 1 Thess. 4.16). The present text recalls Zechariah 14.5 ("the LORD my God will appear with all the holy ones" NEB), where angels are almost certainly meant. Mft ("all his holy ones") and GeCL ("his heavenly following") appear to understand the present text in this way. So does Best, though he comments: "The argument is evenly balanced and 'saints' is a real alternative; there is almost nothing to be said for the view that both are intended" (153). On the other hand, nowhere else does Paul call angels "saints" or "holy ones," while this is one of his favorite names for Christians. In Colossians 1.26 he uses the same expression "his saints" (TEV "his people") in this way, the pronoun "his" reinforcing the idea of "holy," that is, "the people who belong to God." On the whole, it seems better to take "saints" as referring to Christians, that is, to human, not supernatural beings. TEV in any case gives the basic meaning.

The thought of Christ coming "with all his saints" raises in the modern reader's mind the question: "So will all Christians have died by then?" Chapter 4.15-17 shows that this is a problem, not only for the modern reader and the translator, but for the original readers also. However, the Greek word for "coming" (cf. 2.19) does not always express the idea of movement towards a given place.

It may be somewhat awkward to translate "surrounded by all the people who belong to him," but one can simply say "all the people who belong to him will be with him."

CHAPTER 4

This point marks the most important division within Paul's First Letter to the Thessalonians. Some of his letters can be divided into two main parts, the first concerned mainly with teaching and the second concerned mainly with exhortation or appeal for action, though the two are never wholly separated. The first part of the present letter has been concerned with the relationship of Paul and the Thessalonians; the second part begins here. From now on, the main emphasis relates to the present and the future, not to the past.

The distinction between the two parts should not, however, be exaggerated in such a way as to make it absolute. Rigaux seems to go too far in suggesting (p. 493) that Paul could have stopped at the end of chapter 3, and in speaking of an "artificial liaison" at the beginning of chapter 4. He may, however, be right (no one will ever know!) in thinking that Paul may have interrupted his dictation at this point.

Here, as in less important transitions, there are both (1) features which mark the beginning of a new section, and also (2) links with, and echoes of, what has gone before.

1. The new beginning is marked by the first three words of the Greek text, which are represented by KJV's "Furthermore then..., brethren."

(a) To begin with the third feature, we have already noted Paul's use of brothers to introduce a new development in his thought (see the notes on 2.1, cf. 2.17; 2 Corinthians 13.11; Philippians 3.1; 4.8; 2 Thess. 3.1).

(b) KJV's "furthermore" (TEV finally) is used also in Philippians 3.1 and 2 Thess. 3.1 to mark a major transition to appeal for action. This usage seems slightly different from the use of this word near the end of a letter (e.g. in 2 Corinthians 13.11; Philippians 4.8), where it does have the meaning "finally." We are not obliged to suppose that Paul's letters were written in so haphazard a fashion that, not much more than half way through 1 and 2 Thessalonians and Philippians, he should repeat the mistake of suggesting that he was about to make his last point. TEV's finally is, however, supported by RSV Mft JB (cf. Phps "to sum up"; GeCL "one thing more"; BJ). The more general transitional function of the word is brought out by KJV's "furthermore" (cf. Lu "furthermore," NEB Knox "and now," Brc "it remains to say," SpCL "now"; cf. TNT Zur Seg Syn TOB DuCL).

(c) KJV's "then" can mean "therefore," indicating a strictly logical development, but the context does not suit this meaning here. The word used here, as in many other passages, reinforces the importance of the transition. It is used in Romans 12.1 and Ephesians 4.1 at the major transition between teaching and appeal for action.

It is not, of course, necessary in translation to employ three distinct features to mark the transition, but some way natural to the receptor language should be found to indicate a major change of theme. DuCL's separate sentence, "And now the following, brothers," is one way of doing this. However, in view of the links between chapters 1-3 and 4-5 mentioned in the next paragraph, an even better translation could be: "In this closing part of our letter, then, we beg and urge you...."

2. The content of chapters 4-5 is not unrelated to that of chapters 1-3. The following links may be noted, especially between 3.10-13 and 4.1-12:

(a) The theme of holiness, which dominates 4.1-8, has already been announced in 3.13, and that of love for the brethren (4.9-12) in 3.12.

(b) The theme of doing even more (4.1, 10) has been anticipated in 3.10 (supply what is needed) and more strongly in 3.12 (grow more and more).

(c) The coming of Christ is a recurring theme in both parts of the letter (1.10; 2.19; 3.13; 4.13-18; 5.1-11), though it becomes more prominent in the second part.

(d) In both parts of the letter, Paul stresses that his authority and that of his companions comes from God and from Christ. This is what gives power both to his teaching (1.5; 2.4, 13) and to his appeals for action (4.2-3, 8).

TEV

A Life that Pleases God

1 Finally, our brothers, you learned from us how you should live in order to please God. This is, of course, the way you have been living. And now we beg and urge you in the name of the Lord Jesus to do even more. 2 For you know the instructions we gave you by the authority of the Lord Jesus. (4.1-2)

RSV

1 Finally, brethren, we beseech and exhort you in the Lord Jesus, that as you learned from us how you ought to live and to please God, just as you are doing, you do so more and more. 2 For you know what instructions we gave you through the Lord Jesus. (4.1-2)

4.1 Finally, our brothers, you learned from us how you should live in order to please God. This is, of course, the way you have been living. And now we beg and urge you in the name of the Lord Jesus to do even more.

Finally must be understood as a transitional, equivalent to a phrase such as "in conclusion." It must not be understood in the sense of "you finally learned."

Sometimes Paul's thought is so concise that it is difficult to follow; sometimes it includes repetition for the sake of emphasis. We find both these features in this verse.

First, there is repetition. There is no significant difference of meaning in this context between beg and urge, but the two words reinforce each other (like Phps' "beg and pray"). There are other ways of conveying emphasis; DuCL, for example, has "we ask you most seriously."

Second, there is a train of thought which is compressed to the point of obscurity. Omitting the transitional words which have been discussed above, the sentence may be broadly analyzed into the following statements, in the approximate order of the Greek: (1) We ask you in the Lord Jesus to behave as you should in order to please God. (2) We already told you how you should behave in order to please God. (3) You are behaving in this way now. (4) We want you to do so still more. Even such a preliminary analysis shows that item (2) comes before the others, both logically and in time, that it is naturally followed by (3), and that (1) and (4) are closely related, (4) intensifying part of the meaning of (1). This is the basis for the restructuring and consequent change of order adopted by GeCL and DuCL. The main emphasis falls on item (4), with a secondary stress on item (1). The Greek conveys this by putting (1) at the beginning of the sentence and (4) at the end. TEV achieves the same effect in different ways. First it "de-emphasizes" item (2) by you learned and item (3) by of course, indicating old or assumed information, and suggesting that the main thrust of the verse is still to come. Then items (1) and (4) are combined, and emphasized by the introductory words and now.

Most translations link in the name of the Lord Jesus with we beg and urge you. This is the most probable interpretation. Paul speaks on behalf of Jesus and with his authority. However, the words the name of are implied, and it is possible to link in ... the Lord Jesus with you, and translate, as Brc does, "...to urge upon you as a Christian fellowship." The order of words in the Greek (literally "we beg you and urge in the Lord Jesus") makes this unlikely, as does the close parallel with by the authority of the Lord Jesus in verse 2.

In a number of languages, it is impossible to translate literally in the name of the Lord Jesus and convey real meaning, because so many languages simply do not use the expression "in the name of" as a reference either to the authority of a person or to the source of a communication. The closest equivalent in some languages is "and now, as persons who speak on behalf of the Lord Jesus, we beg you earnestly." It may also be possible to relate "the Lord Jesus" to this urgent request by making him the ultimate source of information, for example, "because of what the Lord Jesus has said, we now urgently beg you." In general, however, it is best to render in the name of the Lord Jesus as an indication of representation, that is, the apostles spoke on behalf of the Lord Jesus as representing him. This is probably the most satisfactory way of indicating that the ultimate authority rests with Jesus, a point which is clearly made in verse 2.

You learned from us is literally "you received from us." Paul refers here and repeatedly later (vv. 2, 6, 11) to teaching he gave during his visit (not to what he has written earlier in this letter). The word "received" is often almost a technical term for the attitude of those to whom the Christian message is handed on (cf. 1 Corinthians 15.1). Paul has received it from Christ (cf. v. 2) and he transmits it to others. NEB brings this out by translating: "We passed on to you the tradition of the way we must live to please God."

How you should live must in some languages be closely related to general conduct, since it is not existence which is in focus, but the manner in which people behave toward one another. It may be necessary, therefore, to translate as "how you should act toward one another," or "how you should act toward people," in order to indicate the broadest possible range of behavior and not merely attitudes toward and actions involving fellow Christians.

How you should live in order to please God is translated literally in RSV.

"To live" and "to please" are not, however, two parallel activities, but they are related as means and purpose, and most translations recognize this. To please God may be rendered as "so that God will be happy," "so that God will look upon what you do as good," or "so that what you do will make God content."

In some languages it is not easy to reproduce satisfactorily a close equivalent of of course. In this context one may introduce the fact of the Thessalonians' having lived in a proper way by saying "I know this is the way you have been living."

The way you have been living is in the present tense in Greek (cf. NEB "you are indeed already following it"), and there is no suggestion that the Thessalonians have just changed their way of life for the worse. Paul is stressing the continuous aspect of their Christian living. This sentence is missing in some manuscripts (cf. KJV), but this omission is almost certainly due to a scribal error.

KJV's "abound more and more" faithfully reproduces a redundancy which is a little strange in Greek, just as in English, and which TEV and many other translations therefore avoid. Paul uses here the same verb which in 3.12 (see notes) was translated make...become...great.

To do even more is an excellent rendering in English, but it poses certain problems in other languages if to do simply refers to living. In fact, it is not an increased amount of living but an increased quality of life which is indicated. Therefore one may need to translate "to do even better," or "to behave toward other people even better."

4.2 For you know the instructions we gave you by the authority of the Lord Jesus.

This verse adds nothing new; its function is to emphasize by repetition (though in other words) you learned from us how you should live and in the name of the Lord Jesus from verse 1. Because of this emphasis, verses 1-2 fulfill something of the same function as a large-type heading in a modern newspaper. Verse 2 looks back to Paul's oral teaching in Thessalonica, but (more important though less explicit) it also looks forward to the more detailed specification of God's will which will begin in verse 3. Paul often tactfully reminds his readers of what he presumes they know already (cf. 1.5; 3.3, 4; 5.2).

You know the instructions we gave you may be rendered as "you know what we told you you should do," or "you know how we told you you should live."

By the authority of the Lord Jesus (cf. Mft) means virtually the same as in the name of the Lord Jesus in verse 1. The variation is one of style, not of content. RSV's literal translation "through the Lord Jesus" (cf. KJV) is unnecessarily misleading. Paul is not saying that Jesus is an intermediary between himself and the Thessalonians. By the authority of the Lord Jesus may be rendered in some languages as "these instructions came from the Lord Jesus" (cf. TNT), "this is just what the Lord Jesus said should be done," or "this is what the Lord Jesus said we should tell you." However, this last expression may suggest a connection between Paul and the Lord Jesus which would be too immediate.

After the introductory verses 1-2, Paul specifies two matters on which he exhorts his readers: sexual morality (vv. 3-8) and Christian fellowship (vv. 9-12).

TEV

3 God wants you to be holy and completely free from sexual immorality. 4 Each of you men should know how to live with his wife[c] in a holy and honorable way, 5 not with a lustful desire, like the heathen who do not know God. 6 In this matter, then, no man should do wrong to his fellow Christian or take advantage of him.

[c]live with his wife; *or* control his body. (4.3-6a)

RSV

3 For this is the will of God, your sanctification: that you abstain from immorality; 4 that each one of you know how to take a wife for himself in holiness and honor, 5 not in the passion of lust like heathen who do not know God; 6 that no man transgress, and wrong his brother in this matter,[c]

[c]Or *defraud his brother in business* (4.3-6a)

Verses 3-6 form a single sentence in Greek. This passage is such a closely knit unit that it will be necessary to discuss verses 3-6a together.

God wants translates the phrase which in Greek is literally "this is God's will." "This" refers directly to "God's will," which is then specified in four ways: (1) to be holy, (2) to be...completely free from sexual immorality, (3) to know how to live with one's wife in a holy and honorable way, and (4) not to do wrong to one's fellow Christian. These and similar infinitives often have the force of imperatives, and may be translated as such ("be holy," etc.) if this is natural. Zur marks the transition from the general (God's will") to the specific (to be holy) by inserting "namely" (quite legitimately, though in unnecessary square brackets). Cf. Phps "God's plan is to make you holy, and that means a clean cut with sexual immorality." To be...completely free from sexual immorality is more specific than to be holy, but not a different point as TEV's and suggests. A comma, or even "that is," is preferable.

Instead of translating the first words literally, "this is God's will," in some languages one may wish to translate "the following is what God wants," or "the things I will mention are what God wants."

"God's will" should not be understood as a remote set of general rules (though it does indicate the content of what God wills, rather than the act of willing). Paul regularly (e.g. 1 Corinthians 1.1) uses this expression in speaking of his personal calling to be an apostle.

There is a tendency for some translators to think that "will" in the phrase "God's will" must reflect some kind of philosophical concept of "inexorable plans" or "predetermined set of circumstances." In this context the emphasis is upon "what God wants" or "what God desires," and so one may translate God wants you to be holy...."

What are the relations between these four specific aspects of God's will for the Thessalonians? This important question cannot be answered until we are clear about the meaning of the individual items. (1) and (2) present no serious problems, but (3) has been and still is understood in radically different ways, and (4) is also open to different interpretations.

1. The word translated to be holy (literally "sanctification," RSV) implies a process which depends on God. On the meaning of holy, see the notes on 3.13. Common language translators have to face the problem of whether holy and related words are part of common language. TEV and FrCL think they are. GeCL translates "God wants your whole life to belong to him," and DuCL "God wants you to lead a life which is devoted to him." It may be difficult to speak of "a life which belongs to God" or even "a life devoted to God." A person, however, may be regarded as belonging to God, and therefore one can translate "to lead such a life as one would who belongs to God," or "to live in such a way as to show that you are devoted to God."

2. God wants you to be...completely free from sexual immorality. The word translated sexual immorality is sometimes translated simply "immorality" (cf. RSV 1st edition and FrCL), but it means more specifically any kind of sexual immorality. It is therefore narrower in meaning than most dictionary definitions of the English word "immoral" (Concise Oxford Dictionary: "Opposed to morality; morally evil; vicious, dissolute"), but in current English there is a strong tendency for sexual overtones to become dominant, while the more precise high-level synonym "fornication" (KJV NEB Knox JB) is becoming archaic and/or ecclesiastical. Phps, as TEV, makes the sexual element explicit: "a clean cut with sexual immorality," cf. SpCL "that no one should have sexual relations outside marriage"; cf. also Mft, RSV 2nd edition "unchastity," TNT. In some languages it may be necessary to be explicit in translating free from sexual immorality, for example, "so that no one will have sexual intercourse with anyone except his or her own spouse." In some instances, however, it is better to employ a term for immorality, and then to state the avoidance of such, for example, "to never live like a dog," "to never go around with other women," or "to never loosen someone else's girdle."

3. Commentators have been divided for many centuries over the meaning, in this context, of the word which TEV translates wife (cf. 1 Peter 3.7). KJV, like the Vulgate, adopts the literal translation "vessel," possibly in the sense of a receptacle for the soul. RSV and Mft (cf. Zur Lu GeCL FrCL TOB SpCL DuCL) agree with TEV in translating wife. NEB Knox Phps JB Brc TNT (cf. Seg Syn BJ) translate "body," which is the main alternative. JB (cf. BJ) regrettably and awkwardly tries to have the best of both worlds by translating "the body that belongs to him." Many translations give the alternative rendering in a note.

The word translated live with implies actually an act of taking possession of or acquiring, and not merely the state of having or possessing. GeCL ("to live together with his wife") and TEV may therefore be too weak, unless the phrase is intended as a euphemism for (b) below. "To get a wife" would therefore mean either (a) "to win a girl to become one's wife" (as in Ecclesiasticus 36.24: "the man who wins a wife has the beginnings of a fortune" NEB), or (b) "to have sexual relations with one's wife," which, together with the following in a holy and honorable way, would make a good contrast with verses 3b and 5. Meaning (a) is the normal meaning of the English expression "to get a wife"; (b) is perhaps the slightly more probable meaning of the Greek in this context, if the translation wife is chosen. If, on the other hand, one translates "body," the entire phrase would mean something like NEB's "each one of you must learn to gain mastery over his body."

Part of the problem is that nowhere else in the New Testament is "vessel" used metaphorically by itself: it is always used in some such defining phrase as "vessel of wrath" or "vessel of the Holy Spirit." Those who prefer the translation "body," however, argue that the "common clay pots" of 2 Corinthians 4.7 (cf. 2 Timothy 2.21) are almost certainly bodies, in the normal biblical sense of human beings in their weakness.

Those who choose the translation "wife" argue that it is more natural to speak emphatically of one's "own wife" (in contrast to the relations outside marriage implied in verse 3) than of one's "own body." However, the word translated "own" is not always emphatic in New Testament Greek (see notes on 2.7). On the other hand, it is argued that the context contains a general appeal, not only to married men, but to the whole Christian community in Thessalonica, and that the translation "body" avoids an abrupt transition.

One solution would be to understand "vessel" as a euphemistic metaphor for the penis (cf. NAB "guarding his member"). This is the most likely translation of the equivalent Hebrew word in 1 Samuel 21.5 (another difficult verse) and parallels in secular Greek are also quoted. There is no parallel in the New Testament, but in view of the subject matter the argument from silence is not strong. The most powerful argument in favor of this meaning is that it would explain the obscurity of the expression, and thus the conflicting interpretations to which it has given rise. Receptor languages differ in the degree of euphemism they employ, in a text of this kind, in speaking of genital organs. If one favors the second of the two solutions, it may be best to choose the translation "body," while recognizing the likelihood that the original reference was narrower. It is interesting to note that in 1 Corinthians 12.23-24 Paul uses the same word for honor as in the present passage ("give greater honor to those parts of the body that lack it").

4. The main difficulty here is in deciding the meaning of the word translated matter (v. 6). This is a general term which can also, in certain contexts, have the specific meaning of "business." Knox (following the Vulgate), Brc GeCL Seg choose this meaning here, but most translators agree with TEV in choosing a more general word. There are two strong arguments in favor of this: (a) there is no parallel to the use of this word in the singular to mean "business" (compare this sense of the English word "affair[s]"); and (b) the translation "business" would involve an abrupt transition from sexual ethics to a discussion of honesty. The two verbs with which matter is associated, do wrong and take advantage, though comparatively rare, may also have general meanings: the first "break a law" or "sin," and the second "defraud, cheat."

Almost all translations which use a general word like matter put the word this before it, in order to make clear the relation to the previous verses. If we adopt this interpretation, we find at this point an implied reference to marriage and the social consequences of sexual immorality. Jews commonly thought of adultery as primarily a sin against the husband of the woman with whom adultery was committed, and this view goes back to the Tenth Commandment ("You shall not covet your neighbor's wife," Exodus 20.17 NEB).

We can now return to the question posed at the foot of page 77: what are the relations between these four aspects of God's will for the Thessalonians? If our understanding of the individual aspects is correct, there is a clear progression in Paul's thought from the general to the specific, with each item related to the one before, and developing part of its meaning. We have noted this kind of movement in several previous passages. (1) God wants to make the Thessalonians completely holy, people whose lives show that they belong to him. (2) In particular, they must avoid sexual immorality. (3) Christians should shine by contrast with pagans in the way in which they control their sexual impulses. (4) If they do this, they will avoid damaging other people's marriages. In other words, Paul warns his readers successively against sin in general, against sexual immorality, against lack of sexual self-discipline, and against adultery.

Paul appeals to the authority of Christ at the beginning and end of this passage (vv. 2, 6b), but in between he stands on common ground with Jews against non-Jews (contrast 2.14-16). This is significant for the translator at two points. First, a negative word like heathen or "pagan" is quite in place in verse 5, as it would not be in 2.16. Second, it would be wrong to translate fellow Christian (literally "brother") in verse 6 in such a way as to overemphasize the distinction between members of the Christian family and others. Paul is speaking to Christians, and by "brother" he does indeed mean fellow Christian, but there is no suggestion that the Thessalonians should behave any differently in this respect towards non-Christians than they would towards other members of the church.

4.4 Each of you men should know how to live with his wife in a holy and honorable way,

In a holy and honorable way is literally "in holiness" (the same word as in verse 3) "and honor" (so RSV). The word translated "honor" means (a) "price" or "value," as in 1 Corinthians 6.20 ("He bought you for a price"), and secondly "honor," "respect," or "esteem." The meaning "honor" or "respect" is needed here, perhaps more specifically "the state of being held in honor" ("respectability" without the ironic overtones of this word in English). If the word "vessel" is translated wife, this phrase will be related to the verb "to get" (to live with). If Paul is referring to the body or a part of the body, the phrase will be related to the noun, as in Knox's translation "Each of you must learn to control his own body, as something holy and held in honour." Holy indicates a relationship with God, and honorable, in this sense, usually a relationship with other human beings. GeCL brings this out by translating "as is pleasing to God and men," and this is particularly natural if "vessel" is understood as "wife."

In addition to the problems of interpretation of verse 4, there are certain difficulties inherent in the expression rendered in the TEV should know how. A literal translation could imply that the people in Thessalonica should know how to be married to a woman in the proper manner, but apparently they did not know! In reality, however, it is not the knowledge which is so important, but the behavior. The focus of attention is not upon marrying a woman, but upon the way a man should behave toward his wife after marriage. Therefore, in some languages this verse is translated as "each of you men should behave toward your wife in a holy and honorable way."

In some languages there is a problem in the use of the singular, when in reality a number of persons are involved. Languages which have distributive plural present no difficulty at this point, but in some languages it may be necessary to say "all men should live with their wives in such a way...." With the use of the plural ("wives"), however, it is important to avoid the implication that each man may have more than one wife.

It may be particularly difficult in some languages to speak of the relation of a man to a woman as being "holy." The Greek term translated "holy" suggests the kind of behavior fitting for the person belonging to God or the kind of behavior which God prescribes. One may therefore translate "each man should behave toward his wife in a way which is right before God and before people," or "...in the eyes of God and in the eyes of people." This type of rendering can be employed since holy is seen to refer primarily to the divine relationship, and honorable to the manner in which people would view such behavior.

4.5 not with a lustful desire, like the heathen who do not know God.

Desire, in Greek as in English, can have both a bad meaning (as here) or a good one (as in 2.17, where it refers to Paul's longing to revisit Thessalonica). Lustful is a translation of the phrase "passion of desire." "Passion," like desire, does not always have a bad sense, but the context clearly requires it here. Lustful desire may be translated as "heart desire" or even "genital desire." In some languages this desire is described as simply "a desire for sex relations," but if this or a similar expression is used, the translation must make it clear that Paul is speaking of a wrong kind of sexual desire.

Who do not know God. The verb know is not the verb used in Romans 1.21 ("they know God"), but there is considerable overlap of meaning between them, and they cannot usually be distinguished in the translation of passages which are so similar as these. The reconciliation of these two texts is a task for the commentator rather than the translator.

The translation of who do not know God can readily lead to misunderstanding since it may imply that these persons "know nothing about God." This is not what Paul is talking about. In this context know must refer to "experience with God" or "acknowledging God in what they do." In some languages an appropriate equivalent may be "they do not reckon with God," or "they do not take God into account." That is, their behavior is without reference to God or to what he has said people should do.

4.6a In this matter, then, no man should do wrong to his fellow Christian or take advantage of him.

In some languages it may be important to amplify the phrase in this matter, so as to make clear that the reference is to the relation between men and women. Therefore, it may be possible to render this transitional phrase as "in the way in which a man conducts himself toward women he should not wrong his brother." If our conclusions in the general notes on this passage are correct, the meaning of "brother" here is properly limited to male fellow-Christians.

Do wrong to his fellow Christian is often rendered as "to cheat his brother" or "to do something against his brother," but it may be necessary in this particular context to render "brother" as fellow Christian. It would be all too easy for persons to understand "brother" in its literal sense, because in this context one is speaking about intimate family relations.

The expressions do wrong to and take advantage of are essentially similar in meaning. The second expression simply reinforces the first. It is, therefore, possible in translation to employ one expression but with some kind of emphatic qualifier, for example, "he should not cheat his brother in anything at all."

TEV	RSV
We have told you this before and we strongly warned you that the Lord will punish those who do that. 7 God did not call us to live in immorality, but in holiness. 8 So then, whoever rejects this teaching is not rejecting man, but God, who gives you his Holy Spirit. (4.6b-8)	because the Lord is an avenger in all these things, as we solemnly forewarned you. 7 For God has not called us for uncleanness, but in holiness. 8 Therefore whoever disregards this, disregards not man but God, who gives his Holy Spirit to you. (4.6b-8)

These verses reinforce by repetition much of the content of verses 1-2.

(a) We have told you this before echoes verse 1.

(b) The contrast between immorality and holiness recalls verse 3. The word for immorality is different in verse 7, but it is also always used by Paul to refer to sexual misconduct. In other authors it may refer more widely to any physically or ritually unclean object or practice.

(c) The insistence in verse 8 on the divine authority of Paul's teaching echoes verses 1-2. This echo not only adds emphasis; it also indicates the conclusion of the paragraph. Despite the continuation of the previous sentence to the end of verse 6, Paul's thought takes a new step with the words we have told you this before, returning from the specific (vv. 3-6a) to the general (as in vv. 1-2).

The grammatical structure of 6b (literally "because the Lord is an avenger ..."), 7 ("for God has not called us ..."), and 8 ("therefore whoever disregards this ...," all RSV) varies, and the introductory words "because," "for," and "therefore" are different in Greek as in RSV (and Brc). However, the introductory words and the sentences they begin are both parallel in meaning; each of them gives a reason why the Thessalonians should respond to Paul's appeal. "For" does not link verse 7 with 6b, but refers back to verses 1-6a, and therefore should probably be omitted in translation to avoid possible misunderstanding. So then in verse 8, on the other hand, is a strong and unusual expression which leads the reader to expect (rightly) that Paul is about to say his last word on the present subject.

4.6b We have told you this before and we strongly warned you that the Lord will punish those who do that.

We strongly warned you may be rendered as "we told you forcefully what would happen," or "we said to you with strong words that you should beware."

The Lord, as usual (cf. notes on 1.2), means Jesus, but Paul's thought (as in 3.11-12 and 4.1-3) moves easily between Jesus and God the Father. Paul will return in 2 Thess. 1.8 to the role of Jesus in judgment.

The background of will punish, which is related to the word for "justice," is the Old Testament idea of retributive justice, whereby a man, a group, or a people was punished, either by God or by a human judge acting on his behalf, in proportion to the crime which had been committed. This was a personal activity, but one related to the law. Modern western culture does not share with the Bible the view of law as based on a personal activity of God. Translators of this and similar texts therefore often have to choose whether to emphasize the idea of just punishment or that of personal hostility. The former is more appropriate, since "avenger" and related words, used by KJV RSV Mft (cf. BJ TOB), have come to be associated with vendettas, gang warfare, and similar illegal activities.

In many languages punish is translated literally as "make to suffer."

Those who do that is literally "concerning all these." KJV understood "these" to refer to people: "the Lord is the avenger of all such" (presumably the "brothers" mentioned, though in the singular). But "these" is much more likely to refer to things, that is, in general terms, to the sins just mentioned. "All" has the effect of making the reference more general: "the Lord will punish those who do this kind of thing." This general reference is brought out by the word "such" in Brc (cf. GeCL FrCL).

There is much overlap of meaning between told you...before and strongly warned you, the second verb being stronger than the first, and the two together stronger than either would be alone. Some translations combine the two: "we have already most solemnly warned you" (TNT cf. RSV), "we told you before with all emphasis" (NEB), "we have already very definitely told you" (Brc cf. FrCL SpCL). The repeated references to Paul's earlier oral teaching suggest that he means "we told you before now" rather than "we told you before the punishment comes." Strongly warned could also mean "bore witness" ("testified" KJV), and Phps expands this interpretation into "we have seen this work out in our experience of life." Phps' interesting rendering does not limit or restrict God's activity of punishing to the "last days," but the coming judgment is such a frequently recurring theme in this letter that Phps' interpretation is unlikely, and it is not shared by other translators.

4.7 God did not call us to live in immorality, but in holiness.

God did not call us makes it clear, as RSV's "has not called us" does not, that Paul is referring to a specific event, not to a state or a process. "Us" clearly includes both the Thessalonians and the evangelists.

Call must not be understood in the sense of "shouting to," but in that of "inviting," that is, "inviting us to be Christians" (cf. 1.4). In many languages it is necessary to change the location of the negative, for example, "for God called us, but not for us to live in immorality; rather, he called us to be holy."

To live in immorality, but in holiness is literally "for immorality, but in holiness." The preposition "for" suggests "this was not the purpose God had in mind when he called us," and "in" suggests "to live in a state of holiness." TEV combines the ideas of purpose and state, and applies them to both immorality and holiness.

To live in immorality may be rendered as "to live immorally," or "to have sexual relations with a person to whom one is not married."

Holiness should refer to the condition of a person who lives as one who belongs to God. Hence it is rendered in some languages as "God called us to live as those who belong to him."

4.8 So then, whoever rejects this teaching is not rejecting man, but God, who gives you his Holy Spirit.

The Thessalonians had received Paul's message about Christ as a word from God (2.13), but Paul now reminds them that if they reject the moral appeal that goes with this message, they are rejecting God. Whoever rejects this teaching may be rendered "whoever refuses to follow this teaching," or, idiomatically, "whoever throws this teaching away." Some languages introduce direct discourse to express rejection, for example, "whoever says no to this that we have taught," or even "whoever says about what we have taught, This is not true."

As in many other instances, it may be necessary to have a positive before the negative, for example, "that man is saying no to God; he is not just saying no to a man." It is true that to reject the message involves rejecting the person who proclaims the message (in this case, Paul), but since Paul speaks on behalf of God (as representing God's authority), the rejected one is really God himself. Accordingly, it may be necessary to introduce an expression such as "just" in order to indicate that "it is not just a man, but it really is God."

Some Greek manuscripts have a word meaning "also" between God, who and gives you his Holy Spirit ("God, who also gives..."). The UBS Greek New Testament has this word in the text but encloses it in square brackets. KJV and Seg include it, but most translations do not.

Translations vary between God, who gives and "God who has given" (Knox cf. KJV GeCL Seg Syn SpCL). Both concepts are included in the meaning of the Greek, which specifies only that the "giving" extends over a period and is not a single event, as Mft's "gave" suggests.

The order of the last words of this sentence in Greek is somewhat unusual (though not as odd in that language as a literal translation suggests): "giving the

Spirit his the holy to you." The effect is to emphasize "to you" and also "holy." Phps conveys this effect by translating "It is not for nothing that the Spirit God gives us is called the Holy Spirit" (cf. SpCL).

Some manuscripts have "us" in place of "you"—a common confusion between similar sounding Greek words. An emphatic you makes better sense. This is the reading supported by most good manuscripts and followed by most translations, but KJV Knox Phps Brc SpCL have "us."

TEV

9 There is no need to write you about love for your fellow believers. You yourselves have been taught by God how you should love one another. 10 And you have, in fact, behaved like this toward all the brothers in all of Macedonia. So we beg you, our brothers, to do even more. 11 Make it your aim to live a quiet life, to mind your own business, and to earn your own living, just as we told you before. 12 In this way you will win the respect of those who are not believers, and you will not have to depend on anyone for what you need. (4.9-12)

RSV

9 But concerning love of the brethren you have no need to have any one write to you, for you yourselves have been taught by God to love one another; 10 and indeed you do love all the brethren throughout Macedonia. But we exhort you, brethren, to do so more and more, 11 to aspire to live quietly, to mind your own affairs, and to work with your hands, as we charged you; 12 so that you may command the respect of outsiders, and be dependent on nobody. (4.9-12)

Paul turns from the subject of sexual morality (4.1-8, cf. 3.13) to that of love for the brethren (cf. 3.12). The structure of these two sections in Greek presents striking parallels. Paul begins by a reassuring reference to what the Thessalonians have already learned (v. 9, cf. vv. 1-2)—a tactful way of approaching a delicate subject—and he appeals for greater effort in the same direction (v. 10b, cf. v. 1b). Next, he gives details of three specific aspects of his appeal (v. 11, cf. vv. 4-6a). Finally, he indicates the basic motivation of his teaching, again with a reference to what the Thessalonians have already heard. The main differences in structure between verses 1-8 and 9-12 are as follows:

1. In the second section, the theme is announced immediately, before the introduction and general appeal. However, two comments are in order here. Firstly, the subject of relationships within the Christian community was probably somewhat less delicate than that of sexual morality. Secondly, there is greater distance, not only in the order of the passage but also in meaning, between the general theme and the specific details in the second section than in the first (see notes on v. 11, below).

2. The second section is shorter than the first. There are probably two reasons for this. Firstly, verses 1-2 form the introduction, not only to the first section (vv. 1-8), but to the entire second part of the letter (chapters 4-5). Secondly, the subject of the second section may have seemed less urgent, as

well as less delicate, than the subject of the first—at least at the time when Paul wrote this first letter, though he returns to this subject with greater emphasis and at greater length in 2 Thess. 3.6-12, which is the best commentary on 1 Thess. 4.9-12.

3. The basis for the teaching in section one is expressed in terms of reason, while the basis for the teaching in section two is expressed in terms of purpose. This distinction is closely related to the fact that the teaching in the first section is based on the nature of God, whereas the action Paul is recommending in the second section is directed to other human beings, both within and outside the Christian community.

4.9 There is no need to write you about love for your fellow believers. You yourselves have been taught by God how you should love one another.

The new theme is introduced by a transitional which KJV and RSV (cf. Lu) inappropriately translate as "but." As we have just seen, no contrast with the previous section is involved, but rather a close parallel. The transition is made by some translators in a brief phrase: "as for love of the brethren" (Knox cf. Seg Syn JB) or "next, as regards brotherly love" (Phps). The first word, translated about, is often used by Paul to introduce a new subject (e.g. 1 Corinthians 7.25; 8.1; 12.1; 16.1). It forms part of the title of many Greek writings, and has almost the function of a section heading here.

It may seem strange to say There is no need to write you about love for your fellow believers and then do just that. This was a common device in ancient times, and is characteristic of the way in which, at times, Paul implies the right kind of behavior in those to whom he writes, even while urging them on to greater effort and better behavior. This impersonal expression may be rendered in some languages as "I do not need to write about love," or "To write to you about love for your fellow believers is really not necessary."

Love for your fellow believers is one word in Greek. Most older translations (KJV cf. Lu Zur Seg Syn) and some more modern ones (Mft Phps cf. TOB) have "brotherly love," a phrase which has passed into current speech and thereby lost much of its specific original meaning. For the first Christians it meant, not figurative brother-like love, but the love of those who had become, in a very real sense, members of the Christian family. Outside Christian writings (e.g. 1 Maccabees 12.10, 17) the word is used only in speaking of men of common physical descent. In the Old Testament, "brother" meant "fellow Israelite," but Jesus called his followers his own (Mark 3.33 ff.) and one another's (Matthew 23.8) brothers, and this usage was carried over into the early church, regardless of differences of nationality and descent. TEV's apparently loose paraphrase is thus much more precise than the literal equivalent "brotherly love" would be. Compare RSV "love of the brethren" (cf. GeCL); SpCL "love between brothers"; JB "loving our brothers"; FrCL, more explicitly, "love between brothers in the faith"; Brc "the love which should be characteristic of the Christian fellowship"; NEB "love for our brotherhood"; TNT "love for our fellow-Christians." It is a quite different word from that used at the end of the verse in love one another, but the meaning in this context is the same. Here as in 3.12 Paul immediately balances a reference to the love of Christians for one another by a reminder of their responsibilities to those who are not believers (v. 12).

If love for your fellow believers is transformed into a verb expression, it may be necessary to say "about how you should love others who also believe in Christ," or "...your brothers who believe in Christ."

You yourselves is emphatic in Greek as in English. The implied contrast is "you do not need us to write to you, because you have been taught by God" (cf. FrCL DuCL). GeCL changes the focus a little by putting the sentence into the active voice: "God himself has taught you to love one another" (cf. SpCL). The word translated taught by God is not used anywhere else in the Greek Bible; just as we speak of people being "self-taught," so Paul says that the Thessalonians are "God-taught." The means of teaching may be either through the guidance of the Holy Spirit or through experience.

It may be necessary in some languages to change the passive expression you yourselves have been taught by God into an active one, for example, "God himself has taught you how you should love one another."

The exact relation between you...have been taught and you should love is uncertain. The Greek is general enough to convey either a relation of means and purpose ("you have been taught in order that you might love") or a relation of means and result ("you have been taught, and as a result you love one another"). The former is much more likely. The Greek does not imply manner: "taught in what way you should love one another," though the how of TEV (cf. FrCL) might be misunderstood in this sense. Mft cf. JB Brc TNT Lu GeCL Syn JB TOB DuCL have simply "taught...to love one another," with a possible slight loss of meaning. The past tense is not explicit, since "God-taught" is an adjective.

If loving one another is not understood as what God taught, but rather as the purpose of what he taught, then one may translate "God himself has taught you so that you should love one another." If the meaning is taken as result, one may translate "God has taught you, and therefore you love one another."

4.10 And you have, in fact, behaved like this toward all the brothers in all of Macedonia. So we beg you, our brothers, to do even more.

The Thessalonians have put their love into practice, not only in their own city, but throughout the surrounding province of Macedonia (cf. 1.8). The Greek means "you are also doing it," but in English, where the expression "doing brotherly love" is awkward, behaved like this is a good common language equivalent (cf. FrCL). DuCL has "you also put love into practice towards..." (cf. GeCL). This is better than "you do this with the brothers..." (cf. SpCL JB). The love of the Thessalonians for Christians in other parts of Macedonia no doubt met with a response, but Paul does not say so here: his concern is with what his readers have been doing.

Because it may be difficult to use a general expression such as behaved like this, one may prefer to use a more specific reference to love of the brethren, for example, "loved all of the brothers in all of Macedonia," or "...all fellow believers...."

The UBS Greek text includes in square brackets a definite article between brothers and in all of Macedonia. If it is included, the meaning would be, as in TEV, the brothers in all of Macedonia. If it is omitted (and the textual evidence seems in favor of leaving it out) the most likely meaning would be "you are behaving like this all over Macedonia, to all the brothers." There is a difference in grammatical form, but the meaning is essentially the same.

The second part of the verse repeats almost verbally expressions used in verse 1. The transitional, translated so, may indicate a contrast, and Phps and NEB accordingly translate "yet" (Brc cf. Lu Seg BJ FrCL have "but"). The contrast is of limited scope, between the love the Thessalonians are showing and the still greater love Paul recommends, and it should not be overemphasized in translation, as JB's "however" tends to do. So is perhaps slightly ambiguous. On a hasty reading, it could be misunderstood as introducing a conclusion or summing up what has been already said; but when the passage is read as a whole, it is clear that Paul's thought is looking forward to the specific advice he has to give in verse 11.

To do even more could be misunderstood if translated literally, even as the same phrase occurring in 4.1 can be misconstrued. Paul does not mean that the Christians in Thessalonica should love more people, since he has already indicated the extent of their love. Evidently it is the quality of their lives (as reflected in verse 11) which is here in focus. Therefore "to do even better" may be a more satisfactory equivalent.

4.11 Make it your aim to live a quiet life, to mind your own business, and to earn your own living, just as we told you before.

The relation between "love for the brethren" in general and the specific instructions contained in this verse is not immediately clear. Paul seems to be more concerned in this verse with the "image" of the Christian community in the outside world than with relationships between individuals within the Christian community. However, in the situation in Thessalonica, the church's external image and its internal relationships must have been closely linked. The church was under pressure from outside, and so any foolish or immature behavior by individuals within the church would have two effects: it would strain relationships with other, more balanced, members, and it would damage the witness of the Christian community to the outside world. It is therefore important in translation to avoid at this point any transitional expression which would suggest that Paul is introducing a fresh subject. For Paul's concern for the "respectability" of the Christian community, see the notes on 4.4.

The three items of instruction which Paul gives in this verse are simply added to one another, as far as the surface grammatical form is concerned. There is, however, a progression within the verse, similar to the progression we have noted in verses 3-6. Each item is somewhat more specific than the one before it. The climax and the most sensitive point are reached with to earn your own living, after which Paul hastens to reassure his readers (rather like a dentist withdrawing his drill!) by the words just as we told you before.

Make it your aim often includes the suggestion of an ambition or a point of honor; GeCL has "consider it a matter of honor" (cf. Seg Syn). The Greek verb may also be translated as "desire very much," "try very earnestly," or "decide this is the way you should...."

To live a quiet life translates a verb which Paul uses only in this text. A related noun is used in 2 Thess. 3.12. In other parts of the New Testament, it can mean "to be quiet," either in the sense of "to rest" (for example, by not working on the Sabbath, Luke 23.56), or in the sense of "not to speak" (e.g. Luke 14.4). The first meaning is explicitly excluded by the context, and the second does not seem appropriate here; therefore a third meaning must be looked for. GeCL translates "lead an orderly life," and this suits the context very well, though close parallels for this meaning are difficult to find. If one asks, "How would the Thessalonians have behaved if they had not followed Paul's instructions on this point?", the phrases immediately following (and later 2 Thess. 3.6-12) seem to suggest the answer, "They would have behaved in such a way as to make themselves justifiably unpopular within the community at large." The ideas of maintaining peace within the Christian community (or even within the individual life) are not excluded, but they are not in the foreground.

In many languages it is easier to describe a boisterous life than a quiet one. Therefore to live a quiet life may be best expressed in a negative manner, for example, "don't go around always making a lot of noise," in which "noise" would imply more than loud sound. It may be appropriate in some instances to translate this advice as "don't go around all the time arguing loudly."

To mind your own business is an idiom with a wide meaning, not being limited to financial or commercial activities. Paul means "go on fulfilling your normal responsibilities." In some languages mind your own business is translated quite idiomatically, for example, "sit in your own shade." Once again, in some languages this concept may be expressed in a negative form; for example, "do not meddle in other people's affairs," or "do not always tell other people how they should do things."

All the infinitives in this verse, make, mind, and earn, like do in verse 10, imply activity over a period of time.

To earn your own living is literally "work with your hands," as in most of the older translations and also in NEB and TNT (cf. TOB SpCL). JB and FrCL agree closely with TEV: Brc has "do an honest day's work"; Phps, "do your work yourselves." DuCL combines the specific reference to manual labor with the wider meaning: "by handwork provide for your own (life-) support." Most of the Thessalonian Christians were no doubt manual workers, but the words "your hands" are not emphasized, and the phrase is defined more closely in the next verse by you will not have to depend on anyone for what you need. TEV is therefore not guilty of transculturating for a society in which manual workers are in a minority.

In some languages to earn your own living can be most effectively translated in a negative manner, for example, "don't expect others to take care of you," "don't make others give you food," or, idiomatically, "don't rest on other people's shoulders," or "don't lie in your hammock all day."

We told you before clearly implies "when we were in Thessalonica." The Greek has the same meaning as the English "to tell someone to do something"; that is, not "to inform," but "to instruct" or "to order." The authority on which Paul has insisted in verses 1, 2, 6, and 8 (as well as earlier in the letter) provides the basis, not only for general preaching and exhortation, but for specific instructions in a particular situation. In some instances it may be useful to translate just as we told you before as "this is just what we before ordered you to do," or even "when we were with you, this is what we told you you should do." The clause "when we were with you" may be the only way in which the fact of a previous order can be clearly indicated, since an adverb like "before" might suggest only a previous letter.

4.12 In this way you will win the respect of those who are not believers, and you will not have to depend on anyone for what you need.

TEV transforms a relation of means and purpose ("in order to win the respect") into one of means and result (in this way you will win the respect), but the two are never clearly distinguished in Greek. The latter seems to be more natural in several western languages, especially when a new sentence is begun at this point (cf. Seg FrCL DuCL; Phps "the result will be a reputation for honesty"; Brc "then the people outside the church will admire your life and conduct"). The original "in order to" is clearly related, not to just as we told you before, but to the appeal to do even more, and to the detailed instruction in verse 11. Paul is not explaining directly the purpose of his teaching, but the purpose of the behavior he is recommending.

The transitional in this way may be effectively translated in some languages as a conditional, for example, "if you do this." The relation to what follows, namely, you will win the respect of those who are not believers, will then express the result. Win the respect of is a rather complex concept which must often be expressed in quite a different way, for example, "you will cause those who are not believers to honor you," or "you will make those who are not believers say, These believers are good people."

Those who are not believers is literally "the (plural) outside." It is very close in form to the English "the outsiders," but does not have the unfavorable implications of this expression. The context shows that Paul means "those outside the Christian brotherhood," and TEV is right to make this explicit. Both pagans and non-Christian Jews are intended.

You will not have to depend on anyone for what you need means literally "so that you may have need" either (a) "of nothing" or (b) "of no one." Meaning (a) is followed by KJV and NEB "may never be in want" (cf. Phps NAB Zur SpCL), and (b) is followed by RSV Knox TNT (cf. GeCL Seg Syn BJ FrCL TOB). DuCL has "knock on no one's door for support"; JB (improbably) "though you do not have to depend on them." The underlying question is really: "What is Paul's main fear for the Thessalonian Christians? That they will go hungry? Or that they will live as parasites on other people, even non-Christians?" The second alternative seems to fit the situation more exactly, but the first is a more frequent meaning of the Greek term used here. Dependence upon other individuals may often be expressed idiomatically, for example, "don't just eat other people's food," "don't go from meal pot to meal pot," or "don't be a guest every day."

TEV	RSV
The Lord's Coming 13 Our brothers, we want you to know the truth about those who have died, so that you will not be sad, as are those who have no hope. 14 We believe that Jesus died and rose again, and so we believe that God will take back with Jesus those who have died believing in him. (4.13-14)	13 But we would not have you ignorant, brethren, concerning those who are asleep, that you may not grieve as others do who have no hope. 14 For since we believe that Jesus died and rose again, even so, through Jesus, God will bring with him those who have fallen asleep. (4.13-14)

Here, as at the transition between earlier sections, there are both (1) differences and (2) points of contact.

1. It is clear both from the form and content of this section that Paul is moving to another subject. Several formal features indicate a new beginning:

(a) There is the common transitional which KJV and RSV, here as in verse 9, awkwardly translate "but." There are, it is true, some elements of contrast, for one might say that here Paul is giving his readers encouragement, whereas in verses 1-12 he has been presenting them with the stern demands of the gospel. Or one might say that previously he has been speaking about his readers' own conduct, but now he turns to the subject of their fellow Christians who have died. However, any such contrast, if it was in Paul's mind at all, is not strongly marked in the original, and therefore it should not be marked in the translation. RSV's "but" does not indicate by itself anything more than a minor transition; it becomes more significant when, as here, it is strengthened by other transitional features.

(b) Brothers, as we have noted before (e.g. 2.1; 4.1), sometimes marks a change of subject.

(c) The expression translated we want you to know (literally "we do not want you not to know") is regularly used by Paul to introduce something new. (See notes on v. 13.)

(d) About, here as in verse 9, indicates the introduction of a new theme.

2. What then leads Paul to move to the new subject at this point? The transition seems abrupt, because this new section does not at first seem to have much to do with what has gone before. The transition from moral appeal (vv. 1-12) to teaching about the Lord's coming (4.12—5.11) is all the stranger, since Paul returns more briefly to matters of conduct in 5.12 ff. Nevertheless, the points of contact are real and significant.

(a) Paul remains in the sphere of exhortation and appeal; he does not go back to discuss his past relationships with the Thessalonians. This section is not an exception to the broad distinction which we have drawn between chapters 1-3 and 4-5.

(b) The need for teaching about the dead has been suggested by the words all who belong to him being found in an emphatic position at the close of the section 2.17—3.13 (see notes on 3.13).

(c) Paul's discussion of love for fellow Christians in verses 9-12 may have raised in his mind the question of the relation between the living and the dead within the Christian community, since the brotherhood is not limited to the living.

(d) Why has Paul been so insistent in verses 9-12 that the Thessalonian Christians should earn their own living and generally live a normal life? 2 Thess. 2.1-4 and 3.6-12 reflect a situation in which excitement about the Day of the Lord was accompanied by a neglect of work and day-to-day duties. Paul's teaching on these two subjects is not so emphatic in 1 Thessalonians, and the subjects are not directly linked. But it is perhaps significant that at this point they are placed side by side.

The links between the present section (4.13-18) and the one which follows (5.1-11) are closer and clearer than the links between this passage and the one before. They will be discussed in the notes on 5.1-11.

Although the subject of this section is quite different, its structure is rather similar to that of the two previous sections, as summarized on page 85. The theme is announced (under the "subtitle" about those who have died) in verse 13, summarized in general terms in verse 14, and specified in verse 15, and again in more detail in verses 16-17. The main structural difference between verses 9-12 and 13-18 is that Paul mentions at an earlier stage (v. 15) the divine authority of his words: what we are teaching you now is the Lord's teaching.

The section is filled, not only with translational difficulties, but also with theological difficulties of which the translator should be aware, even though they may not directly affect the shape of his translation. It is therefore even more important than usual to consult general commentaries in addition to this handbook.

4.13 Our brothers, we want you to know the truth about those who have died, so that you will not be sad, as are those who have no hope.

The literal "we do not want you not to know" is used by Paul in Romans 1.13 and 2 Corinthians 1.8 to introduce a new piece of information. In Romans 11.25; 1 Corinthians 10.1; 12.1, the same expression introduces something which is not part of the basic Christian message as outlined, for example, by Peter in Acts 2.14-39 and by Paul himself in 1 Corinthians 15.3-5, but which is important for a fuller understanding of the scope of Christian truth and life. In Romans 11.25 it is a question of the "mystery" or "secret truth" (TEV) of how God has used the stubbornness of Israel as part of his plan for other nations. In 1 Corinthians 10, Paul speaks of the hidden, Christian significance of the rescue of the Israelites from slavery in Egypt. And in 1 Corinthians 12, he introduces a much-needed piece of teaching on the gifts of the Holy Spirit. The present passage is also a piece of advanced teaching, about the (still obscure) subject of the state of Christians between death and resurrection.

In translating the present passage, the double negative "we do not want you not to know" is transformed into the positive we want you to know by Mft ("we would like you...to understand") and Knox ("make no mistake"). JB's "we want you to be quite certain" is a little too strong. Brc has "I do not want you...to get wrong ideas," and Phps "we don't want you...to be in any doubt" (cf. GeCL DuCL). Paul himself uses an equivalent positive expression (which is perhaps slightly stronger) in 1 Corinthians 11.3 and Colossians 2.1 (cf. Philippians 1.12).

Here as elsewhere in this letter, it is very likely that "we" means Paul and his companions, though Brc disagrees.

The truth is implied, for there is no suggestion in the text that false views about the dead were circulating among the Thessalonians. Paul is fighting fear and anxiety rather than wrong ideas firmly held. The Thessalonians had seen Christians die, just as Paul himself had seen Stephen stoned to death. They needed reassurance that death would not prevent Christians from sharing in whatever God had in store for them.

What Paul wants the Thessalonian Christians to know is what happens to those who have died. In many languages, the truth can best be expressed as "what happens to" or "what really happens to," for example, "we very much want you to know what really happens to those who have died."

Those who have died, here and in verse 14 (but not in v. 16), is literally "those who are asleep" (RSV cf. KJV Lu), or, according to a slightly less well-supported reading, "have fallen asleep" (cf. Zur Knox?). "Sleep" is used in many passages to mean "die" (e.g. Job 14.12; Daniel 12.2-3; 2 Maccabees 12.43-45; John 11.11-13; 1 Corinthians 15.18,20). This is certainly the meaning here, as the literal equivalent in verse 16 shows. Many translations (JB GeCL Syn BJ TOB FrCL SpCL) agree with TEV in removing the figure of speech, sometimes putting it in a footnote. Seg (rather less helpfully for anyone hearing the passage read aloud) does the reverse, putting "those who sleep" in the text and "the dead" in a note. Mft ("those who are asleep in death"), Phps ("those who 'fall asleep' in death"), and Brc ("those who sleep death's sleep"), cf. NAB, keep the metaphor, but explain it in the text. Knox ("those who have gone to their rest") and DuCL ("those who have crossed over") use equivalent metaphors. The question for the translator is whether, in his receptor language, it is more usual to speak of death directly, or to use a figure of speech. The answer to this question varies not only between languages, but between temporal periods and between social groups using the same language. In many languages, especially those spoken in face-to-face societies, there is much less of a tendency to use figurative expressions than in most European languages, but the amount of such figurative language, even in English, differs greatly from time to time.

Some persons have wished to make a special point of the literal Greek rendering "those who are asleep" to imply that these are only "resting in death, looking forward to the judgment," and that therefore they have not gone on to heaven. But it is unwise to read into this kind of an idiom a special doctrine of the future life. (In 1 Kings 22.40 the metaphor of sleep is used in speaking of the death of the bad King Ahab, and it was also used by pagans in the ancient world.) The safest and most accurate way of translating the Greek is to say "those who have died."

The relation between we want you to know and so that you will not be sad is one of means and purpose. As indicates a comparison, but the nature of the comparison needs to be carefully defined. Those who have no hope is literally "the others" or "the rest, who do not have hope." These are the same group of people whom Paul has just called "those outside" (v. 12), that is, those who are not members of the Christian community. The contrast is not between kinds or degrees of grief, but between two groups of people; that is, Christians, who have reason to hope, and non-Christians, who do not. Translations should therefore be avoided which suggest that Paul's concern is simply to say that Christians should not be as sad as non-Christians. Phps' "like men who have no hope" does not bring out sufficiently clearly that Paul is contrasting real groups of people. NEB's "like the rest of men, who have no hope" (cf. DuCL) is better. On hope, see the notes on 1.3.

It is important to avoid a translation which would imply that the clause so that you will not be sad is directly related to the immediately preceding clause those who have died. To avoid this misunderstanding, it may be necessary to repeat the expression "we want you to know," for example, "we want you to know what happens to those who have died; we want you to know this so that you will not be sad."

Sadness is often expressed by an idiomatic phrase, for example, "with tears in your eyes," "with your stomach in pain," "with your heart throbbing," or "with your face fallen." It is better not to use an expression which would imply ritual mourning or weeping, even though this is a natural type of rendering in a context which speaks about death.

The comparison introduced in the last clause, as are those who have no hope, may be rather difficult to express in some languages. In fact, a conditional clause may be necessary, for example, "if you do not know about this, you will be like those who have no hope," or "...you will be sad just like those who do not look forward with confidence."

In many languages it is not possible to speak of "hope" without indicating what is the goal of the hope. In this context it is hope for life after death, and it may be necessary to say "those who do not hope for life after death." In some languages it would be more appropriate to speak about "those who have no hope for heaven," or, even better, "no hope to be with God."

4.14 We believe that Jesus died and rose again, and so we believe that God will take back with Jesus those who have died believing in him.

This verse gives the reason why Christians should not grieve as non-Christians do. The relation with verse 13b is marked in Greek by a conjunction meaning "for," which TEV, in accordance with current English usage, omits, leaving the relation implied. Throughout the New Testament, Christian hope for the future is closely related to the past events which form the basis of faith, that is, the death and resurrection of Jesus. So it is here.

The relation between the two halves of this sentence, beginning we believe that Jesus and so we believe that God, is not quite clear. Several factors need to be taken into consideration.

1. Paul is expressing himself in a very concentrated way, and some links in the chain of his argument are omitted. This becomes clear if we set it out in the following way, adding in brackets the ideas which seem to be needed to make the parallel complete:

A_1 We believe	B_1 so we believe
A_2 that Jesus died	B_2 that...those who have died believing in him
A_3 and rose again	B_3 (will rise again)
A_4 (and will come back)	B_4 and God will take them back with Jesus.

DIAGRAM 3

A_4 is implied in B_4 (with Jesus) and stated explicitly in verse 16. B_1 is not explicit in the Greek text. B_3 is not explicit till verse 16.

2. We have noticed in previous passages how easily Paul makes the transition between speaking about Jesus and speaking about God. In fact, Paul more often says "Jesus was raised," implying "God raised Jesus," than he says Jesus ...rose again (the words for "raised" and rose are quite different in Greek). The parallel would have been clearer if Paul had followed his normal usage here, but he may be quoting a fixed saying already current in the church. Nevertheless, the underlying parallel is clear, namely, that God raised Jesus and God will also raise those who believe in Jesus.

3. KJV (cf. Lu Zur Seg) follows the form of the Greek closely by translating "if we believe that Jesus died and rose again." This is ambiguous in English,* since it does not tell us whether or not the condition is fulfilled. There

*Compare the sentence: "If you think Brown is the best candidate, you will vote for him." Only the wider context (or possibly the intonation) would show whether or not the person addressed did in fact think Brown was the best candidate. To clear up the ambiguity, it would be necessary to choose between (a) "If, as you do, you think Brown is the best candidate...," (b) "If you thought that Brown was the best candidate...," implying "you do not think so," and (c) "If you happen to think that Brown is the best candidate...," leaving the question open.

is no doubt, however, that the Thessalonians shared the fundamental Christian belief that Jesus did die and rise again. The form of the Greek suggests taking the condition as a fact. There are various ways of making this fact clear. TOB (cf. Syn) has "if, in fact, we believe," which is equivalent to "if, as we do, we believe." RSV has "since" instead of "if." Phps (1st edition) has: "if, after all, we believe." All these renderings are possible. The simplest solution is that chosen by JB TEV NEB Brc GeCL FrCL, that is, to make two separate statements, leaving the relation between them to be expressed at the beginning of the second.

4. What, then, is the relation between verse 14a and 14b?

(a) As we have seen, it is not satisfactory to see it as one of ground and condition. "We believe that God will bring believers with Jesus, on condition that we believe that Jesus died and rose again" does not properly represent the relation.

(b) Nor is it simply a comparison, as SpCL has ("as we believe that Jesus died and rose, in the same manner we believe"), though this is the normal meaning of the word which TEV translates so. A glance at Diagram 3 is enough to show that the items listed in the second column are not only (and not primarily) similar to those in the first column, but the second group really depends on the first.

(c) The relation between 14a and 14b is best understood as one of reason and result; but even this needs to be more closely defined. We believe in 14a indicates a presupposition (it is almost an aside). The second we believe is not expressed in the Greek text. Paul is therefore not relating one act of believing to another (as in Phps "if we believe that Jesus died and rose again from death, then we can believe that God . . . ," cf. Seg). Brc's otherwise excellent translation runs into difficulties at this point: "We believe that Jesus died and rose again. We therefore also believe that in the same way God will bring with Jesus those who died in the Christian faith." The whole point of the passage is that the Thessalonians do not yet believe the second point, and this translation would require either a different meaning for the two occurrences of "we," or some vague and unusual meaning such as "Christians believe." Paul is rather relating one act of God, which the Thessalonians already know about, to another, the consequence of the first, about which they have not yet been taught. The meaning may be paraphrased as "Jesus died and rose again. (We all believe this already.) Therefore, this assures us that God will take back to himself those who have died believing in him." Unfortunately, as we have seen in paragraph 1, the consequence is indirect, but Mft may be right in translating "since we believe that Jesus died and rose again, then it follows . . . ."

Two more problems remain. First, the words translated believing in him are literally "through Jesus" (RSV). They may be related either (a) to will take back which would give the meaning "through Jesus, God will bring with him those who have fallen asleep" (RSV cf. Mft "by means of Jesus," Lu Seg Syn TOB "by Jesus and with him"); or (b) to those who have died believing in him (literally, as in v. 13, "those who have fallen asleep through Christ"). In this case, "through Christ" would have the same meaning as the more frequently used expression "in Christ," discussed in the notes on 2.14. This would make a convincing parallel to those who have died believing in Christ in verse 16. This interpretation is followed by KJV Knox JB Phps Brc NEB TNT (cf. GeCL FrCL SpCL DuCL), as well as by TEV.

The final problem is the meaning of take back. Literally the Greek word means "will bring" or "will lead," but in English "bring" includes the idea of movement toward a given point of reference. In this context "bring" therefore would imply "God will move down from heaven to earth with Jesus and with those who have died believing in him." Is this what Paul means? There are strong reasons for thinking that it is not.

(b) The meaning of the word translated will take back varies according to the context. Sometimes the infinitive may mean simply "to go." Usually, it implies movement with someone else and on someone else's initiative, like the English "lead." It does not, however, always imply movement towards a point of reference. In Acts 20.12, for example (contrast Acts 5.26), it involves movement away from the point of reference, and TEV accordingly translates "they took the young man home." That the meaning varies according to the context is recognized by the translators of BJ, who change "will bring" of their 1st edition to "will take away" in their 2nd edition in their rendering of the present verse.

(b) There is no suggestion here or in the wider context of God the Father's coming from heaven to earth.

(c) Nor is there any suggestion that the dead are already in heaven (cf. Matthew 27.52 f.).

(d) Verse 16, which fills out the meaning of verse 14, suggests that the movement is in the opposite direction: Those who have died believing in Christ will rise to life first.

In translation, the point of reference must be made clear. In the context, this is the earth, where we are in verse 15. The translation would therefore be something like "God will take" (or "take back") "to himself." Very few translations make this clear, as TEV does, but DuCL has "God will draw to himself, together with Jesus, those who have died as Christians," and NAB has "will bring forth with him from the dead." Some translations avoid the problem by eliminating the idea of movement completely. GeCL has "God will...give (them) life with Jesus" (cf. SpCL).

In some languages one encounters serious problems in trying to translate literally rose again. In the first place, "to rise" may not express the concept of "coming back to life." It might only mean to sit up from a lying position or to stand up from a lying or a sitting position. Furthermore, "again" can be confusing, since it may imply merely rising up a second time, rather than coming back to life from death. This means that in many languages it is necessary to say that "Jesus lived again," "Jesus became alive again," or "Jesus died and then became alive."

The conjunction so may require a more elaborate equivalent in order that the precise connection will be clearly indicated. A literal translation might suggest that "because of our belief about Jesus, therefore we believe that God will do...." As already pointed out, this is not the proper connection. It may be preferable to translate "because Jesus died and rose again, therefore we believe that God...."

To avoid the wrong implication of "will bring with Jesus" (cf. NAB), it may be useful to use a causative, for example, "will cause them to be with Jesus."

Those who have died believing in him indicates a relation often described as "attendant circumstance"; in the present instance the people were believing in him at the time they died. This relation may be expressed as "those who were believing in him when they died," or "those who believed in him and died." It would be wrong to suggest a concessive relation, such as "those who died even though they believed in him." This idea may be precisely what was troubling the Thessalonians; they may have thought that true Christians would not experience physical death, and so were quite disturbed by the fact that some of their number had died.

TEV

15 What we are teaching you now
is the Lord's teaching: we who are
alive on the day the Lord comes
will not go ahead of those who have
died. 16 There will be the shout
of command, the archangel's voice,
the sound of God's trumpet, and the
Lord himself will come down from
heaven. Those who have died believing in Christ will rise to life
first; 17 then we who are living
at that time will be gathered up
along with them in the clouds to
meet the Lord in the air. And so
we will always be with the Lord.
18 So then, encourage one another
with these words. (4.15-18)

RSV

15 For this we declare to you by
the word of the Lord, that we who
are alive, who are left until the
coming of the Lord, shall not precede those who have fallen asleep.
16 For the Lord himself will de-
scend from heaven with a cry of
command, with the archangel's call,
and with the sound of the trumpet
of God. And the dead in Christ
will rise first; 17 then we who
are alive, who are left, shall be
caught up together with them in the
clouds to meet the Lord in the air;
and so we shall always be with the
Lord. 18 Therefore comfort one
another with these words. (4.15-18)

These verses raise two general problems for the translator. First, he needs to recognize that Paul's main purpose, as he has stated in verse 13 and will repeat in verse 18, is not to give his readers further information, but to prepare them for the coming of Christ, and to calm their fears about this great event. Any further teaching he gives is a means to this end. This should be brought out in translation, wherever possible, by the use of language with a warm emotive content. GeCL, for example, begins verse 15 with the words "you need have no fear." (These words also have another function, which will be discussed in the notes on verse 15.) TEV has encourage one another (v. 18), and Brc "comfort and encourage."

The second problem is closely related to the first. In this passage, Paul is speaking of events which are outside direct human experience. He therefore uses a high proportion of figurative language, much of it borrowed, with some adaptation, from the Jewish apocalyptic tradition which had its roots in the Old Testament (especially in Daniel and Ezekiel), developed rapidly in the centuries immediately before the birth of Jesus, and continued into the New Testament (especially, but not only, in Revelation). Some of the details of Paul's picture (e.g. references to trumpets and clouds) are common throughout this literature. It is difficult to assign either a literal or a theological meaning to such features. On the other hand, they have taken on a symbolic value as happenings associated with the end of the age, and they should therefore be retained in translation, unless they would present difficulties in the receptor language. To look for equivalent but different images in the receptor culture (assuming that it has its own traditions about the end of the age, which are rather rare outside the Jewish-Christian-Islamic tradition) is perhaps not impossible, but in practice it raises the usual difficulties of cultural transposition. The references to time (for example, first in verse 16 and then in verse 17) need not be understood literally, but they must be taken seriously into account in the translation, not simply omitted.

4.15 What we are teaching you now is the Lord's teaching: we who are alive on the day the Lord comes will not go ahead of those who have died.

What we are teaching you now is the Lord's teaching raises the same question that "for this other reason" raised in 2.13. The verse literally begins "for this to you we say." Does the word "this" (TEV what) refer backward or forward? Is the Lord's teaching contained in verse 14 or in 15b ff.? The answer to this question is not immediately clear, since verses 15-17 repeat in more specific terms the content of verse 14. However, it is practically certain that "this" refers forward to the sentence which follows. Paul has announced his theme briefly in verse 14; now, as he prepares to expand it, he makes a solemn appeal to the authority of Christ. GeCL here, as in 2.13, makes this clear by reversing the two parts of verse 15: "You need have no fear: those who have already died will not be at any disadvantage compared with us, who are still alive when the Lord comes. For this, I can appeal to a word of the Lord." FrCL solves the problem by beginning "here is...," an expression which in French is regularly forward-looking. TEV's colon after the Lord's teaching has the same function, but when the passage is read aloud, the punctuation needs a sensitive reader to interpret it with the appropriate intonation. TNT expands the text and divides the sentence: "We are now telling you something which the Lord himself said. It is that those of us who are alive...."

To make clear that the Lord's teaching refers to what follows, one may use TEV's wording or a similar one, for example, "what we are going to tell you is just what the Lord taught." Otherwise, the transposition of this first clause to the end of verse 15 may be the most satisfactory solution, for example, "we who are still alive when the Lord comes, will not go ahead of those who have already died. This is just what the Lord himself taught."

4.15

The identification of participants in this verse raises linguistic problems which have important theological implications. The first we (in we are teaching you) is defined by the word you; it means Paul and his fellow evangelists. There is no need, as we have seen in many other passages, to limit the reference to Paul alone, as GeCL does. The second we (before who are alive on the day the Lord comes) is most naturally understood as including both Paul and his companions on the one hand and his readers on the other. Here (as is not always the case) the grammatical structure of the Greek sentence corresponds to the semantic relations between its parts. Paul's principal concern, expressed in the main verb, is that those who are still living when the Lord comes will have no priority over those who have already died. Paul is not concerned to make any dogmatic statement, either about which of his readers will still be alive at that time, or about whether he will himself still be alive. The we is quite general (and Phps is not justified in omitting it completely, translating "those who are still living..."). Paul may have assumed, as the Thessalonian Christians did (see 2 Thess. 2.1-3), that Jesus would come soon, and that he, Paul, would be alive at that time. But the question of Paul's own survival is not for the moment in focus.

The Lord's teaching is literally "a word of the Lord." "Word" clearly means here a whole "message" rather than a single word; and "of the Lord" means "from the Lord" rather than "about the Lord." Paul is not quoting any recorded saying of Jesus. Nor does he seem to be quoting any particular saying which has since been lost. It would certainly be difficult to decide where to insert quotation marks to identify an assumed quotation. Paul may be giving the general content of Jesus' teaching about the end of the age, such as was later recorded in such passages as Mark 13. GeCL's literal translation "a word of the Lord" (cf. Seg Zur Syn Lu DuCL) is therefore probably too specific; teaching (cf. FrCL SpCL TOB) or "message" (Brc Phps) is to be preferred. Mft's "we tell you, as the Lord has told us" is an attractive restructuring which brings out the similarity in the Greek of "we say" and "word," as TEV's we are teaching and teaching also do.

The Greek connecting word "for" (translated by KJV RSV Mft) is rightly omitted in modern English and some other languages.

Verse 15b, and probably verses 16-17 also, contain the teaching referred to in 15a. The connection is shown in Greek by a "that" (cf. KJV RSV) which has the same function as the colon in TEV. The verse continues, in literal translation, "we, the living, the left-behind to the appearing of the Lord, will not precede those who have fallen asleep." "We" is emphatic, in contrast to "those who have fallen asleep." "Not" is also emphatic, showing that Paul's main concern is to show that Christians who have died will benefit from the coming of Jesus, just as much as those who are still alive. Several translations combine "living" and "left-behind" in some such phrase as "we who are left alive" (NEB); TEV omits the second element. Exactly the same expression is used in verse 17. TEV's the day is not expressed in this verse in the Greek.

On the word for "appearing," see the notes on 2.19. On sleep as a metaphor for death, see the notes on verse 13.

GeCL restructures the sentence so as to make the dead, rather than the living, its subject: "Those who have already died will...be at no disadvantage ...." The meaning is the same, but this translation brings out more clearly the fact that Paul's main concern, and that of his readers, is for the Christians who have died. Note that in doing this, GeCL removes the metaphor which TEV translates go ahead of. Alternatively, TEV's spatial metaphor may be replaced by a temporal metaphor without distorting the meaning, for example, "we who are alive when the Lord comes will not be with him any sooner than those who have died."

4.16 There will be the shout of command, the archangel's voice, the sound of God's trumpet, and the Lord himself will come down from heaven. Those who have died believing in Christ will rise to life first;

In verses 16-17, the figurative language becomes even more marked. Paul draws a picture of a meeting of Jesus, first with those who have died and then with those who are still alive. The "place" of this meeting is the air (v. 17). In the Greek world view, this was a technical term for the middle level between the earth and the space in which the stars were thought to move, called "the ether." It is not clear how far Paul shared this view of the world. He never uses the word "ether"; no one else in the New Testament uses the word "air." When Paul uses "air," it sometimes has a more general sense than it seems to have here. In this passage, the general picture is clear and can normally be translated without the help of cultural annotations. The dead are snatched up from the ground, and the Lord comes down from heaven to meet them in some "place" between. Expressions of space and time need not be understood literally, but they should be taken seriously in translation.

These central events are accompanied by others. The shout of command translates a single word which may also have the more general meaning of a loud cry. "It belongs to the language of sailors, hunters and jockeys" (Rigaux). It is not clear from the text who is shouting. GeCL makes it clear that it is God, and this makes good sense for receptor languages which prefer or require an explicit statement about the agent. Similarly, the text does not state explicitly that it is God who blows the trumpet, though this may be implied. The text states only that the trumpet belongs to God.

A literal translation of TEV would be very difficult in some languages, since in them one cannot speak of shouting a command without indicating who is the agent. Furthermore, placing the phrase the shout of command immediately before the archangel's voice might imply that it is the archangel who does the shouting. The closest equivalent in some languages is simply "God will shout a command, the archangel will speak, and people will hear God's trumpet." It is possible in some instances to avoid indicating the agent by introducing the sounds by the phrase "people will hear," for example, "people will hear a loud command, the voice of the archangel, and God's trumpet."

Since in verse 17 it says that the believers will meet the Lord in the air, it would be wrong to translate "the Lord himself will come down" in such a way as to imply that he will come down to the surface of the earth. It is simply that "the Lord will come down out of heaven." The translation should not specify precisely how far down he comes, though in some languages it may be useful, in order to avoid other complications, to say "will come down from heaven into the air."

Those who have died believing in Christ is literally "the dead in Christ." The metaphor of sleep, used in verses 13 and 15, is replaced here by the normal literal expression. The text does not focus on the fact of their having believed in Christ at the moment of death, for after death also they are "in Christ." Paul simply means "dead Christians," "the Christian dead." It is most natural to connect "in Christ" with "those who have died." The alternative construction, "those who have died will rise in Christ first," is much less likely. Throughout this passage, Paul is thinking only of Christians who have died. TEV's to life is implied in the text. These words remind us of the literal meaning behind the metaphor of rising.

For some of the problems involved in translating who have died believing in Christ, see the note on verse 4.14.

The phrase will rise to life must be translated in many languages as simply "come back to life" or "live again."

The temporal expression first implies a comparison, and this is brought out clearly in the beginning of verse 17, but in some languages the temporal relation is better expressed by a transitional alone, such as "then," for example, "those believers in Christ who have died will come back to life, and then we who are living at that time...."

4.17 then we who are living at that time will be gathered up along with them in the clouds to meet the Lord in the air. And so we will always be with the Lord.

The effect of this verse is to reinforce Paul's message that no Christians, neither the dead, nor those who are still alive, will be separated from Christ at the time of his coming. We who are living at that time (literally "we [emphatic], the living, the left-behind," exactly as in verse 15) will be with them, that is with the Christians who have died; and all Christians will from then on be always with the Lord—a statement which contrasts strikingly with the various kinds of figurative language which have gone before.

The words translated along with most commonly mean "at the same time as" (cf. Zur Lu). This conflicts slightly with the preceding first and then, but in a passage using so many figures of speech, this is not a serious problem. Consistency in the use of figurative language is not one of Paul's strong points anyway (cf. e.g. Romans 11.16-24). The words translated along with (see also 5.10) may, however, also mean "in the same place as," and this may be the most natural basis for translation here, for example, "we will all be gathered up to be with them, and to meet the Lord in the air."

We...will be gathered up includes the idea of being violently caught or snatched away (that is, from earth; cf. Acts 8.39). There are two problems involved in translating we...will be gathered up along with them. First the passive expression may be difficult, since an agent is implied, and in some languages it may need to be expressed. The obvious agent in this context is God, so one may translate "God will gather us up together." Second, the implication of meeting Jesus in the air may suggest a term for "gathering" which would mean "lift up together" or "snatch up." Such a term, however, could imply violence, as when the police or soldiers seize a thief. In some translations, therefore, a causative expression is used: "God will cause us to come together."

It would be wrong to translate in the clouds in such a literal way as to suggest that the Christians will be "hidden from sight." The apparent meaning here is "up where the clouds are." This coincides with the meaning suggested by the phrase in the air, rendered in many languages simply as "in the sky."

The word translated meet is an unusual one. In secular Greek, it is used in referring to ceremonies held on the occasion of a state visit, and especially to the inauguration of a ruler or important official. But the idea of going out to meet God is also found in the Old Testament (e.g. Exodus 19.10-18). The general idea is that of a solemn, not a casual or accidental, meeting. For some languages the appropriate connotations of a word translating meet may be contained in a term suggesting "to greet the Lord in the sky," or "to gather round the Lord in the sky."

There is a difference, both in the Greek words and in their meanings, between so in this verse and so then in verse 18. The term translated so summarizes what has gone before, while the word translated so then indicates a relation of means and result. The context shows very clearly that we here includes all Christians.

We will always be with the Lord is in some languages best expressed as "we will always remain with the Lord," or "...continue with the Lord." In some instances this may be rendered "we will always stay where the Lord is," or even "we will always accompany the Lord."

4.18 So then, encourage one another with these words.

This concluding sentence recalls verse 13, where Paul first stated his desire to meet his readers' anxieties. Encourage is the word which is translated "help" in 3.2, and "encourage" in 2.12 and in the exact parallel 5.11. The word can also mean "comfort" or "console." However it is translated, it should relate to be sad (literally "be pained") of verse 13. That is, now that the Thessalonians have been given a new understanding of one aspect of the Christian faith, they need no longer grieve over the final outcome of those who have died. What Paul tells them and assures them can change their sadness into confident hope; they can be comforted and encouraged by this teaching of the Lord's, and they are to comfort, encourage, and give hope to one another.

In choosing a translation for encourage, it is important to select a term which will be in contrast with sad in verse 13. In some cases one may wish simply to translate "remove the sadness from one another with these words," or "with these words cause your hearts no longer to tremble."

CHAPTER 5

TEV

Be Ready for the Lord's Coming

1 There is no need to write you,
brothers, about the times and occasions when these things will happen. 2 For you yourselves know
very well that the Day of the Lord
will come as a thief at night.
3 When people say, "Everything is
quiet and safe," then suddenly destruction will hit them! It will
come as suddenly as the pains that
come upon a woman in labor, and
people will not escape. 4 But you,
brothers, are not in the darkness,
and the Day should not take you by
surprise like a thief. 5 All of
you are people who belong to the
light, who belong to the day. We
do not belong to the night or to
the darkness. (5.1-5)

RSV

1 But as to the times and the
seasons, brethren, you have no need
to have anything written to you.
2 For you yourselves know well that
the day of the Lord will come like
a thief in the night. 3 When people say, "There is peace and security," then sudden destruction will
come upon them as travail comes
upon a woman with child, and there
will be no escape. 4 But you are
not in darkness, brethren, for that
day to surprise you like a thief.
5 For you are all sons of light and
sons of the day; we are not of the
night or of darkness. (5.1-5)

The relation of 5.1-11 to previous sections is easier to see than the development of Paul's thought within the passage itself. A transition to a new subject is marked in the same ways as in 4.9, 13.

(a) The first word of the section in Greek (as in v. 9) is about. This has the function of a subtitle, roughly equivalent to "the time at which the Lord will come."

(b) Then comes the frequent transition which KJV RSV and Phps (cf. SpCL) translate "but." There is an element of contrast here: "You needed further teaching about Christians who have died, but you know already that the end will come unexpectedly." The main function of the word, however, is to indicate that Paul is moving to another subject, and for this reason most modern translations omit it.

(c) Finally, the word brothers, here as, for example, in verse 13, helps to mark the introduction of a new theme.

The close relation between 5.1-11 and 4.13-18 is marked formally by the repetition of encourage one another in 4.18 and 5.11. In the present section, Paul returns to the subject of non-Christians (the others in v. 6, probably also people in v. 3) which he has not touched since 4.13 (those who have no hope). The transition to the negative aspects of Christ's coming, judgment, and destruction, is natural.

Here, as in other passages, Paul pays his readers the compliment of referring to what they know and practice already (vv. 1, 11). However, it is not mere diplomacy when he says that there is no need to write to them about the date of Christ's coming (though the situation has changed by the time he comes to write 2 Thessalonians). This is a fairly common rhetorical device. In fact, Paul simply states, using a simile which was not original (see notes on v. 2), that the Day of the Lord will come as unexpectedly as a thief comes at night. Within verse 4, Paul passes on to a passage of moral teaching, the beginning of which is marked by brothers (again) and an emphatic but you. From this point onward, Paul's main concern is no longer with the Day of the Lord, but with a contrast between Christian and non-Christian living, in which the image of day and night takes on a different meaning.

5.1 There is no need to write you, brothers, about the times and occasions when these things will happen.

Times and occasions represent two Greek words which in some contexts are clearly differentiated, times referring to time as recorded by clocks and calendars, and occasions referring to the "psychological moments" at which the time is ripe (especially, for God to act). However, this distinction is not always maintained, particularly in such a set phrase as this, in which the two words are used together. GeCL therefore combines them, translating "the point in time," cf. DuCL "the precise moment." In many languages it is quite impossible to distinguish between times and occasions, and so it is often necessary to translate "about the day when these things will happen."

In there is no need to write you, it may be necessary in some languages to indicate who would do the writing (if there were a need for it); this would, of course, be Paul. These things is a reference back to the coming of the Lord (4.15; 5.2). It may be necessary, therefore, to translate "there is no need for me to write to you about the precise moment when the Lord will come," or "... come back."

5.2 For you yourselves know very well that the Day of the Lord will come as a thief at night.

You yourselves know very well (NEB, cf. TOB "perfectly well") emphasizes both you and know. At the moment, the point of the comparison with a thief is that he comes as unexpectedly as the Day of the Lord will come (cf. SpCL "will surprise you"). The idea that the thief comes to do harm is not implied until later. The concept of the Day of the Lord goes back at least to Amos 5.18, 20, where it is already linked with the contrast between light and darkness; but whereas in the Old Testament, "the Lord" was God (that is, Yahweh or Jehovah), for Paul, here as in almost all other passages, "the Lord" is Christ.

The translation should make it clear, first, that the comparison is between two events, the coming of the Lord and the coming of a thief; and secondly, that something which is to happen, and is therefore unknown, is being compared to something which has already happened frequently, and is therefore well known. The addition of the future verb will come indicates clearly that the Day of the Lord is an event in the future. The verb "comes" could be added after thief, since it is implied. GeCL makes the point of comparison explicit by translating "will come as unexpectedly as a thief in the night."

The image of the thief may be influenced by the saying of Jesus later recorded in Matthew 24.43; Luke 12.39. The same image is used later in 2 Peter 3.10; Revelation 3.3; 16.15. Paul does not need to search for original ways of expressing teaching with which his readers were already well acquainted.

The Day of the Lord will come as a thief at night is far more difficult to translate than one might think. The comparison is between two events, but in the first instance it is "time that comes" and in the second instance it is "the thief that comes." In many languages it is impossible to speak about "a day coming," though one can say "a person will come on a certain day." If, however, one translates "the Lord will come as a thief comes at night," the comparison may seem to point, not to the unexpectedness of the coming, but to stealthiness or bad intent. Here it may be necessary to say "the Lord will come as unexpectedly as a thief who comes at night" (cf. Phps), or "the Lord will come when no one expects him, just as a thief comes when no one is expecting him."

5.3 When people say, "Everything is quiet and safe," then suddenly destruction will hit them! It will come as suddenly as the pains that come upon a woman in labor, and people will not escape.

The word translated when usually, but not always, means "whenever"; but "whenever" clearly will not do here, since the Day of the Lord does not come every time people talk of peace and security (virtually two synonyms). But the idea of repeated action need not be excluded in translation, and various English versions may suggest this by the use of the so-called progressive form. Brc has "when people are talking of how peaceful and secure life is"; Knox "It is just when men are saying, All quiet, all safe, that..."; Phps "When men are saying 'peace and security'"; TNT "Just when people are saying how peaceful and secure everything is...";—cf. Mft "when 'all's well' and 'all is safe', are on the lips of men"; cf. Jeremiah 6.14; Ezekiel 13.10; Matthew 24.37-39. But the emphasis here is not on the repeated action of thinking that all is well, but on the factor of indefinite time.

Some languages need to make it clear that say refers to a future activity, that is, "when people will be saying." GeCL translates: "when people begin to say."

People translate an impersonal "they say," but the latter part of the verse suggests that Paul is thinking specially of non-Christians, and he states this more explicitly in verse 4 by the emphatic but you, and in verse 6 by the others.

In some languages it is necessary to make quiet and safe more clearly related to those who talk about such a condition, for example, "when people will say, No one is rioting and we are safe," or "...Everyone is peaceful, and we need not have any fear."

Destruction translates a word which in the New Testament (1) always refers to destruction by some supernatural power, and (2) never implies complete annihilation. The meaning is close to "punishment" or even "God's judgment."

Those who refuse to believe are punished, but (or therefore) do not cease to exist. It is difficult to combine both these elements in translation, and the impersonal use of destruction (avoiding the direct statement "God will destroy them") makes things even more difficult. Mft's "Destruction" (with a capital D) shows that he was conscious of the problem, but using a capital letter does not solve it. JB has "the worst suddenly happens," and some French translations have "ruin," both of which avoid the suggestion of annihilation.

In some languages one cannot say "destruction will hit them," because destruction is itself an event. One can be hit by objects but not by an event such as destruction. The closest equivalent may be "then suddenly they will suffer terribly," or "they will be in great trouble."

The latter part of the verse introduces successively a new comparison and a new idea: the pains that come upon a woman in labor. TEV (cf. Phps) brings out clearly a reference to the final stages of pregnancy which is required by the context. A woman who is about to give birth is in Greek simply "a pregnant woman." The major point of the comparison is the suddenness both of the birth pangs and of the Day of the Lord. TEV emphasizes this by suddenly at the beginning of the clause (then suddenly), as the Greek, and also be repeating it in the next sentence (as suddenly as), where it is not found in the Greek. A slight overemphasis of this element is perhaps needed, since Paul probably returns in verse 4 (see the notes on that verse) to the unexpectedness of the Day of the Lord. In people will not escape, the word not is emphasized. One may also translate "then destruction will hit them as suddenly as the pains that come upon a woman who is about to give birth, and they will not escape."

It is always possible to talk about "escaping" from prison or from confinement, but it may be difficult to speak of "escaping" from destruction. If in the previous clause destruction will hit them is rendered something like "suddenly they will suffer terribly," then people will not escape may be rendered as "people will most certainly suffer," or "it is not possible that people will not suffer."

Since Paul is not referring to the intensity of pain in childbirth but to the fact that such pain is unexpected, it may be possible to translate "the suffering will surely come, and when one is not expecting it, just like the suffering that comes to a woman who is about to give birth."

5.4 But you, brothers, are not in the darkness, and the Day should not take you by surprise like a thief.

Paul's use of figurative language raises several problems here. First, there is a transition from the Day in the sense of an unknown time at which God will bring history to its climax, to the day (v. 5) as an image of the openness of Christian living. This transition is indicated in TEV by capitalization of Day in the first sense, but this device is inadequate to convey the distinction to anyone who only hears the passage read aloud. The second sense of day is well established by verse 5. The implication in verse 4 is that Christians have nothing to fear from that final Day in which everything will be known and judged, because they already live lives in which there is nothing to hide.

Second, the image of a thief reappears in a sense which cannot be defined until a decision is taken about the meaning of the word translated take ...by surprise. This verb, in the meaning required by the context, may include the following elements: (1) being seized, so that one cannot escape; (2) being overtaken or surprised (as a traveler in Mediterranean latitudes could be overtaken unexpectedly by the sudden arrival of night); (3) suffering harm. All elements fit the present context well, but which is the translator to choose as central? (1) takes up the idea expressed in verse 3b, (2) reverts to the idea of verses 2-3a, and (3) takes up the thought of verse 3a (destruction). Most translations agree with TEV in taking (2) as central, and this may well be correct. However, (1) is the common meaning of the verb where the context does not define it in some other way (but compare John 12.35).

If the translator chooses such an expression as "seize" or "catch," he must be careful to make the two terms of the comparison clear. The meaning would not be: "the Day should not catch you as a thief is caught,"* but "the Day should not seize you as a thief seizes someone" (for example, the occupant of the house he is about to rob).

The relation between the two parts of this verse is left open or implicit by TEV (cf. FrCL), which links them only by and. The relation indicated by the Greek is one of reason and result, for example, "you are not in darkness, and so you should not be surprised...," or "since you are not in darkness, you should not be surprised...."

You...are not in the darkness is a figurative expression, and as such it may be difficult to render literally in some languages, since darkness may have nothing to do with either ignorance or the wrong kind of life. It may be important to change this metaphor into a simile, for example, "but you do not live as it were in the darkness," or "...in the night." One may also translate as "but you do not live as those who are ignorant of God and who sin."

It is impossible to say in some languages "the day will take you by surprise," since surprise is not something that a person experiences with regard to a particular day. Therefore, one may need to restructure this latter part of verse 4 to read "and therefore you will not be surprised when the day of the Lord comes, as a thief might surprise someone when he (the thief) grabs him."

5.5 All of you are people who belong to the light, who belong to the day. We do not belong to the night or to the darkness.

All is emphatic. The Greek has the conjunction "for" (omitted in TEV), which explains the relation of 4a to the preceding verse. People who belong to the light, who belong to the day translates a Greek text which is literally "sons

*One Coptic and two Greek manuscripts, probably misunderstanding the text in this way, have "thieves" instead of "thief," corresponding to the plural "you." Mft follows their reading in his text, and NEB mentions it in a footnote. It is almost certainly wrong, though Metzger may go too far in calling it "near nonsense" (p. 633).

of light you are, and sons of day." The expression "sons" goes back to a Hebrew idiom used to identify personal characteristics (cf. Acts 4.36, where the name Barnabas is translated literally "son of encouragement," TEV "One who Encourages"). The literal translation, followed by most traditional and many modern versions, has little meaning or impact in non-Semitic languages.

We do not belong to the night or to the darkness emphasizes verse 5a by putting the same idea in negative form. It also marks the inclusion of Paul and his companions by the change from you to we, which is maintained until verse 11. DuCL attractively translates "we have nothing to do with the darkness of night." We, of course, includes both senders and readers of the letter.

This verse seems quite simple in an English translation such as TEV, but the concepts are extremely difficult to communicate effectively in some languages. It may not make sense to say people who belong to the light or we do not belong to the night. It is possible to speak of an object as belonging to a person, but how can a person belong to light? Nevertheless, in order to introduce the contrasts occurring in verses 6-8, at least some reference to "light" and "darkness" and "day" and "night" is required in verse 5. In some cases one may translate "all of you are people who live just as though everything were done in the light of day," or "...do everything as though it were done in the light, that is in the daytime." The second part of verse 5 is simply a negative reflection of the first part, and can be translated in some languages as "we do not live like people who always carry on at night or in the darkness," "...who do what they do at night or in the darkness," or "...when no one can see."

TEV	RSV
6 So then, we should not be sleeping, like the others; we should be awake and sober. 7 It is at night when people sleep; it is at night when they get drunk. 8 But we belong to the day, and we should be sober. We must wear faith and love as a breastplate, and our hope of salvation as a helmet. 9 God did not choose us to suffer his anger, but to possess salvation through our Lord Jesus Christ, 10 who died for us in order that we might live together with him, whether we are alive or dead when he comes. 11 And so encourage one another and help one another, just as you are now doing. (5.6-11)	6 So then let us not sleep, as others do, but let us keep awake and be sober. 7 For those who sleep sleep at night, and those who get drunk are drunk at night. 8 But, since we belong to the day, let us be sober, and put on the breastplate of faith and love, and for a helmet the hope of salvation. 9 For God has not destined us for wrath, but to obtain salvation through our Lord Jesus Christ, 10 who died for us so that whether we wake or sleep we might live with him. 11 Therefore encourage one another and build one another up, just as you are doing. (5.6-11)

The introductory expression so then may be translated as "since all this is true," or "since this is surely so." Paul now begins to draw moral consequences from the principles he has just stated. It is only in the light of the structure of the whole passage that the translator can decide the meaning of individual words, especially the key word translated be . . . sober. On a first reading, it may seem that Paul's main concern is to warn his readers against drunkenness, as he does in passing in Ephesians 5.18. However, this is by no means certain. (1) Everywhere else in the New Testament, the verb "be sober" is used figuratively, with the meaning "be self-controlled," "exercise self-restraint," or "avoid excess." Early in the second century A.D. Ignatius wrote to Polycarp (2.3) "be self-controlled, like an athlete of God." This exhortation gives the normal meaning of the verb, that is, not merely avoiding drunkenness, but being "in training," avoiding all kinds of excess. (2) This meaning fits in well with the meaning of be awake in verse 6. Paul clearly does not mean that his readers should literally not take any sleep until the Day of the Lord comes, but that they should be alert and ready. (3) Verse 7 is therefore an aside, in which, exceptionally and by way of illustration, Paul uses the words night, sleep, and get drunk in their literal meanings. (4) This interpretation of the passage is confirmed by the following verses, which deal with the Christian's relationship to God and to other Christians rather than with matters of personal conduct.

If this interpretation is correct, verse 6b should be translated "we should be alert and self-controlled" (Phps "let us keep awake, with our wits about us"; cf. Brc "we must be sleeplessly and soberly on the watch"). Verse 8a would then be translated "but we belong to the day, and we should keep ourselves in control."

5.6 So then, we should not be sleeping, like the others; we should be awake and sober.

TEV recognizes that the construction "let us" (RSV), used as a first person plural imperative, is becoming old-fashioned in English. This construction, which closely follows the form of the Greek, is also abandoned by NEB JB Knox Mft Brc, cf. GeCL FrCL SpCL DuCL (here but not in v. 8) and Zur (in v. 8 but not here).

The others are those who were described in 4.12 as "those outside" (TEV those who are not believers). The phrase as a whole suggests that they are so well known as to need no more explicit identification.

We should not be sleeping should not be interpreted as meaning that Christians should not sleep. The reference here is to lazy sleeping or lack of alertness. Perhaps the meaning can be expressed as "we should not be sleepily unconcerned." This would then make it possible to contrast "sleepiness" with the "alertness" implied in "being awake."

In many instances a translation of sober will emphasize "controlling oneself," which may be expressed in a variety of ways, for example, "being able to say no to one's desire," "thinking everything straight," "keeping one's head right," or "making one's thoughts conform."

5.7 It is at night when people sleep; it is at night when they get drunk.

The grammatical structure of this verse in Greek is balanced, but the meaning is not. A fairly literal translation would be "for the sleepers sleep at night, and the drunkards get drunk at night." Paul is not interested here in distinguishing those who sleep and get drunk from those who do not, but in mentioning two of the activities associated with night. TEV effectively focuses attention upon the factor of time by introducing both the sleeping and the drunkenness with the phrase it is at night. Other languages may use "at night people sleep; at night they get drunk," or "people sleep at night and get drunk at night."

5.8 But we belong to the day, and we should be sober. We must wear faith and love as a breastplate, and our hope of salvation as a helmet.

After the aside of verse 7, Paul now returns to his main theme. Verse 8a repeats part of 6b, with an emphatic transitional but we to mark the contrast between Christians and the others. The Greek (literally "but we, being of the day, let us be self-controlled") implies a relation of reason and result: "since we belong to the day, let us exercise self-control."

For the expression we belong to the day, see the discussion under verse 5; for we should be ... sober, see verse 6. There should, of course, be a close correspondence between the expressions used in verse 8 and the same expressions used in previous verses, since verse 8a summarizes the complex figures of speech which begin with verse 4.

Since the beginning of this chapter, Paul has been writing sentences which, for him, are comparatively short.* The emotive tone has been correspondingly lower, partly because he has been mentioning those who stand outside the personal relationship which links him with his readers. Now he begins to write once more about the faith which they have in common, and the emotive tone rises in verses 9-10 to a climax of the whole section (4.13—5.11). The process begins in verse 8, although the sentence has formally begun with verse 7, which we have identified as an aside from the point of view of its meaning.

Paul several times compares the Christian's spiritual resources with arms and armor (Ephesians 6.13-17; Romans 13.12; 2 Corinthians 6.7; 10.4; cf. Isaiah 11.5; 59.17; Wisdom 4.17-20). He makes no attempt to be consistent in comparing the various Christian virtues with the various pieces of military equipment. Here faith, love, and hope are mentioned in the same order as in 1.3 (see the notes on that verse). Typically, Paul now urges his readers to exercise qualities which, at the beginning of his letter, he has praised them for already possessing (cf. also 3.12; 4.1).

Hope of salvation: salvation is the object of hope (cf. GeCL "hope for salvation"). This phrase is the pivot on which the following verse turns and to which it is related in an unfolding sequence.

These figures of speech, which liken certain Christian virtues to armor,

*In the UBS Greek text, verses 1-6 consist of four sentences of between 16 and 26 words each, while verses 7-10 form a single sentence of 55 words. Verse 11, like 4.18, which it resembles in other ways, is a short, emphatic, concluding sentence.

are extremely difficult to translate meaningfully into some languages. There are several reasons for this. In the first place, armor is quite unknown in some cultures, and therefore there are no terms for pieces of armor nor can people readily imagine how armor was used. In the second place, it is extremely difficult to liken events or states implied in "trusting" and "loving" to something as concrete as a breastplate. In the third place, faith and love must often be expressed by verbs, and this makes the comparison far more difficult. An equivalent of 8b in some languages would be "you must trust and love God: then you will be wearing, as it were, a protection for your body." It simply does not make sense in some languages to talk about "wearing faith and love." Furthermore, it is the function of the breastplate which must be made clear; otherwise any meaningful connection between "faith" and "love" on the one hand, and the "breastplate" on the other, will be lost.

Our hope of salvation may be rendered in some languages as "we should look forward confidently to our being saved," or "...to God's saving us." Then the phrase as a helmet may be translated as "this will be like a protection for our heads." The need for the breastplate and the helmet is, of course, because of the spiritual conflict with Satan, but this aspect is not specifically brought out in this passage as it is in Ephesians 6.16-17.

5.9 God did not choose us to suffer his anger, but to possess salvation through our Lord Jesus Christ,

The words translated did not choose (cf. Phps; RSV NEB Knox Brc [cf. Mft] "has not destined," KJV "hath not appointed," JB "never meant us to experience the Retribution") have been understood in rather different ways, as the various English translations just quoted show. The ordinary meaning of this common verb is "to put." One of its extended meanings is "to put in a particular position or office," and thus "to appoint." "To destine" is the meaning chosen here by many commentators and translators, but it is rare elsewhere. It is not the more usual word for "choose" (found, for example, in 1 Corinthians 1.27), nor is it the word for "predestine" (found in Romans 8.29-30 and Ephesians 1.5, 11). The closest parallel is Acts 13.47 (quoting Isaiah 49.6), where TEV translates "I have made you a light for the Gentiles." The Greek verb does not imply choosing certain persons from among a larger group, and the reference to the future contained in the English "destine" is found, not in the Greek verb itself, but in the following words, "for wrath." In order to avoid as far as possible all these outside associations, there is much to be said for keeping close to the ordinary meaning of the verb, and translating "God did not put us here in order to condemn us." "Here" (that is, "in the church," not "in the world") is implied. "In order to condemn us" brings out the clear implication that the "wrath" is God's (TEV does this by inserting his).

If one wishes to avoid a direct translation of choose, it may be possible to employ an expression such as "God did not deal with us as he has...," or "God has not done what he has done to us in order to condemn us."

To possess may mean "to hold in possession" or "to gain possession of."

How one translates this verb will depend on whether salvation is understood as a present possession or a future hope. This question is settled decisively (1) by hope of salvation in verse 8, which implies a future event, and (2) by the parallel to suffer his anger, which has a future reference. The wider context, too, looks forward to the final and complete salvation which believers will experience at the coming of Christ. Salvation is therefore here a future hope, and to possess means "to gain possession of."

To suffer his anger may be rendered in some languages as "in order to condemn us and make us suffer at the last judgment," or "just so that he could make us suffer." The phrase to possess salvation may seem clear in English, but it is quite impossible in some languages where "to possess" may refer only to objects and not to a state such as is implied in salvation. If one translates the first part of verse 9 as "God did not deal with us as he did in order to make us suffer at the last judgment," it may then be possible to translate the second part as "but he did what he did in order to save us through our Lord Jesus Christ."

In placing the negative in verse 9a, it may be necessary to shift it from God's activity to the suffering, for example, "God dealt with us as he did, not in order to make us suffer, but in order that we would be saved through our Lord Jesus Christ." In some cases it may be necessary to introduce the positive statement before the negative one, for example, "God dealt with us as he did in order that we would be saved through our Lord Jesus Christ. He did not purpose that we would just suffer."

Through our Lord Jesus Christ expresses secondary agency. It is God who is the primary agent in salvation, and this is made possible by means of the Lord Jesus Christ. This secondary agency is expressed in some languages by "in order that God would save us; our Lord Jesus Christ did it."

5.10 who died for us in order that we might live together with him, whether we are alive or dead when he comes.

To say that Christ died for us is an apparently simple statement, but it raises great problems of theological interpretation, and some (fortunately smaller) problems for the translator, centering on the meaning of the word for. Greek uses two main prepositions in similar contexts, and it is dangerous to press too hard the distinction between them. The one used here (huper) tends to have a fairly general meaning: "on behalf of" or "for the sake of," rather than "instead of" or "in place of." The implication here is that Christ died in order that those who believe in him might benefit in some way. Paul goes on immediately to say in what way: the purpose of Christ's dying is that all believers might live together with him forever (cf. 4.17). Might is required in English after in order that.

The phrase for us (in the clause who died for us) expresses a benefactive relation; that is, we are the beneficiaries of the fact of Christ's dying. Some languages even have a benefactive case, and that would be the appropriate form to use in this context.

Whether we are alive or dead is literally "whether we are awake or asleep."

"Sleep," both here and in 4.13 and 15, is a metaphor for death, and this determines the meaning of "to be awake." This verb does not have the specific meaning here that it has in verse 6, that of being alert for the coming of Christ, but it has the wider meaning of remaining alive (that is, until the time of his coming). Here Paul cleverly uses two terms which he had been using to speak of alertness but which at this point he transposes to mean "alive/dead." In this way he brings us back to 4.13. When he comes (cf. FrCL) is implicit in the text.

Whether we are alive or dead is rendered in some languages as "it makes no difference whether we are alive or dead," or "whether we are alive or dead, it is all the same." When he comes must be closely related to "being alive or dead." Therefore one may translate the entire expression as "whether we are alive or dead when he comes, that will not make any difference."

5.11 And so encourage one another and help one another, just as you are now doing.

So refers back directly to verses 9-10, but also more generally to all the encouragement Paul has been giving his readers throughout the chapter, just as so then in 4.18 refers back to the entire section 4.13-17.

One another...one another. No doubt for stylistic reasons, Paul uses two different expressions in Greek, but they have the same meaning, and therefore need not be distinguished in translation. Help is a literal equivalent for Paul's metaphorical "build one another up" (cf. JB "keep on strengthening one another"). Both verbs, encourage and help, suggest continued action over a period of time, and this is made explicit by the following words, just as you are now doing (cf. 4.10). This clause may be rendered as "that is, of course, just what you are now doing," or "you are, of course, doing just that."

TEV

Final Instructions and Greetings

12 We beg you, our brothers, to pay proper respect to those who work among you, who guide and instruct you in the Christian life. 13 Treat them with the greatest respect and love, because of the work they do. Be at peace among yourselves.

14 We urge you, our brothers, to warn the idle, encourage the timid, help the weak, be patient with everyone. 15 See that no one pays back wrong for wrong, but at all times make it your aim to do good to one another and to all people.

16 Be joyful always, 17 pray at all times, 18 be thankful in all

RSV

12 But we beseech you, brethren, to respect those who labor among you and are over you in the Lord and admonish you, 13 and to esteem them very highly in love because of their work. Be at peace among yourselves. 14 And we exhort you, brethren, admonish the idle, encourage the fainthearted, help the weak, be patient with them all. 15 See that none of you repays evil for evil, but always seek to do good to one another and to all. 16 Rejoice always, 17 pray constantly, 18 give thanks in all

circumstances. This is what God
wants from you in your life in
union with Christ Jesus.
19 Do not restrain the Holy
Spirit; 20 do not despise inspired
messages. 21 Put all things to the
test: keep what is good, 22 and
avoid every kind of evil.
23 May the God who gives us
peace make you holy in every way,
and keep your whole being--spirit,
soul, and body--free from every
fault at the coming of our Lord Jesus Christ. 24 He who calls you
will do it, because he is faithful.
25 Pray also for us, brothers.
26 Greet all the believers with
a brotherly kiss.
27 I urge you, by the authority
of the Lord, to read this letter to
all the believers.
28 The grace of our Lord Jesus
Christ be with you. (5.12-28)

circumstances; for this is the will
of God in Christ Jesus for you.
19 Do not quench the Spirit, 20 do
not despise prophesying, 21 but
test everything; hold fast what is
good, 22 abstain from every form
of evil.
23 May the God of peace himself
sanctify you wholly; and may your
spirit and soul and body be kept
sound and blameless at the coming
of our Lord Jesus Christ. 24 He
who calls you is faithful, and he
will do it.
25 Brethren, pray for us.
26 Greet all the brethren with
a holy kiss.
27 I adjure you by the Lord that
this letter be read to all the
brethren.
28 The grace of our Lord Jesus
Christ be with you. (5.12-28)

Paul ends his letter with a series of brief instructions, and two prayers or benedictions (vv. 23, 28). As in the rest of chapters 4 and 5, Paul appeals here for action: some of it (e.g. vv. 12, 15) outward and visible, some of it (e.g. vv. 16, 18) inward and spiritual.

The relation of this passage to earlier sections is marked by (1) the transitional which RSV translates "but" (misleadingly, since no contrast is implied), KJV translates "and," and TEV omits; (2) the repetition of we beg from 4.1; and (3) the use of brothers (as in 4.13; 5.1, 25, and other places) to help mark the beginning of a new section or subsection. Phps translates "we ask you too," but the "too" is unnecessary and awkward, since the last use of we beg is so far away, and Paul has meanwhile presented so much material of a different kind.

The internal structure of the section is rather loose, but it is possible to see some kind of development. Verses 12-22 may be divided into four subsections, as TEV indicates by paragraphing. Verses 12-13 are concerned with the relationships between members and leaders of the community; verses 14-15 with the responsibility of Christians to one another and to non-Christians; verses 16-18 with the fervor of a Christian's inner personal life; and verses 19-22 with the Holy Spirit and the effects of his work. Then, in verse 23, comes a first prayer, closely linked with the expression of confidence in God in verse 24. Verse 23 is more complex than other sentences in this part of the letter, and forms a natural climax. Verses 25-28 are not at all closely related to what has gone before, and they read like one of the postscripts Paul sometimes adds to his letters in his own handwriting (cf. Galatians 6.11; Colossians 4.18; 2 Thess. 3.17).

5.12

Commentators disagree about whether, throughout this passage, Paul is addressing the whole Christian community in Thessalonica, or whether in verses 14-15 he is speaking only to the leaders. It seems better not to make a rigid distinction. There is no conclusive evidence that the brothers in verse 12 are not the same as the brothers in verse 14, and verse 15b clearly applies to everyone.

5.12 We beg you, our brothers, to pay proper respect to those who work among you, who guide and instruct you in the Christian life.

We beg (cf. 4.1) translates a word which can mean either "to ask a question" or "to ask someone to do something." The context makes it clear that the second meaning is intended here. To pay proper respect translates a single word which normally means "to know." Here it has the meaning of "to recognize" (Phps), "respect," or "appreciate the worth of" (see 4.4), and it refers to those who guide and instruct you in the Christian life. Paul means that the Thessalonians are to pay the respect which is due to them as leaders or guides. Phps "get to know those who work so hard among you" oddly implies that the "spiritual leaders" were not already well known to those whom they led. Work suggests hard labor. The corresponding noun is used in 2.9, where Paul is speaking about manual work; in 3.5, where he is speaking of his work as an apostle; and in 1.3, where both everyday work and specifically Christian activities may be implied. Here the context shows that Paul is referring to work involved in the leadership of the Christian community.

As RSV's rather literal translation shows, the verbs work, guide, and instruct are linked only by "and": "respect those who labor among you and are over you in the Lord and admonish you." TEV shows correctly that work is a general term, and that guide and instruct refer to specific aspects of the leaders' work.

The translator has to choose between two possible meanings of the word which TEV translates as guide: (1) "to be at the head of," and (2) "to be concerned about," or "care for" (in each case, the Christian community). 1 Timothy 5.17 is a clear example of the first meaning (TEV has "leaders" there, as TNT has in the present verse), and Titus 3.8, 14 is an evident case of the second. Those who prefer the second meaning here argue that the surrounding verbs work and instruct refer to voluntary work which could be done by any member of the community. However, this is by no means certain, particularly as far as instruct is concerned. Like the older translation "admonish," instruct often implies warning or blame; it is not the most common word for "teach." In 1 Corinthians 4.14 and Colossians 1.28, the same word refers to one of Paul's own functions as an apostle and evangelist; in Colossians 3.16 it is a question of Christians instructing each other.

Are we then to think of "ordinary" Christians working hard at caring for one another and warning one another when necessary? or of leaders in the community who issue instructions and warnings from a position of special responsibility? The form of the sentence as a whole (those...who...) seems to point to a particular group within the Christian community. However, Paul does not in this passage use any of the words, such as "bishop," "elder," or "deacon," which later became titles to describe particular offices in the church. The translator should beware of reading back into this passage the more formal hierarchical structures of a later period. GeCL uses a compound word which means "those who preside over the community" and adds a note comparing them to the officials of the synagogue mentioned, for example, in Matthew 5.22 (cf. Mft "presiding over you"). The meaning of the whole sentence (omitting "in the Lord" for the moment) is therefore that the Thessalonians are to show the respect due to those who have the hard task of leading the community and issuing any warning or reproof which may be necessary. There is no suggestion that those who work, those who guide (or lead), and those who instruct (reprove, warn) are different people. GeCL "Honor all who exert themselves for you, those who preside over the community, and all who show you the right way" is slightly misleading, since it suggests different groups.

It would obviously be wrong to translate beg as a request for some object or special consideration. This is a matter of "urgently asking" or "urging."

To pay proper respect may, of course, be translated merely as "to give honor to," but one may come a little closer to the meaning of the original in translating "to recognize as important," or "to acknowledge the value of those who...."

Since who work among you can be so readily misunderstood as an expression of manual labor, it may be better to use some such expression as "do so much for you."

The final clause, who guide and instruct you in the Christian life, may be introduced by a phrase "these are the ones who...." To guide may be rendered as "be your leaders," and instruct you as "tell you what you should do."

5.13 Treat them with the greatest respect and love, because of the work they do. Be at peace among yourselves.

This verse begins in Greek with "and," but this conjunction is better omitted, not only because of the preference in many languages for shorter sentences, but because "and" tends to lead the reader to expect something new, distinct from what has gone before. In fact, verse 13a largely repeats verse 12. Work is a common word, unrelated to work in verse 12, and without the suggestion of effort or hard labor. Paul is clearly thinking here, not of the work these individuals do in order to earn their living, but of their function as leaders in the church.

Treat them with the greatest respect may be translated as "honor them very much," or "show them how important you think they are."

Treat them with...love can be rendered in some languages only as "love them," but in certain instances a translation such as "show great appreciation for them" may be closer to the meaning of this context.

Because of the work they do may be best expressed in some cases as "because of all the ways in which they help you," or "because of all that they do," thus avoiding any specific reference to work which might imply physical labor.

5.14

BJ (1st ed.) JB Syn Mft Phps NEB GeCL all begin a new paragraph at be at peace among yourselves, and one or two translations try to make explicit a connection with what follows. Syn suggests a contrastive relation: "Be at peace among yourselves. However, we beg you, brothers, warn...." Phps, on the other hand, thinks of a relation of means and purpose: "Live together in peace, and our instruction to this end is to reprimand...." If be at peace among yourselves is placed at the end of the preceding paragraph, it will refer to good relations between the church leaders and the rest of the Christian community.* If this admonition is placed at the beginning of a new paragraph, it will refer to tensions among the members (cf. v. 15a). Formally, however, verse 14, with its we urge you, the transitional "and" or "but," and brothers, appears to begin a new paragraph. If 13b is placed, as in most translations (including BJ 2nd ed.), at the end of the preceding paragraph, it forms a good bridge between verses 12-13 and 14-15. The underlying thought, somewhat expanded, is most probably "you should maintain good relations with your leaders, but also with one another generally; and we must therefore go on to urge you to warn the idle" etc. Peace in Hebrew and Jewish-Christian thought was more than the absence of conflict. Nevertheless, Brc's rendering of verse 13b should be noted as an example of "over-translation": "Nothing must ever be allowed to interrupt your personal relationships with each other."

Be at peace implies a state, not a specific act of peace-making or reconciliation; "live at peace" (NEB cf. DuCL FrCL GeCL SpCL) expresses this clearly. A positive quality such as peace can best be expressed in some languages as the negation of a bad quality or condition, for example, "live together without quarreling," or "live together without feeling against one another."

This is the first of a long series of imperatives in verses 13-22 which suggest continuous or repeated action over a period. This effect is strengthened by the use of such words as at all times (vv. 15, 17) and always (v. 16).

5.14 We urge you, our brothers, to warn the idle, encourage the timid, help the weak, be patient with everyone.

We have already noted the similarities between the beginnings of verses 12 and 14 (cf. also 4.1). The words beg and urge are typical of those passages in which Paul appeals for action; cf. also 4.10, 18; 5.11 (and 5.27, where a different word is used in the Greek). There is little difference of meaning between the words translated urge here, and beg in verse 12; GeCL translates them by the same word: verse 12 "we ask you," and verse 14 "we further ask you." We have seen no reason for thinking that Paul, at this point, suddenly turns to address the leaders of the community. We must therefore suppose that the leaders were not the only people who had the right and responsibility to warn others. Paul uses here the word which in verse 12 was translated instruct. Since the

---

*A number of manuscripts, reflected in the Vulgate, make this explicit by their reading "be at peace with them," i.e. the leaders, but this is almost certainly not the original text.

admonition Paul directs to the Thessalonian Christians consists of four different activities, one may translate the introductory expression as "these things are what we urge you, brothers, to do."

The word translated idle is found only here in the New Testament, but a related verb and adverb are used in 2 Thessalonians 3.6, 7, 11, where the context makes it quite clear that Paul is speaking of a refusal to work. The central meaning of the adjective in secular Greek is "not in good order." It is used to describe an undisciplined army, and also someone who is not at his post of duty. Which element of meaning is dominant here? Is Paul thinking of "those who will not accept discipline" (Brc), or of "those who do not want to work" (SpCL)? The first alternative is supported by KJV and Phps ("unruly"), NEB ("careless"), cf. GeCL Seg Zur Syn Lu BJ (2nd ed.) TOB; the second alternative is supported by Mft ("loafers") and JB ("idlers") cf. DuCL BJ (1st ed.). The immediate context is too indefinite to settle the question, but Paul's wider concern in both letters to the Thessalonians suggests the second alternative (cf. 4.11). Idle is not to be understood as "the unemployed," "those who have no work," or even "those who do not work," but rather as "those who refuse to work" (cf. SpCL).

In this context, warn implies a strong admonition not to behave in a particular way. A satisfactory translation may be simply "tell those who are idle that they must not be so," "tell those lazy people that this is not right," or "speak strongly to the lazy persons."

Encourage the timid. Both encourage and timid translate rather uncommon words in Greek. Paul has used "encourage" in 2.12, where TEV translates comforted. The word sometimes means "to console (someone who is mourning)." Paul may be thinking of the Thessalonians' fears concerning death, which he has tried to meet in 4.13-18. The word translated timid not only refers to those who are nervous in personal contacts, but to people who are easily frightened. TOB renders "give courage to those who have little of it."

A literal translation of encourage the timid could result in precisely the wrong meaning, namely, "encourage the timid to be more timid." A more satisfactory equivalent may be found in a rendering such as "give courage to those who are fearful," "take away the fear from those who are afraid," or "give confidence to those who are afraid."

The four imperatives in this verse move in widening circles, from the specific problems of the Christian community (unwillingness to work and lack of courage) to a more general concern for the weak and patience with everyone. Within this setting, it is difficult to decide whether the weak are (as in Romans 14) weak members of the Christian community or people outside it. It is usually possible to leave both alternatives open in translation. In any case, it is clear that Paul's use of the word weak, here as in Romans 14.1-2, does not imply any condemnation. Like the timid, the weak are people who need help, no doubt because they are immature or inexperienced. Since it is impossible to know precisely the meaning of weak in this context, it may be best to use a descriptive phrase which will fit with the meaning of "help," for example, "help those who need help," or "help those who are lacking in some way."

Be patient with everyone may be expressed idiomatically, for example, "speak softly to everyone," "move slowly with everyone," or negatively, "do not speak sharply to anyone," or "do not shout at anyone."

5.15 See that no one pays back wrong for wrong, but at all times make it your aim to do good to one another and to all people.

In this verse, as at the end of verse 14, Paul's concern widens to include non-Christians. No one and to all people make this clear. To one another means "to fellow-Christians."

English, like Greek, can naturally use the metaphor see in the sense of "take care" or "make sure." In New Testament Greek, as in modern English, the metaphor is dead or dying, but it continues in certain negative expressions, for example, "see that (something) does not happen." It is therefore often appropriate to translate it by a literal equivalent. (See also the notes on 5.19 for the translation of metaphors.)

See that no one pays back wrong for wrong may need some restructuring. This is particularly the case with the introductory expression see, for example, "prevent people paying back wrong for wrong," or "do not permit people to pay back wrong for wrong." On the other hand, it is possible that this admonition is directed to each individual, in which case one can translate "no one should pay back wrong for wrong."

The phrase pays back wrong for wrong is a very condensed expression involving a number of complex relations. These are expressed in various languages in quite different ways, for example, "exchange one bad deed for another bad deed," or "give back a bad deed when one has received a bad deed." It may, in fact, be necessary to be even more explicit, for example, "No one should do wrong to someone else just because that person has done wrong to him."

Greek dictionaries commonly distinguish between the words for good used here and in verse 21. The word used here tends to mean "morally good" or "physically sound," while the word used in verse 21 tends to mean "good to look at, attractive, beautiful." In this context, however, they have virtually the same meaning, and TEV therefore translates them both by good.

At all times may be translated as "always," but since in Greek it is a relatively strong term in an emphatic position, one may translate it as "regardless of the circumstances" or "regardless of what happens."

Make it your aim may be translated as "try earnestly" or "endeavor strongly."

To do good to one another may be equivalent to "help one another."

5.16-18 Be joyful always, (17) pray at all times, (18) be thankful in all circumstances. This is what God wants from you in your life in union with Christ Jesus.

The verse divisions in this section are inconsistent. The three imperatives in these verses are no more and no less closely linked than the four imperatives of verse 14. This is what God wants from you in your life in union with

Christ Jesus refers to all the imperatives, not alone to be thankful in all circumstances.

Be joyful always. Paul has already mentioned the joy of the Thessalonian Christians (1.6) and the joy he had received from them (2.20; 3.9). There is nothing contradictory about his now telling them to be joyful; it is another example of the "do even more" motif which occurs in various passages (e.g. 4.10). In some languages it is anomalous to command anyone to be joyful, since the experience of joy is regarded as being dependent upon outside circumstances over which one has no control. The implication of Paul's statement is that real joy depends upon one's relation to God, which is permanent and unchanging. Since the Thessalonians were admonished to give evidence to this important and lasting relation, an equivalent in some languages may be "always wear a happy face," "let your happy heart be known," or "let the song within your insides be heard."

Pray at all times is literally (KJV) "pray without ceasing." There is an element of rhetorical exaggeration here, as in Romans 12.12 and Colossians 4.2 (cf. Ephesians 6.18). Rigaux comments: "(Paul) does not ask them to recite prayers all day long; he asks that they should feel the need of turning to God, not only when important things are happening but at all times." Paul means "never give up praying" (cf. GeCL). Pray is a general term which includes all forms of prayer, not only petition and intercession for oneself and others. In order to avoid the implication that the believer should be constantly in prayer to God, one may say "be ready to speak to God at all times," or "speak to God on any and all occasions."

Be thankful (cf. 1.2; 3.9). In translation it may be necessary to specify that the thanksgiving is addressed to God. Circumstances is not explicit in the text, and it is equally possible that "at all times" is intended. The Greek is quite general, and the translation should therefore not be too narrow in its reference. The meaning of verses 16, 17, and 18 is closely parallel, though for stylistic reasons the words are different in the original. Be thankful in all circumstances may be equivalent in some languages to "be thankful to God regardless of circumstances," or "...despite whatever may happen."

This is what God wants from you in your life in union with Christ Jesus. This sentence raises two problems, the first related to from you and the second related to in union with Christ Jesus. RSV reflects the form of the Greek.

On the first question, translators are generally divided into three groups. The first group, represented by TEV JB Knox Brc TNT (cf. DuCL FrCL GeCL SpCL), thinks that Paul is speaking about what God demands of or from the Thessalonians, namely, a life full of joy, prayer, and thanksgiving. TNT, for example, translates "this is what God wants you to do as Christians." The second group, represented by RSV Mft Phps NEB Zur, thinks that Paul is referring to what God wills for them, that is, what he intends and makes possible for them. NEB, for example, translates "this is what God in Christ* wills for you."

*The omission of the word "Jesus" is not well attested in the manuscripts.

The third group, including KJV (cf. Lu Syn Seg TOB), chooses a vague compromise solution, "this is the will of God in Christ Jesus concerning you."

The first solution fits in well with Paul's long series of imperatives and makes a good transition to verse 19: "This is what God expects of you; (19) therefore...." On the other hand, the second solution also makes a good transition to verse 19. On this interpretation, verses 18b-19 would describe, not what is required from the Thessalonians, but (like 1.3-6 on a wider scale) what becomes possible through the working together of Father, Son, and Holy Spirit. The second alternative is also a slightly more natural translation of the Greek. However, TEV's solution cannot be ruled out. The third solution tends to produce an unclear translation with less impact than the original, in which from you or "for you" is in an emphatic position at the end of the sentence.

The translator's decision on this first problem will influence his translation of "in Christ Jesus." TEV's in your life is not explicit in the text. The choice is between (1) linking "in Christ Jesus" with "God" or "will of God" and (2) linking this phrase with "you." The first alternative would fit in better with NEB's solution of the first problem; the second alternative would be more natural if TEV's solution of the first problem were chosen. The options may be summarized as follows:

	A (TEV)	B (NEB)	(KJV)
1 what God wants	from (or of) you	for you	concerning you
2 in Christ	in your life in union with Christ Jesus	what God in Christ (Jesus) wills	B2

DIAGRAM 4

If A is chosen, other possibilities, in addition to TEV's in your life in union with Christ Jesus, are Brc's "the way in which God wishes you who are Christians to live," FrCL's "your life with Jesus Christ," GeCL's "that is what God wants from those who are bound together with Jesus Christ," or simply "from those who belong to Jesus Christ."

This is what God wants from you in your life in union with Christ Jesus may require some restructuring, for example, "this is how God wants you to live as persons who belongs to Christ Jesus." This latter expression may be necessary since "in Christ Jesus" may seem quite meaningless. If one attempts to follow the NEB interpretation, namely, "this is what God in Christ wills for you," a problem arises since the three admonitions which immediately precede are not things which are given to persons, but things which the persons themselves should do. The equivalent would be more or less "this is the kind of experience which God wants for you." The phrase "in Christ" would then express that this is the provision which God, who was in Christ or who operated through Christ, was desirous of providing for the believers. In some languages the closest equivalent may be "God did this by means of Christ," or "God does this by means of Christ."

"Jesus Christ" and Christ Jesus are commonly used by Paul without any distinction of meaning; the translator should feel free to use the more natural order in the receptor language. Christ here, as normally in Paul's writings, is a name, not the title "Messiah" (see the notes on 1.1).

5.19-22 Do not restrain the Holy Spirit; (20) do not despise inspired messages. (21) Put all things to the test: keep what is good, (22) and avoid every kind of evil.

A good part of the meaning of these five imperatives is lost if we do not first understand the relations between them. The first clear distinction is between the two negative commands of verses 19-20 and the three positive commands of verses 21-22. In Greek the two groups are separated by an adversative "but" (omitted in many manuscripts, probably accidentally incorporated into the next word). Within each group, Paul moves from the generic to the specific; despising inspired messages is a special case of restraining the Holy Spirit. Keeping what is good and avoiding every kind of evil are the two consequences of putting all things to the test.

The question then arises: Does the second group of commands, like the first, refer to "inspired" activities, or does it have a wider meaning? When Paul says put all things to the test, does he mean "everything which claims to be an inspired message," or is he advising his readers in general terms not to take anything at its face value? NEB makes the first possibility explicit in its text: "Do not despise prophetic utterances, but put them all to the test and then keep what is good in them and avoid the bad of whatever kind," and the second possibility in a footnote: "...Put everything to the test: keep hold of what is good and avoid every kind of evil." The first alternative makes stronger sense of the context, though NEB's text is perhaps too emphatic.

Do not restrain the Holy Spirit. TEV and GeCL make explicit the word "Holy" in this context. The word is implicit in the original Greek, but for the reader of a common language translation it is better to make it explicit.

Restrain is a nonmetaphorical translation of a text which contains the metaphor of putting out a fire (cf. RSV "do not quench the Spirit"). The Holy Spirit was sometimes described as a flame or fire (see Acts 2.3). Translators deal with this metaphor in four different ways. (1) KJV RSV Lu Zur Seg Syn BJ TOB keep the metaphor as it stands, leaving the image of the comparison implicit. (2) Others make the image of comparison explicit: "never damp the fire of the Spirit" Phps (cf. Mft GeCL SpCL). (3) NEB Knox TNT FrCL replace the original metaphor by a different one: "stifle" or "put an obstacle in the way of." (4) TEV JB Brc GeCL replace the metaphor by a literal expression or, in the case of GeCL, by a dead metaphor. The first choice is the least likely to be clear, outside the original setting of the primitive church. The choice between the three other possibilities depends on the resources of the receptor language. Generally speaking, a nonmetaphorical translation should be chosen only if (2) and (3) prove to be difficult or misleading.

Something of the metaphorical significance of the phrase "do not quench the Spirit" may be reflected in other types of metaphors, for example, "do not hold back the Spirit," "do not tie the Spirit down," "do not make the Spirit shut up," or "do not tell the Spirit, That is enough."

Inspired messages are literally "prophecies," but TEV avoids this term, since it has narrowed its meaning to that of "prediction," foretelling the future. TEV restores the full meaning of the original, which meant an inspired and intelligible message, as distinct from speaking with tongues, which for Paul is inspired but not normally intelligible. Despise includes the ideas of treating something as of no account and of rejecting it with contempt.

There are some difficulties involved in translating inspired messages. If one calls them "messages that come from God," then obviously there is no special point of putting them to the test and keeping what is good while rejecting the rest. The same would be true if one called them "messages which come from the Holy Spirit," for such a phrase would indicate that all such messages are valid. The only way in which these problems may be avoided in some languages is to say "messages given by those who claim to speak on behalf of God." Such an expression defines the role of "the prophet," in its New Testament sense, and provides at least a basis for the warning in verse 21.

Put...to the test is quite a common word in both New Testament and secular Greek. It is used, for example, in speaking of a moneychanger testing the genuineness of a coin. Inspired messages are to be tested in a similar way, to see whether their inspiration comes from the Holy Spirit or from the powers of evil (cf. 1 Corinthians 14 and especially 1 Corinthians 12.3). All things probably means "all inspired messages" (cf. the general notes on vv. 19-22). On what is good, see the notes on verse 16.

Put all things to the test must often be translated in this type of context as "try out all of these messages," or "test all of these messages to see if they are right." No particular way is indicated as to how the messages can be tested, and therefore perhaps a general expression must be used, for example, "decide whether these messages are true," or "decide whether these messages really do come from God."

Keep what is good should not be understood in the sense of "keeping hold of" and "treasuring up." The implication is rather that the believers should obey the good admonitions or instructions. Accordingly, a rendering such as "do that which is good," "follow that which is good," or "put into practice that which is good" may be appropriate.

Avoid must not be understood as "getting out the way of," but rather as "refusing to do" or "having nothing to do with."

Every kind of evil is the way in which almost all translations understand the text which KJV renders "all appearance of evil." In Greek the word evil may be either masculine or neuter, and so in some contexts it may also mean "an evil man," but the contrast with good in verse 21 excludes that possibility here.

The meaning every kind is found only here in the New Testament. In Luke 3.22 and 9.29 it means "appearance," and this is the meaning given to it by an early 2nd century writing, the Didache (3.1), which expands this text into "flee from all evil and from all that is like it." If KJV's interpretation is chosen (and it is not impossible), the translator should guard against the misunderstanding that Paul is warning only against apparent, and not against real, evil. "Keep away from even the appearance of evil, in any form" would avoid this danger. However, TEV gives the simplest and the most probable meaning.

It is often difficult to speak of every kind of evil, because some languages have classifications of objects, but not classifications of qualities such as may be implied by the term "evil." In this context, however, evil refers, not so much to an abstract quality as to evil action or behavior; therefore one may render this admonition as "refuse to do anything which is evil," or "refuse to act in any way which even seems bad."

5.23 May the God who gives us peace make you holy in every way, and keep your whole being—spirit, soul, and body—free from every fault at the coming of our Lord Jesus Christ.

God is emphatic and means "God himself." The God who gives us peace makes clear the relation between God and peace implied in the Greek construction "the God of peace." On peace, see the notes on 1.1 and 5.13. Paul is using the word in the sense of the Hebrew shalom, a total material and especially spiritual well-being which God gives. GeCL brings this out to some extent by translating "God who gives us his peace." Though some persons might want to see in this phrase a reference to the reconciling function of God in "making peace," that is not the meaning in this context. It is rather a reference to "God who provides fully for us." One should certainly avoid the meaning of "God who stops the fighting"!

Make you holy in every way is literally "make you completely holy." Christians are already holy (3.13) in the sense that they belong to Christ, but they need to share more completely in his life and being. The word whole reinforces the idea of completeness. Being (cf. TOB note) is implied in the text, which uses a singular adjective.

In many contexts it is easy to translate "holy" as "a person who belongs to God," thus avoiding the meaning of "holy" as ritual performance or taboo. In the present context, however, it is difficult to say that "God will make you belong to himself," since the Thessalonians were already related to God as his possession. In some languages the concept of holiness is so closely related to the character of God himself (as being one of his most distinctive characteristics) that one can justifiably render holy in the present context as "make you like himself in every way," "save you from sin," or "make you completely good." Such a paraphrase would be used, however, only in circumstances where there is simply no term for "holy" which would fit this type of context.

This is the only place in which Paul makes the threefold distinction: spirit, soul, and body. In such a passage as this, which is close to poetic or liturgical language, it is not surprising that Paul does not define precisely the relations between these three elements. Lu seems to think that the first includes the second and third: "your whole spirit, together with soul and body," but this sense is unlikely.

It is clear from the context that spirit is here a part or aspect of human nature, that the Holy Spirit is not referred to. In biblical thought generally, each of the three terms designates the whole of man seen from a particular point of view, spirit being the inner man who thinks and worships, soul being equivalent to life in its outward manifestations, and body being man in his weakness (though not explicitly in his sin). Here, as often, Paul is using Greek words with Hebrew meanings. It is neither possible nor necessary to burden the text, or even the footnotes of a translation, with a complete analysis of the meanings of the Hebrew words. Paul's overriding purpose is to pray that every aspect of his readers' existence may belong completely to God, and so be kept safe at the coming of Christ. The translator should therefore feel free to choose a variety of terms (not necessarily three) which in the receptor language refer to various aspects of human nature.

The expression keep your whole being—spirit, soul, and body is extremely difficult to translate adequately in many languages. This is not merely because a language may not have three words such as "spirit," "soul," and "body" to represent three parts or aspects of the personality. It is rather because the words which a language does have are differently related to the concept of "your whole being." Many languages have no expression for "being." In reality, this term refers, not to an abstract "being," but to existence or life. For this reason, in many languages one must translate "keep your whole life...free from all fault."

As an explanation for or amplification of "whole life," one may introduce these various aspects of the personality, namely, "spirit," "soul," and "body." On the other hand, the Greek term translated "soul" is often rendered as "life," and a more natural translation in some languages would be "keep your whole life, spirit, and body." In this way one can include all that is spiritual and material in one's existence. For many languages this is more effective and meaningful, as well as more accurate, than an inclusion of three terms which might be either confusing or misleading.

Free from every fault translates a single word which includes the meaning of not being blamed for anything, that is, of not deserving any blame (cf. 3.13). In the background is the picture of the coming of Christ for a trial in which Satan will accuse and Christ will judge. Paul does not simply mean that the Thessalonians are to be kept safe until the coming of Christ; Christ's coming is itself the supreme test which those, and only those, whom God has made holy can meet without fear. Keep...free often involves a causative expression, for example, "cause you to be blameless," "cause to happen that no one can blame you," or "...can accuse you about anything."

At the coming of our Lord Jesus Christ may be rendered as "when our Lord Jesus Christ comes again," or "when our Lord Jesus Christ shows himself." The choice of terms will depend upon the way in which one translates the same type of expression in other passages in 1 Thessalonians. On coming, see the notes on 2.19 (cf. 3.13; 4.15).

May . . . God . . . keep correctly translates a passive, "may your whole (being) . . . be kept," implying an activity of God.

5.24 He who calls you will do it, because he is faithful.

For Paul, he who calls you is always God the Father (cf. 2.12; 4.7). Here, as in 23b, Paul follows Jewish practice in referring to God without naming him directly. TEV reverses the order of the sentence (cf. RSV) for two reasons. First, there is a tendency in Greek for the greatest emphasis to occur at the end of the sentence, whereas in English the greatest emphasis tends to occur at the beginning. Second, TEV is able, by reversing the order, to bring out more clearly the relation of result and reason expressed in because (implicit in the text). He who calls you will do it may require some shift in tenses, since the present calls might imply that God was at that very moment calling to the Thessalonians. This is a reference to what God constantly does, but for this to refer to the specific experience of the Thessalonians, it may be necessary to use a perfective tense, for example, "he who has called you will do it." As in other contexts, call may suggest here a wrong meaning if it is translated literally. A translation should not suggest "shouting" but "inviting," expressed in some languages as "God who has spoken to us to become his."

He is faithful means "he is reliable," "he keeps his promises." The same God is at work from the moment at which the Thessalonians are called until the coming of Christ. This may be semantically restructured as "you can always trust him," or "you may be sure he will always do what he has said."

5.25 Pray also for us, brothers.

Brothers marks a transition, perhaps (see general notes on vv. 12-28), to a postscript in Paul's own writing (see also notes on v. 27). Also is omitted in many good manuscripts, included in the 1st and 2nd editions of the UBS Greek New Testament, and placed in square brackets in the 3rd edition. It may have been added by a copyist who was thinking of Colossians 4.3. If it is original, it refers back either to verse 23, with the meaning "pray for us, as we have just prayed for you," or more remotely to verse 17, with the meaning "pray at all times, and remember also to pray for us."

Languages differ in the positions within sentences in which they introduce the names of persons or references to persons directly addressed. Throughout this book of 1 Thessalonians, the tendency is to place the term translated brothers immediately after some initial expression, often a transitional device. In this context in verse 25, however, it occurs in Greek at the beginning. In some languages any item of direct address must occur at the beginning of a sentence. A literal translation of the TEV order could be confusing, since "us" could be immediately combined with "brothers" and thus imply "pray for us who are brothers." This is not the meaning, and hence special care must be exercised in the location of "brothers." If it is necessary to state in translation to whom the "brothers" are related, "our brothers" should be used in preference to "my brothers" (BJ 1st ed.).

5.26 Greet all the believers with a brotherly kiss.

A brotherly kiss is literally "a holy kiss." This verse and verse 27 presuppose that Paul's letter will be read aloud when all the members of the church come together for worship. This is brought out by NEB's translation "the kiss of peace" (cf. DuCL), but this suggests to the modern reader a feature of certain forms of worship, such as the Roman Catholic mass or the liturgy of the Church of South India. In the earliest Christian communities, the "holy kiss" was more like a spontaneous greeting between friends. It does not seem to have had any precedent in synagogue worship.

Phps' "Give a handshake all around among the brotherhood" represents a brave attempt to find an equivalent custom in a western culture, but TEV's solution of a difficult problem (cf. FrCL GeCL) is to be preferred.

In areas of the Middle East where the kiss of greeting is widely used, there is no difficulty in rendering the translation of this verse more or less literally, for example, "greet all the brothers with the kind of kiss one would bestow upon a brother." But in many parts of the world kissing is regarded as exclusively an expression of amorous or erotic interest. Under such circumstances one cannot use a literal expression for "kiss." One equivalent may be "greet fellow believers in the same way you greet members of your family," or "greet fellow believers affectionately."

5.27 I urge you, by the authority of the Lord, to read this letter to all the believers.

This is one of the few places in this letter in which Paul distinguishes himself from his companions. He may have written the last few lines with his own hand.

Urge represents a strong term in Greek. An equivalent in some languages may be "I command you" or "I tell you that you should."

The authority of (cf. SpCL) is implied in the text. FrCL and DuCL have "in the Lord's name" (cf. Knox JB Brc TNT). It is not the same Greek expression which occurs in 4.2, but it is in many respects similar and may be rendered in some languages as "as one who represents the Lord." The Greek expression may be literally translated as "I adjure you by the Lord," or "I put you under a solemn oath, calling upon the Lord as witness," but this more technical meaning hardly fits the context, and it may be that one should translate "I strongly urge you to read this letter to all the brothers, since that is what the Lord would want."

The Lord, here as usually in Paul's writings, is Jesus, not God the Father, as Phps translates it.

5.28 The grace of our Lord Jesus Christ be with you.

Here as at the end of all his letters, Paul replaces the brief greeting, common in secular letters of the period, with a specifically Christian benediction. For the key word grace, see notes on 1.1. GeCL restructures the sentence to read "May Jesus Christ, our Lord, keep you in his grace."

This final statement in this First Letter to the Thessalonians is essentially a kind of prayer, and therefore must be put into such a form in some languages, for example, "I pray that our Lord Jesus Christ may be gracious to you," "... may show his goodness to you," or "...may show you his love and kindness." The use of both "love" and "kindness" is an attempt to reproduce the two major components of meaning which exist in the Greek term translated grace.

The final "Amen," found in many manuscripts, is included in KJV SpCL Mft Knox. It was probably added through the influence of liturgical usage. Different manuscripts add a variety of notes, of which KJV translates one: "The first epistle unto the Thessalonians was written from Athens." Other manuscripts have "from Corinth." None of these notes even claims to be part of the original text.

2 THESSALONIANS

INTRODUCTION

This Handbook is based on the assumption, for which reasons will be given in the notes on the various sections, that the general plan of this letter is as follows:

Greeting (1.1-2)
A. Thanksgiving, and teaching about what God is doing (chapters 1-2)
   1. The Judgment at Christ's Coming (1.3-12)
      (a) thanksgiving (1.3-4)
      (b) the final judgment (1.5-10)
      (c) prayer (1.11-12)
   2. The Wicked One (2.1-12)
      (a) warning against false teaching (2.1-2)
      (b) correct teaching (2.3-12)
   3. You Are Chosen for Salvation (2.13-17)
      (a) summary (2.13-15)
      (b) prayer (2.16-17)
B. Call for action, and teaching about what men should do (chapter 3)
   1. Pray for Us (3.1-5), including further prayer for the Thessalonians
   2. The Obligation to Work (3.6-15), including warning against lazy people
   3. Final Words (3.16-18), including blessing and signature

This is, in general, the plan followed by most modern translators and commentators. Two important variations from it will be discussed later: (1) Rigaux's commentary takes 3.1-5 with 2.13-17, under the title: "Salvation is assured to the brethren: conduct to be followed." (2) GeCL divides chapter 2 at verse 8, not at verse 13, and inserts a section heading at verse 8: "The chosen will be saved."

There are many points at which 2 Thessalonians repeats and reinforces the message of the first letter. The reader of the notes on 2 Thessalonians will therefore need to refer back rather often to the notes on 1 Thessalonians. It is also important to refer to the general commentaries mentioned in the Short Bibliography, pp. 213-215. These give further information, especially on such matters as whether or not this letter was written by Paul, its date, the circumstances under which it was written, and the theological importance of its message. Such matters may not directly affect the translation of particular verses, but they should be carefully considered by the translator as he begins his work, since they may affect the attitude in which he approaches his task. These notes will assume that the Second Letter to the Thessalonians, like the first, was written by Paul (see the notes on 1 Thess. 1.1 for the role of Silas and Timothy), and that chronologically it followed the First Letter.

CHAPTER 1

TEV	RSV
1 From Paul, Silas, and Timothy-- To the people of the church in Thessalonica, who belong to God our Father and the Lord Jesus Christ: 2 May God our Father and the Lord Jesus Christ give you grace and peace. (1.1-2)	1 Paul, Silvanus, and Timothy, To the church of the Thessalonians in God our Father and the Lord Jesus Christ: 2 Grace to you and peace from God the Father and the Lord Jesus Christ. (1.1-2)

As in the case of Paul's First Letter to the Thessalonians, the statement of presumed triple authorship, that is, from Paul, Silas, and Timothy, may be misleading, for it is obvious from the letter itself that Paul is the real author. It may be necessary in some languages to translate "from Paul, together with Silas and Timothy," or "from Paul, with Silas and Timothy joining in," or "I, Paul, am writing to you with the help of Silas and Timothy." It is often necessary to introduce a verb such as "write to" or "send this letter to" in order to combine the statement of authorship with an indication of those to whom the letter is directed.

There are only two differences between these verses and 1 Thess. 1.1 (see the notes, pp. 1-3).

First, the word our is added (God our Father), clearly including both the senders of the letter and those who will receive it. The appositional expression God our Father must be expressed in some languages by means of a relative clause, for example, "God, who is our Father." Some translators feel that it is necessary to identify the figurative meaning in our Father and mark it as a simile, for example, "God, who is like a Father to us." However, this is usually not necessary.

The second addition is less readily seen in TEV than in the more literal RSV:

1 Thess. 1.1b	2 Thess. 1.2
Grace to you and peace.	Grace to you and peace from God the Father and the Lord Jesus Christ.

TEV restructures the sentence in 2 Thessalonians, using the word give to bring out the meaning of the preposition "from."

In a number of languages it is relatively meaningless to say "grace to you and peace from God our Father and the Lord Jesus Christ." Since this is essentially a petition expressing a desire for God's response and blessing, it must sometimes be represented as a prayer, for example, "I pray that God the Father and the Lord Jesus Christ may give you grace and peace," or "...be gracious to you and cause you to experience peace."

In both verse 1 and verse 2, God our Father and the Lord Jesus Christ are closely linked by the use of a single preposition: literally "in God our Father and the Lord Jesus Christ" in verse 1, and "from God our Father and the Lord Jesus Christ" in verse 2. Brc's translation, "who belong to God our Father and to the Lord Jesus Christ" (v. 1), and "from God the Father and from the Lord Jesus Christ" (v. 2), does not convey this close link. However, in some languages it is grammatically essential to repeat the preposition (cf. FrCL of v. 1, and SpCL of both verses).

While the weight of the Greek manuscript evidence seems to favor "God the Father" as the more correct reading, many manuscripts do have God our Father. In some languages the translator will have no choice, since kinship terms such as "Father" must have an expressed possessor.

Though it may very well be that the expression grace and peace reflects Christian greeting in its Greek and Semitic forms, it is certainly not enough merely to say "greetings to you." The fact that grace and peace are to come from God our Father and the Lord Jesus Christ indicates clearly that Paul has something more in mind than mere Christian greeting. It is sometimes very difficult to find the appropriate translation of grace and peace for this type of context. Some translators employ "may God the Father and the Lord Jesus Christ show you their love and call you to be at peace," or "...be kind to you and cause you to rest within your hearts." In this type of context "peace" is not so much the peace of reconciliation with God as the normal blessing which comes to a man who is a child of God.

Commentators have often noted that Paul's Second Letter to the Thessalonians is less warm and affectionate than his First Letter. This is generally true, and many of the indications of emotion which were mentioned in the notes on the first letter are absent or less frequent in the second. There are, however, exceptions to this general rule. In proportion to their length, Paul addresses his readers as brothers as often in the second letter as in the first. The emotive tone of 2 Thess. 1.3-12 is also as high as that of the first letter.

One indication of high emotive content in Paul's letters is the length of his sentences. In the original Greek, the sentence length is generally greater than in most modern languages, but it is particularly great when Paul's argument or appeal reaches a climax. In 2 Thessalonians, only three sentences are more than two verses in length. One of these (2.8-10) is central to the main theme of the first part of the letter, and another (3.7-9) is central to the main theme of the second part. By far the longest sentence in the whole letter is in this section: it runs without a break from verse 3 to verse 10. It is no coincidence that this is also the passage in which Paul expresses most strongly his affection for the Christians in Thessalonica, and his confidence that, despite all the attacks upon it, their faith will continue to stand firm.

Different languages have other ways of indicating high emotion. For example, GeCL puts an exclamation mark at the end of the first sentence, and emphasizes the evangelists' "boasting" in verse 4 by putting it at the beginning of the sentence ("with pride we tell..."). Knox uses a rhetorical question in verse 6 ("or do you doubt that there is justice with God...?").

TEV

The Judgment at Christ's Coming

3 Our brothers, we must thank
God at all times for you. It is
right for us to do so, because your
faith is growing so much and the
love each of you has for the others
is becoming greater. 4 That is why
we ourselves boast about you in the
churches of God. We boast about
the way you continue to endure and
believe through all the persecutions and sufferings you are experiencing.

5 All of this proves that God's
judgment is just and as a result
you will become worthy of his Kingdom, for which you are suffering.
6 God will do what is right: he
will bring suffering on those who
make you suffer, 7 and he will
give relief to you who suffer and
to us as well. He will do this
when the Lord Jesus appears from
heaven with his mighty angels,
8 with a flaming fire, to punish
those who reject God and who do not
obey the Good News about our Lord
Jesus. 9 They will suffer the punishment of eternal destruction,
separated from the presence of the
Lord and from his glorious might,
10 when he comes on that Day to receive glory from all his people and
honor from all who believe. You
too will be among them, because you
have believed the message that we
told you.

11 That is why we always pray
for you. We ask our God to make
you worthy of the life he has called you to live. May he, by his
power, fulfill all your desire for
goodness and complete your work of
faith. 12 In this way the name of
our Lord Jesus will receive glory
from you, and you from him, by the
grace of our God and of the Lord[a]
Jesus Christ.

[a]our God and of the Lord; *or* our God and Lord. (1.3-12)

RSV

3 We are bound to give thanks to
God always for you, brethren, as is
fitting, because your faith is
growing abundantly, and the love of
every one of you for one another is
increasing. 4 Therefore we ourselves boast of you in the churches
of God for your steadfastness and
faith in all your persecutions and
in the afflictions which you are
enduring.

5 This is evidence of the righteous judgment of God, that you may
be made worthy of the kingdom of
God, for which you are suffering--
6 since indeed God deems it just to
repay with affliction those who af-
flict you, 7 and to grant rest
with us to you who are afflicted,
when the Lord Jesus is revealed
from heaven with his mighty angels
in flaming fire, 8 inflicting vengeance upon those who do not know
God and upon those who do not obey
the gospel of our Lord Jesus.
9 They shall suffer the punishment
of eternal destruction and exclusion from the presence of the Lord
and from the glory of his might,
10 when he comes on that day to be
glorified in his saints, and to be
marveled at in all who have believed, because our testimony to
you was believed. 11 To this end
we always pray for you, that our
God may make you worthy of his
call, and may fulfil every good
resolve and work of faith by his
power, 12 so that the name of our
Lord Jesus may be glorified in you,
and you in him, according to the
grace of our God and the Lord Jesus
Christ. (1.3-12)

In a number of languages it may be necessary to change rather radically the form of the section heading The Judgment at Christ's Coming. If a verb for "judging" is necessary, one may need to make a full sentence such as "God will judge people when Christ returns." Others might prefer as a section heading "God will judge people rightly" or "God will make no mistake in judging people."

In order to render this relatively complex section satisfactorily, it is important to recognize the progression of thought. In the first paragraph Paul speaks about his abundant confidence in the faith of the people in the church of Thessalonica, as evidenced in the way in which they have suffered persecution. The mention of this suffering persecution leads immediately into the second paragraph. Paul can point out how, as the result of sufferings, the Christians at Thessalonica are in a sense prepared for God's righteous judgment. It also makes possible the contrast which Paul introduces between these Thessalonian believers and those who do not believe and who therefore will suffer the punishment of eternal destruction—something which will not happen to those who have believed the message which Paul has proclaimed to the people. In verse 10 Paul echoes the theme of the faith of the Thessalonians which he first introduced in verse 3, and thus prepares the way for the third paragraph in this section, in which he introduces his plea that the believers in Thessalonica should live a life worthy of their calling. These three themes: faith, judgment, and living out the implications of one's faith in God, form an excellent introduction to the remaining two chapters, where Paul treats in very practical ways the implications of these themes.

1.3 Our brothers, we must thank God at all times for you. It is right for us to do so, because your faith is growing so much and the love each of you has for the others is becoming greater.

Our brothers, here as in many other places, serves the double function of indicating affection and marking the beginning of a new section. Here the word comes rather later than usual in the Greek sentence, but some translations move it either right to the beginning (TEV TNT DuCL SpCL) or nearer the beginning (e.g. Brc Lu Seg), to give greater emphasis or a smoother style. In a number of languages it may be necessary to render our brothers as "our fellow believers," "those who believe together with us," or "you who are also believers." In some translations it may be even necessary to employ a general term with the meaning of "relative," rather than the more specific term "brother," in a context such as this. "Brother" would seem, in some languages, to eliminate women from the fellowship of the believing community.

This verse is similar to 1 Thess. 1.2 (see the notes, pp. 5-6). There is no difference in Greek between the first always in that verse and at all times in this verse. We must thank God at all times is stronger and more formal than the simple we always thank God of the first letter. Must implies moral obligation and personal duty, rather than being forced to do something because of outward pressure. Mft translates "we are bound," Knox "we owe a constant debt," and Brc "it is nothing less than a duty." Phps' translation, "Nowadays I always thank God for you not only in common fairness but as a moral obligation!", combines the Greek expressions corresponding to TEV's must and it is right, though reversing the order. There is, however, nothing in the Greek corresponding to "nowadays," which appears to read into the translation a particular interpretation of the difference between 1 Thess. 1.2 and 2 Thess. 1.3.

Thankfulness is often expressed in translation in somewhat idiomatic forms, for example, "our hearts are so happy," "we speak about kindness," or "our heart is full to you."

For you means "concerning you"; the faith of the Christians at Thessalonica is the subject or content of Paul's thanksgiving. Knox's misleading translation, "on your behalf," appears to be based on the Latin. It is not followed by the more modern Roman Catholic translations, such as JB, or by interconfessional translations such as TOB and DuCL, which are based directly on the Greek text. In some languages for you must be expressed as a causative relation, for example, "we must give thanks to God at all times because of you," or "...because of what you have done," or even "you are the ones who cause us to be obliged to give thanks to God at all times."

It is right for us to do so is literally "as is right" (or "proper"). This phrase emphasizes the idea of obligation contained in we must thank God. The translation of GeCL and DuCL, "we have every reason to do so," goes a little further than the explicit meaning of the text, but makes a natural transition to the next part of the verse, in which Paul does state the reasons why he and his companions feel they must give thanks. It may be difficult to render literally it is right for us to do so, since the reference of "it" could be misleading. One may need to translate "when we give thanks, we are doing what is right," or "such giving of thanks is right."

The word rendered because or "for" in most translations may also mean "that" (cf. Zur), which would give the meaning: "We thank God...that your faith is growing." This rendering is less likely, but the difference in meaning is slight. Phps leaves the logical connection to be inferred by the reader, which is perfectly natural in current English: "...I always thank God for you.... Your faith has made such strides...that we actually boast about you."

There is a difference of metaphor, but little difference in meaning, between the expressions translated is growing so much and is becoming greater. Is growing so much suggests organic growth, for example, the growth of a plant. It is a rare and emphatic word, one of Paul's compounds using the Greek prefix huper-, which is the equivalent of the English and Latin super-. Just as in Romans 8.37 Paul describes Christians as "more than conquerors" (literally, they will "superconquer"), so here, he says that the Thessalonians' faith is "super-growing." Is becoming greater is a commoner and therefore less emphatic expression, which suggests the idea of a container being filled.

In several languages one cannot say your faith is growing, but one can say "you believe more and more," or "you increasingly trust in Christ." Similarly, love must be expressed in some languages as a verb, and therefore one must sometimes render the final clause of this verse as "the way in which you love one another is becoming greater," or "you love one another more and more."

The love each of you has for the others is more emphatic in Greek than in most translations. It is literally "the love of each one of you all for one another" (cf. Rigaux).

In the second part of this verse Paul mentions faith and love (see also 1 Thess. 1.3), but not hope. The general commentaries suggest possible reasons for this omission.

1.4 That is why we ourselves boast about you in the churches of God. We boast about the way you continue to endure and believe through all the persecutions and sufferings you are experiencing.

That is why translates a word which, in this context, indicates that the apostles' boasting is the result of the Thessalonians' growth in faith and love. We and you are close together in the original. As we have seen in the notes on 1 Thessalonians, Paul often uses this way of suggesting a close personal relationship. As usual in these letters, "we" is not just another way of saying "I"; Paul constantly associates Silas and Timothy with himself.

In some languages it may be necessary to specify at the beginning of verse 4 precisely what constitutes the reason for the boasting. It may be necessary to say "because of your trust and love, we ourselves boast about you." In other languages it may be more appropriate to introduce verse 4 with a conjunction such as "therefore" or a phrase such as "as a result."

In this verse and in the following verses, Paul repeats several expressions which he used in his first letter, though sometimes in a rather different context. Boast recalls the boasting of 1 Thess. 2.19, where Paul speaks of boasting at the last day, but here the boasting is present (contrast 1 Thess. 1.8b). The translator's problem is to find an expression which conveys (1) pride, and (2) speaking, without (3) the negative component of speaking well about one's own achievements (the Concise Oxford Dictionary gives "extol oneself" as the first meaning of the verb "to boast," and "vainglorious statement" as the first meaning of the noun "boast"). Mft "we are proud of you" (cf. JB) leaves out (2), and Seg "we glorify ourselves" (cf. Lu Syn Zur) fails to avoid (3). TNT's "speak with pride" and GeCL "with pride we tell" (cf. SpCL) are preferable. It is possible in some languages to suggest the component of pride in the meaning of boast by translating "we are always talking about you in the churches of God," or "we are always glad to talk about you."

The Greek locative preposition translated in TEV as in may have any one of three meanings: (1) Its commonest meaning, and the one chosen by most translations, is "in" or "within," indicating simply location (KJV Phps RSV cf. DuCL FrCL GeCL SpCL Seg Zur). (2) The same word, when followed by a noun in the plural, may mean "among," as in JB NEB (cf. BJ Lu). Knox attractively restructures the sentence to bring out this meaning and translates "as we visit the churches of God." (3) Finally, the word may also mean "to," emphasizing the delivery of a message by Paul to the churches. This interpretation is clearly followed by TNT: "This makes us speak with pride to the other churches" (cf. Syn) and seems to be the basis for Brc "we cannot help telling God's other congregations how proud we are of you." 1 Corinthians 7.17 and 2 Corinthians 8.1 are possible parallels; in both these places, TEV translates "in." This translation seems rather static, and on the whole, perhaps the third meaning suits the context best. In any event, the meaning is simply a locative designation for the place and hence of the persons involved in the communication.

It is sometimes essential to translate the churches of God as "the other churches of God." Otherwise the implication would be that either Paul and his companions had boasted about the faith of the Thessalonians to the people within the church of Thessalonica itself, or that the church of Thessalonica was not to be included among the churches of God. The phrase the churches of God poses an additional problem since it might be rendered in such a way as to refer to the buildings where the congregations met, rather than to the congregations themselves. If one wishes to emphasize the membership of the churches, it may be necessary to say "when speaking to the people of the other churches of God." On the churches of God, see 1 Thess. 2.14 (pp. 41-42). In rendering the phrase churches of God, it is important to make clear that these churches belong to God, avoiding any rendering which would suggest churches which God attends.

The Greek does not repeat we boast about. TEV does so in order to divide the sentence, but the other common language translations do not find this necessary.

About the way you continue to endure and believe is literally "about your endurance and faith." On both these qualities, see 1 Thess. 1.3 (pp. 6-8). TEV changes the original nouns into verbs, since the context shows clearly that the Thessalonians' endurance and faith are expressed in active resistance in the face of persecutions and sufferings. These two words are often linked together (for example, in Mark 4.17, where the order is reversed and the nouns are in the singular). On sufferings, see 1 Thess. 3.3 (pp. 54-55).

It would be possible to interpret to endure and believe as referring to "the endurance of faith," that is, "continuing to believe" or "...to trust." It is better, however, to assume that endure refers primarily to continuing faithfulness to God and believe to continuing trust. These meanings may be expressed in some languages as "how you stand firm and continue to believe."

You are experiencing translates a rather unemphatic verb which, according to the context, can mean undergoing persecution, "bearing with" someone, or even listening patiently to a speech. Mft, like TEV, translates unemphatically "in which you are involved." DuCL and GeCL omit the verb altogether and translate "in all persecutions and sufferings."

Through all the persecutions and sufferings you are experiencing may be rendered simply as "during all the times that you are persecuted and are caused to suffer." However, the contrast between enduring faith and the persecutions which would tend to diminish faith may be expressed in some languages as "the way you continue to endure and to believe, despite all the ways in which you are persecuted and suffer."

1.5 All of this proves that God's judgment is just and as a result you will become worthy of his Kingdom, for which you are suffering.

From this point onward Paul's thought moves steadily toward the main theme of this letter: the last days and the final judgment. However, these events are not wholly in the future; what has been happening to the Thessalonians, and the way in which they have reacted, are directly related to the coming climax of history and the final victory of Christ. The exact relation between present and future events raises not only theological problems but problems of translation. These are not made any easier by the fact that, although many of the expressions Paul uses in this passage have a future meaning, it is not until verse 9 that he uses a verb in the future tense.

In this passage, Paul uses his favorite device of repeating the same ideas in increasing detail, so as to emphasize them and produce an emotive climax. In Diagram 5 (page 140) RSV is used to show the basic structure of the original text, which will normally need modification in translation. This diagram illustrates a number of significant points.

1. The activity of God is closely linked with that of Christ. In verse 7 the passive statement "the Lord Jesus is revealed" is equivalent to "God reveals the Lord Jesus," and it should be so translated in languages where the passive voice is rarely used or does not exist.

2. Similarly, the translator may need to make it clear that the implied agent of "that you may be made worthy" in verse 5 is God; that "to be glorified" in verse 10 implies that "his saints" will glorify Christ (cf. TEV to receive glory from all his people, and v. 12, the name of our Lord Jesus will receive glory from you); and that "was believed" in verse 10 means that the Thessalonian Christians believed the message.

3. The verbs which are underlined in the diagram are the only ones whose tense is explicit in the original. Nevertheless, it is clear that Paul is drawing a double contrast between present and future, and between the Thessalonian Christians and their persecutors. The Christians suffer now, but they will share the kingdom in the future. The persecutors cause suffering now, but they will themselves suffer in the future. The translator should try where possible to bring out, in the form as well as the content of his translation, this complex network of contrasts.

4. The main emphasis falls, towards the end of the passage (vv. 8-9), on the punishment of the persecutors. Indeed, the power of evil is a recurring theme in the letter as a whole.

The first group of problems for the translator concerns the relation of verse 5a to verses 4 and 5b. Within this group, the first difficulty, and perhaps the easiest to solve, is one of punctuation, since the oldest Greek manuscripts have no punctuation marks. The UBS Greek text puts a comma at the end of verse 5, and although individual commentators have at times suggested a different punctuation (see the general commentaries), translations generally agree with TEV in taking the comma as the equivalent of a major pause. By far the most natural procedure is to begin a new sentence at this point.

The first part of verse 5 is rather abrupt: literally, "proof" (better, "evidence"; the exact meaning will be discussed later) "of the righteous judgment of God." What is this "proof"? Some translators find it in something which

Verse	Logical connections	God/Christ	Thessalonian Christians	Persecutors	Other Christians
5	This is evidence of	the righteous judgment of God, (implied)	that you may be made worthy of the kingdom of God, for which you are suffering--		(also? -- see notes)
6	since indeed	God deems it just to repay		with affliction those who afflict you,	
7		and to grant when the Lord Jesus is revealed from heaven with his mighty angels in flaming fire, inflicting	rest...to those who are afflicted,		with us
8		(implied)		vengeance upon those who do not know God and upon those who do not obey the gospel of our Lord Jesus.	
9		(implied)		They shall suffer the punishment of eternal destruction and exclusion from the presence of the Lord and from the glory of his might,	
10	 because	when he comes on that day to be glorified in his saints, and to be marveled at	 to you was believed.		(implied) in all who have believed, our testimony

DIAGRAM 5

Paul has mentioned earlier: either (1) the persecutions (e.g. Mft "they are proof positive of God's equity"); or (2) the Thessalonians' endurance and faith (e.g. Phps 1st ed. "these qualities show..."; but compare 2nd ed. "[God] intends to use your suffering to prove you worthy of his kingdom"); or the Thessalonians themselves (e.g. TNT "you are a clear example..."); or (3) the whole of what Paul has just been discussing (e.g. JB "it all shows that God's judgment is just"). Other translators find the "proof" in something Paul mentions later. Knox, for example, translates "it will be a proof of the just award God makes, when he finds you worthy of a place in his kingdom." A third group of translations do not make it clear whether the word "proof" is related to something in verse 4 or something later in verse 5. It is difficult to be certain whether RSV's "this is evidence" and TEV's all of this proves are intended to look backward or forward. In fact, the Greek text may be interpreted as pointing in both directions.

JB's solution (cf. Brc and [less explicitly] KJV FrCL BJ Seg Syn Zur) seems the most satisfactory, that is, a general backward-looking reference to the situation Paul has just been describing. How this situation constitutes evidence or proof of God's righteous judgment is a question which takes us to the frontier between translation and exegesis. One possibility is: When people of such faith as the Thessalonians have to endure such fierce and undeserved persecutions, it is a clear sign that God must soon intervene in judgment, to reward the believers (cf. v. 5b) and to punish those responsible for the persecution (cf. v. 6). This interpretation fits well with the wider context (see also vv. 7-8). (Best's interpretation, "Paul says: 'I have boasted about you; this is a sign that God will count you worthy then'" [p. 255], seems somewhat forced in that it gives rather too great prominence to Paul's "boasting.")

If we followed such an interpretation as that suggested above, it would be difficult to accept the translation "proof." The only place this particular word is used in the whole of the Greek scriptures is here, though it is related in form and meaning to a word used in Philippians 1.28, where TEV translates "will prove." The difficulty is that "proof" (especially if used with a verb in the present tense, such as "this is proof," or the verb proves, as in TEV) seems to refer to something which is already clear for everyone to see; but the context shows that this is not the case. The persecutions and the Thessalonians' persistent faith belong to the present; but it is the main point of the entire letter to show that the final judgment does not belong to the present. On the other hand, such translations as "this is a sign" or "this shows" are regarded by some as being too weak; there are other expressions which Paul could have used if this were all he meant. Best's "sure sign" (cf. Rigaux) and GeCL "thereby already now God's righteous judgment shows itself" combine effectively, though in different ways, the present and future elements of Paul's message at this point.

Throughout this passage Paul makes repeated use of two groups of related words: (1) "persecutions" (v. 4), "suffering" and "suffer" (v. 6): "suffering" in verse 5 is related in meaning but not in form; (2) "righteous" (v. 5), "right" (v. 6), and "punish" (v. 8). The function of these repetitions is to maintain the momentum, and thereby the emotive level, of this long Greek sentence. In translation, it will not always be possible to reproduce this effect, but any loss can usually be compensated for in other ways. For example, GeCL "Gottes gerechtes Gericht" ("God's just judgment") contains alliteration and other echoes which are not present in the original.

One of the difficulties with a literal rendering of "proof" is that it suggests merely some kind of verbal demonstration. Paul evidently has much more in mind. Perhaps the closest equivalent would be "clear evidence." If one is to relate this to the persecution and suffering which the Thessalonians have endured, one may say "the fact that you have suffered so much shows clearly" or "...assures us." This may then be followed by a verbal form of God's judgment is just as "that God will judge justly."

Judgment is the act of judging rather than the verdict which the judge gives. The distinction is not always significant, but in this case it is, since Paul is mainly thinking of the events which will precede and accompany the end. God's judgment is just may be rendered in some languages as "God will judge people as he should," "...as they should be judged," or "on the basis of what they truly deserve."

As a result translates a Greek construction which may indicate result (as in TEV cf. FrCL and Rigaux), purpose (as in JB "the purpose of it is," cf. Mft Brc TOB etc.), or some vaguer connection (as in TNT "and in the end you will be counted worthy," cf. BJ Best etc.). It is impossible to be certain, and in any case purpose and result, especially with God as the subject, are almost indistinguishable in many biblical contexts. It may be convenient to begin a new sentence at this point and to treat verse 5b as a fuller statement of what Paul has already said in verse 5a. This is typical of Paul's style. The translation would then run: "all this is a sure sign of God's righteous judgment. The result will be...."

It is important that one indicate clearly that as a result refers to what the Thessalonians had experienced. This relation is best expressed in some languages simply as cause, for example, "Because of what you have experienced, you will become worthy of God's Kingdom."

The verb translated will become worthy may have this meaning, but its literal, as well as its more common meaning, is "will be counted worthy." The passive is a common indirect way of referring to God, and Knox makes this explicit: "when he finds you worthy of a place in his kingdom"; cf. Mft "he means to make you worthy of it" and Phps. If some such translation as "count worthy" (cf. TNT) or "find worthy" (Knox) is chosen, it will be necessary to avoid any suggestion of a legal fiction by which God would treat as worthy those who really were not. Some translators render worthy simply as "good enough for." But this introduces an element which is really foreign to the context. A more appropriate equivalent would be "deserving of" or "deserving the recompense of."

On his Kingdom, see the notes on 1 Thess. 2.12. GeCL translates this phrase as "God's new world"; TEV FrCL SpCL TNT TOB add glossary notes. In a number of languages his Kingdom must be expressed in terms of God's rulership; that is to say, "worthy of God ruling over you," "deserving to have God as your king," or "...as your ruler." Though some persons might insist that this reference to God's Kingdom does have temporal and spatial qualifications, the focus here seems to be essentially upon the believer's relation to God—not simply upon some time or place in which God will eventually rule completely.

For which you are suffering. In Greek as in English, for is a word which covers a wide area of meaning. Here, the most likely meaning is not "on behalf of" but "because of." It is particularly important to avoid the implication that the suffering of the Thessalonian believers would advance the Kingdom in some manner. Rather, it was because of their faithfulness to God as the king of their lives that they were suffering. One must also avoid the implication that the Thessalonians were suffering for the sake of getting into the Kingdom as though their suffering had as a goal their becoming good enough to be admitted into God's Kingdom.

The Greek is literally "for which you also are suffering." TEV and many other translations omit the word "also." Some kind of comparison is intended. There are two main possibilities: (1) Paul is comparing the Thessalonians' suffering with that of others, including himself and his companions. This would fit in well with the words and to us as well (literally "with us") in verse 7. However, Paul does not refer anywhere else in this chapter to his own sufferings. (2) The word "also" may simply link two statements about the kingdom: (a) "God reigns, and he will judge you worthy to share in his reign" (v. 5a), and (b) "it is because of his reign, because you acknowledge God as king, that you are suffering now" (v. 5b). BJ (cf. Rigaux Best) understands "also" in the first way: "the kingdom of God for which you also are suffering"; but JB, its English counterpart, implicitly takes "also" in the second way: "it is for the sake of this" (i.e. the kingdom) "that you are suffering now" (cf. Knox DuCL). If the word "also" is omitted, as in TEV, the second meaning tends to be implied. Some translations are ambiguous, but ambiguity should be avoided if possible. You are suffering, as already indicated in Diagram 5, is a real present tense. Knox's translation, "for which you are prepared to suffer," has no basis in the Greek.

1.6 God will do what is right: he will bring suffering on those who make you suffer.

TOB begins a new section here and NEB a new paragraph, but this verse is closely linked with verse 5, repeating and partly expanding it. It is true that there is a distinction, for Paul's main concern is moving away from the situation of the Thessalonians to general teaching about the last days. But the two subjects are not separated, and there are references to "you" in verses 7 and 10.

The Greek begins with a word meaning "since" or "if it is true that." It is like the "if" in the sentence "If there is such a thing as justice, John will come to a bad end," which strongly implies that there is justice in the world, and that therefore John will come to a bad end. Most translations replace the "if" by an emphatic statement, e.g. BJ "for it will indeed be the effect of God's justice to render tribulation to those who inflict it on you."

TEV's God will do what is right is followed by a colon which points the reader (though not necessarily the listener) forward to the second part of the sentence. In this way a logical relation is implied. The punishment of the persecutors and the relief (v. 7) of those who suffer unjustly now are examples or consequences of the fact that God will do what is right. The literal meaning of the Greek is "since (it is) just with God." TEV's restructuring reflects the fact that it is fundamental to biblical teaching (1) that God is just, and (2) that his justice or righteousness expresses itself in action, in doing what is right.

God will do what is right is expressed in many languages as "God will do what he should." A modal element such as "should" suggests correctness of action. However, it is important to relate this directly to what follows, and therefore in some languages the following clause is introduced by a conjunction such as "for"; for example, "God will do what he should, for he will bring suffering on those who made you suffer." In other languages it may be more appropriate to translate "God will do what is right. That means he will bring suffering...."

He will bring suffering on those who make you suffer is literally "to pay back trouble to those who trouble you." "Pay back" is an emphatic word which suggests a reciprocal action such as giving in return. In 1 Thess. 3.9 Paul uses the same word in speaking about giving thanks. TEV leaves the reciprocal action to be understood, as it clearly can be, from the context. Suffering and suffer suggest in Greek some crushing pressure or oppression, either on the body or on the mind. Paul does not specify which, but probably both are included.

It is often impossible to say he will bring suffering, but a causative expression is almost always appropriate, for example, "those who make you suffer he will cause to suffer in return." By introducing some such expression as "in return," one may emphasize the reciprocal factor suggested by the Greek text itself. The reciprocal activity may, however, be merely implied, for example, "he will cause to suffer those who cause you to suffer."

1.7 and he will give relief to you who suffer and to us as well. He will do this when the Lord Jesus appears from heaven with his mighty angels,

For the whole of this verse, compare 1 Thess. 3.13. Relief is not the word which, in verse 2, TEV translates "peace" but "one which indicates the absence of tension and trial" (Best). Paul's use of repetition (noted in the introduction to vv. 5-10) suggests that the relief is connected with life in the kingdom of God (see vv. 5 and 10). However, its immediate meaning is rather negative, an end to the suffering just mentioned in verse 6b.

TEV's he will give relief to you who suffer and to us as well could be misunderstood as involving a contrast between "you," who suffer, and "us," who do not. This is certainly not the meaning of the Greek, which is simply "and to you the troubled relief with us." Though there is, in a sense, a distinction made between you who suffer and us, in reality there is a comparison, for both, in another sense, are included in the relief which is going to come. Therefore, it may be more appropriate in some languages to translate "he will give relief to you who are suffering now, and to us also," or "...both to you who are suffering now, and also to us."

One may, however, find it difficult to render literally will give relief to. This is more likely to be rendered as a causative expression, for example, "cause you to experience comfort," "cause you not to suffer," or "cause your suffering to stop."

He will do this is not in the Greek; TEV adds it in order to begin a new sentence. Paul starts at this point a description of the last days which is full of images drawn from the Old Testament and from later apocalyptic writings which were circulating at that time. There is no need to avoid these images if they are natural in the receptor language. Indeed, some modern translations introduce additional figures of speech (e.g. Brc "when the Lord Jesus bursts from heaven onto the stage of history"; Phps 1st ed. "the final denouement"; but cf. 2nd ed. "the final appearance").

Though in English the present tense is often used to refer to a future event, as in the clause when the Lord Jesus appears from heaven, it is usually necessary in translation to use a distinct reference to the future, for example, "when the Lord Jesus will appear from heaven," or "when the Lord Jesus will come down from heaven and show himself."

His mighty angels is literally "the angels of his power." The translator has to decide whether "his" goes with "angels" or with "power." "His angels of power" could be the equivalent of "his powerful angels," as in TEV (cf. KJV RSV Brc NEB TNT DuCL FrCL GeCL SpCL). "The angels of his power" (Mft JB cf. BJ Seg Syn TOB Zur) is unclear and therefore lacking in impact. As Rigaux says (p. 627), "The angels and the power are two different entities, but it is not possible to specify the relation between them." Knox boldly restructures to give "with angels to proclaim his power." This has the extra advantage of reminding the reader that an angel is normally a heavenly being sent by God on a particular errand or mission. TEV gives a clear and simple translation of a phrase whose exact meaning is uncertain.

With his mighty angels must be expressed in some languages as "his mighty angels will accompany him." One must avoid in a rendering of mighty an expression which will merely imply that they are physically strong or muscular. In some languages the most appropriate equivalent will be "his angels who have great power," or "his angels who can do mighty acts."

1.8 with a flaming fire, to punish those who reject God and who do not obey the Good News about our Lord Jesus.

With a flaming fire is literally "in a fire of flame." These and the following words recall Psalm 79.6; Isaiah 66.15; Jeremiah 10.25; and perhaps Exodus 3.2. The translator has first to decide whether this phrase goes with the end of verse 7 or with the rest of verse 8. If with the end of verse 7 it will be understood that the fire will serve to light up the Lord Jesus when he comes; it will be associated with revelation. If, however, this phrase goes with the rest of verse 8, the fire will serve to destroy the wicked. SpCL takes the words back into verse 7 and translates "when he comes from heaven among flames of fire with his powerful angels." TNT leaves the question open by making "there will be flames of fire" a separate sentence. Several other translations, including TEV, produce a similar effect by putting commas before and after the phrase, leaving the reader to decide where the more important break in meaning occurs. JB links the phrase with what follows: "he will come in flaming fire to impose the penalty...." It is difficult to be certain. The first possibility recalls more clearly the revelation of God to Moses in the burning bush of Exodus 3.2; the second reflects the usage in Psalm 79.6 and Isaiah 66.15.

Since in many languages the phrase with his mighty angels must be expressed as a separate statement, one may be required to render with a flaming fire also as a separate sentence, for example, "there will be a flaming fire," or "there will be a fire which will flame up." This can still be related to the coming of Jesus by saying "when he comes there will be a flaming fire."

The following words, to punish, are rather easier to understand than to translate. RSV's literal translation is "inflicting vengeance." The best commentary is Hebrews 10.30: "I will take revenge, I will repay" (TEV), quoting Deuteronomy 32.35. Old Testament teaching on vengeance can be generally summed up in three points: (1) Because God is just, he has the right to punish those who do wrong and to avenge those who are harmed by others' wrongdoing. (2) God normally does this by disinterested human agents, such as judges, whom he appoints. (3) It is therefore quite wrong for anyone else to "take the law into his own hands" and avenge himself.

The translator's problem is therefore to show that the vengeance in question is the just action of God, not a private vendetta. (A similar difficulty was noted in 1 Thess. 1.10; 2.16, in speaking about God's wrath or anger. In English, "wrath" and "vengeance" are slightly higher level equivalents of "anger" and "revenge," though "wrath" is more archaic than "vengeance.") TEV's punish leaves out the specific element of paying someone back for a wrong done. GeCL has "judges"; JB (cf. Best) "to impose the penalty"; Brc specifies "to execute divine vengeance."

The verb to punish is most frequently translated as "cause to suffer." Such a rendering fits in well with verse 6, in which God causes suffering for those who have caused the believers to suffer. A number of languages, however, do have very specific terms for punishment, for example, "whip," "beat," "torture," but none of these should be employed in this type of context. It is preferable to use a more generic expression which does not need to be interpreted in a strictly literal manner.

The reader of some translations, including TEV, may ask: "Why should God punish those who reject him? Are they not people to be helped rather than punished?" The answer to this problem lies in the words translated reject. Literally the words mean "do not know," but the word "know" normally means, not intellectual knowledge of a fact, but a relationship with a person (cf. Mark 14.71; John 7.28; 2 Corinthians 5.16 [TEV translates "judge"]; Titus 1.16). In Luke 1.34 (where TEV's "I am a virgin" is literally "I do not know a man") a different, but semantically related, verb is used. "Not to know God" means, therefore, refusing to enter into a relationship with him. For this reason, several translations have "refuse to recognize God" (Brc cf. Phps 2nd ed. SpCL) or "refuse to acknowledge God" (NEB cf. Knox). DuCL, more simply, translates "did not want to know God"; GeCL "do not honor God"; Mft "ignore God." TEV correctly understands a refusal to recognize or acknowledge God as a rejection of him. This rejection of God is expressed in a number of languages idiomatically, for example, "push God out of their thoughts," "give God no place in their hearts," or "refuse to open the door to God."

Next, the translator has to decide whether the ones who reject God and the ones who do not obey the Good News are the same people or not. The form of the Greek slightly suggests two different groups, and some commentators try to identify them, but the evidence is not decisive. Translations, both old and modern, are fairly evenly divided, with JB (cf. KJV Mft? Knox? Phps DuCL GeCL SpCL Syn TOB) suggesting a single group ("all who do not acknowledge God and refuse to accept the Good News..."—"all" is not in the Greek), and BJ (cf. RSV Brc TNT FrCL Lu Seg Zur) suggesting two groups ("those who do not know God and those who do not obey the Gospel"). TEV leaves the question somewhat open, for one can interpret the those as referring to one group who are described in two ways. On the other hand, one can understand the those as being carried over and implied before the second who in such a way that two groups are specified. If TEV repeated the those, two groups would be indicated, whereas if TEV omitted the second who, only one group would be indicated. If one wishes to indicate more clearly that only one group of persons is being spoken about, it may be necessary to render "to punish those who refuse to acknowledge God, that is, those who do not obey the Good News about our Lord Jesus," or "...these are the very ones who...."

The English word obey, used by many translations, raises certain problems.

(1) Obey means "to do what one is told," and one normally speaks of obeying an order or someone who gives an order. Obey the Good News sounds strange, because Good News almost by definition implies a statement, while obey implies an order. The outlines of Christian preaching, found in Acts 2.14-39; 3.13-26; 1 Corinthians 15.3-7, and similar passages, often end with a call for people to repent and believe (e.g. Acts 2.38; cf. 3.19), but they consist largely of telling the story of Jesus' birth, death, and resurrection, the coming of the Holy Spirit, and the return of Jesus as judge.

(2) When we compare the English obey with the Greek word which it translates, we find, not surprisingly, that while the range of meaning of the two terms overlaps, it is not completely the same. English obey, unless it is followed by some such word as "willingly," does not suggest any inner agreement or commitment to a course of action—you do what you are told, whether you like it or not. This is sometimes so in Greek also—in Mark 1.27, the demons are forced to obey Jesus. But more commonly, as in the present passage, the context refers to a personal and willing response. New Testament writers speak of "obeying" or responding to the faith (Acts 6.7), the gospel (here and in Romans 10.16), or the apostles' message (2 Thess. 3.14). The same word, which is related to the word for "hear," may also be used of someone answering a knock on the door

(Acts 12.13), and even (though not in the New Testament) of God or a judge "hearing" and responding favorably to someone's prayer or plea.

(3) For these reasons, a few translations avoid the word obey in this verse. JB has "refuse to accept"; cf. DuCL "have rejected" (the Dutch word is also used of refusing an invitation); GeCL "do not listen to"; SpCL "pay no attention to."

As already suggested, it is quite impossible in many languages to speak about "obeying the Good News." In some instances one can speak about "obeying what the Good News says," but even this may sometimes be very difficult. The closest equivalent may be "live in accordance with the Good News." However, since in both expressions, who reject God and who do not obey the Good News, there is either an explicit or implied rejection or refusal, it may be important to introduce this fact explicitly in both clauses, translating the second one, for example, "refuse to follow the Good News," or "reject living according to the Good News."

For the Good News, see the notes on 1 Thess. 1.5; and for Lord, see 1 Thess. 1.1. About our Lord Jesus (cf. FrCL and SpCL) is clearer than the traditional translation "of our Lord Jesus," which could also mean "from our Lord Jesus," a much less likely meaning here.

While the term Lord, in the phrase our Lord Jesus, is basically a title, it should not be rendered merely as an honorific qualification of Jesus. To avoid doing so, it may be necessary in some languages to speak of "the Good News about Jesus, who is our Lord." On the other hand, in some languages there is no term for "Lord" which means an individual who rules over another or to whom one gives complete obedience. Therefore our Lord Jesus may be rendered in some languages as "Jesus whom we obey" or "Jesus who rules over us."

1.9 They will suffer the punishment of eternal destruction, separated from the presence of the Lord and from his glorious might,

They is a general word, "such people" as Paul has just described.

The word for punishment normally means a penalty imposed by a court of law.

The word here rendered suffer is less emphatic than the unrelated words for "suffer" which Paul uses in verses 5 and 6. It means simply "undergo." Mft translates "they will pay the penalty."

Eternal destruction is a difficult phrase, not only from the theological point of view, which does not concern us directly here, but also for the translator. Destruction suggests that the persecutors will cease to exist, but if this were so, how could their destruction be eternal except in the sense of "final" or "permanent"? This same word for destruction could be translated "disaster" in 1 Thess. 5.3, and NAB translates it "ruin" here. Eternal is often used in the New Testament in speaking of the age to come or the last days. "Eternal life" is not simply life which goes on forever, but life of a quality associated with the age to come. Eternal destruction is the opposite of this. In 1 Thess. 4.17 Paul describes the life of the age to come by saying simply "we will always be with the Lord." Conversely, eternal destruction is to be separated from the presence of the Lord. The persecutors will be punished in such a way that "all that makes life worth living is destroyed" (H. A. A. Kennedy, quoted by Best, p. 262).

Eternal destruction must be rendered in some languages as a verb phrase, for example, "he will destroy them forever." This expression may be related to what precedes as "they will be punished; God will destroy them forever," or "God will cause them to suffer; he will punish them by destroying them forever." Note, however, that this eternal destruction is further defined by the phrase which follows, namely, separated from the presence of the Lord.

Separated from represents a common Greek preposition which has a wide range of meanings. KJV Mft Zur translate it rather vaguely as "from." Knox thinks that it is God's presence which causes the destruction and translates "the presence of the Lord, and the majesty of his power, will condemn them to eternal punishment," but he adds a note giving another interpretation. It is more natural to understand the word "from" as referring (metaphorically) to space, and this is the meaning in Isaiah 2.10, 19, 21, of which this verse is a quotation. Most translations understand in this way: separated (cf. GeCL), JB "excluded" (cf. Phps), NEB "cut off," Brc TNT "banishment" (cf. DuCL), "far from" (cf. FrCL SpCL Lu BJ Seg Syn Zur).

The phrase separated from the presence of the Lord serves to further define the meaning of eternal destruction. One may therefore introduce this expression as "this means they will be separated from the presence of the Lord." In some languages, however, it is extremely difficult to use a passive expression such as separated without indicating precisely who does the separating and the mode of the separation. One must say in some instances "God will close them off from where the Lord will be." In many instances, of course, the Lord must be rendered as "our Lord."

The presence of the Lord is a nonfigurative equivalent of the Greek "the face of the Lord," which is not very natural in current English. The Lord, as usual in Paul's writings, means Jesus (cf. v. 8), though in the passage in Isaiah which Paul is quoting, the Lord naturally refers to God. His glorious might is literally "the glory of his might," and could also mean "the glory which comes from" or "is caused by his might." On "glory," see 1 Thess. 2.12; cf. 2.6, 20. In some translations his glorious might has been rendered merely as "his wonderful strength." But this is often not satisfactory. How can one be separated from someone's strength? It is possible in some instances to reverse the attribution and to speak, not of "glorious might," but "great wonderfulness"; that is to say "God will shut them away from the great wonderfulness of our Lord." In some cases this may be best indicated by "and they will never see how very wonderful he is," or "...never experience his great wonderfulness."

1.10 when he comes on that Day to receive glory from all his people and honor from all who believe. You too will be among them, because you have believed the message that we told you.

See also the notes on 1 Thess. 5.2 (pp. 105-106) and 2 Thess. 1.12 (pp. 154-155).

When he comes. The Greek suggests a single event at an indefinite time in the future.

On that Day is emphatic in Greek, because it comes right at the end of this long sentence (vv. 3-10). Many translations, including TEV, make the flow of the sentence smoother by moving on that Day to an earlier position; others preserve the emphasis by making this phrase a separate sentence (Knox "yes; there will be justice when that day comes," cf. BJ "thus it will be on that day"). If on that Day is not closely related to the rest of the verse, the reader may be left asking "On what day?" For the original readers, the phrase on that Day would have been easy to understand because of its use in the Old Testament, where it means the same as "the day of the Lord." Isaiah 2, a passage from which Paul has just quoted, uses this expression repeatedly. Christians reinterpreted "the day of the Lord" to mean the day on which the Lord Jesus would come again, and GeCL makes this explicit by translating "that happens on the day on which he comes." Several translations, including TNT and TOB, add a note to explain the associations of "that day"; the capital letter used by TEV (cf. FrCL) and DuCL "the great Day," show in other ways that "Day" has a special significance here.

Because of the special significance given to that Day, it may be necessary in some languages to use qualifying expressions, for example, "on that special Day" or "on that very important Day." Note, however, that verse 10, though very closely linked to verse 9, may introduce complications in some languages, especially if phrases such as eternal destruction, separated from the presence of the Lord, and his glorious might are all expressed as complete clauses. It may therefore be necessary to begin verse 10 as a separate sentence, for example, "All this will happen when he comes on that special Day...."

It should be noted that to spell Day with a capital letter does not help the person who only hears the passage read aloud. Capitals generally should be used in accordance with the usage of the receptor language, but they are not very effective in distinguishing shades of theological meaning. There is a tendency in some languages, including English and French (cf. FrCL TOB, but not BJ) for the use of capitals to decline.

To receive glory...and honor. Virtually all translations take this to mean that the purpose of Jesus' coming again is to receive glory and honor. However, New Testament Greek, under Hebrew influence, does not distinguish clearly between purpose and result, and it would make equally good sense if Paul meant that the result of Jesus' coming, in the impressive way described in verses 7b-9, would be to make all believers give him honor and glory. In Revelation 16.9, where the Greek construction is similar, TEV translates "(men) would not turn from their sins and praise his greatness," and the second part of this sentence is sometimes understood as the result of the first.

The Greek is literally "when he comes to be glorified in his saints" (cf. KJV RSV). The word for "glorify" is an unusual compound, repeated in verse 12, literally "in-glorified in his saints." This emphasizes the word "in" and makes it important to establish its exact meaning. The possibilities may be grouped as follows: (1) "in (the assembly) of his saints" (cf. Psalm 89.7), "when his people are gathered together," hence "among his people" (cf. NEB "glorified among his own and adored among all believers"). (2) "By means of" or "because of the saints" (cf. Brc translation of 12a: "the name of the Lord Jesus will be glorified because of you," and TOB of verse 10a: "glorified in the person of his saints"). This is not necessarily the same as "by the saints," and some commentators suggest that the angels would glorify God when they see what he has made of the saints. This interpretation, however, is unnecessarily complicated, since the identity of those who give glory is not stated either here or in similar Old Testament passages (e.g. Isaiah 45.25). Several translations, including FrCL and GeCL, therefore take the verse to mean that Jesus will come "to be honored (glorified) by all his saints"; TEV and DuCL use active verbs to give the same meaning. If the translator chooses an equivalent of "by," the context will still show clearly that a community is intended.

On people (literally "saints"), see the notes on 1 Thess. 3.13. Here, however, the words all who believe show clearly that human believers and not angels are intended. The whole passage contrasts the fate of persecutors and believers. NEB translates "his own"; Brc "his own dedicated people"; TNT "those who belong to him."

The word translated honor is a verb which may suggest a range of emotions going from astonishment and fear to reverence and wonder. Both the parallel with glory and the wider context suggest something more than mere surprise or shock. Brc has "welcomed with...awe and wonder," and Best has "marvelled at."

A literal translation of to receive glory from all his people and honor from all who believe might suggest two different actions by two distinct groups. In reality, what will happen on the day of the Lord's return is essentially a single event expressed in this parallel form. To avoid the impression that there will be two events and two groups of persons, it may be necessary to translate "to receive glory and honor from all his people, that is to say, from all who believe in him."

The expressions receive glory and receive...honor may be regarded as substitute passives. It may be important to restructure this sentence in some languages as "when he comes on that special Day, all his people will give him glory, that is to say, all who believe in him will show him honor." In this type of context "to give him glory" may be expressed in some languages as "to lift up his name," "to praise him with powerful words," or "to show how wonderful he is." In many languages a verb such as "honor" may be expressed as "to praise" or "to say great things about."

Believe in verse 10a and have believed in verse 10b both refer to acts which took place at a particular point in the past, probably the point at which Paul's readers first became Christians. You too will be among them (cf. other common language translations, Brc "and by you too," TNT "you too are included") is not in the Greek, but is inserted in order to start a new sentence and to link with the rest of the passage words which, in the original, form a rather awkward parenthesis (KJV uses marks of parenthesis at this point). It may be important to indicate clearly those among whom the believers in Thessalonica are to be, and thus one may need to say "you too will be with those who will honor the Lord."

In some cases, however, it may be sufficient to say "you too will be there with them."

Message is the normal word for "witness" or "testimony." As an apostle, Paul counted himself among the witnesses to Christ's resurrection (cf. 1 Corinthians 15.8 f.), though not, of course, to his earthly life. The last part of verse 10 is literally "because our testimony to you was believed" (RSV). Most modern translations change this into the equivalent active form. It may, however, be more natural to render because you have believed the message that we told you simply as "because you believed what we told you." If one specifically wishes to emphasize the element of "testimony," one can say "because you believed what we told you, things that we ourselves personally knew about."

Verses 11-12 sum up and partly echo what Paul has already said, but they present certain problems of their own. In order to see these problems more clearly, it is useful to list the main phrases repeated from earlier verses, using for this purpose RSV's more literal translation. Unbroken underlining points to the Greek words which are repeated from the previous verses. Broken underlining in the corresponding expressions points to Greek words having the same stems.

1.11-12 (RSV)	1.2-10 (RSV)
We always pray for you, that our God may make you worthy of his call, and may fulfil every good resolve and work of faith by his power, (12) so that the name of our Lord Jesus may be glorified in you, and you in him, according to the grace of our God and the Lord Jesus Christ.	(3) We are bound to give thanks to God always for you...because your faith is growing...and the love of every one of you for one another is increasing.... (7) with his mighty angels... (5) that you may be made worthy of the kingdom of God... (8) the gospel of our Lord Jesus... (10) when he comes...to be glorified in his saints.... (12) Grace to you...from God the Father and the Lord Jesus Christ.

It is clear from this analysis that most of the echoes in verses 11-12 come from verses 2-10 (with the important exception of "glorified" in verse 10), before Paul's attention turns to the final judgment. This, together with the present tense we always pray (v. 11), suggests that Paul's thought is returning from the future to the present. This means that the "call" (v. 11) is the call from God to which the Thessalonians responded at the beginning of their Christian life, and that the glorifying of the name of Jesus (v. 12) is something which is to happen in the present as well as in the future.

1.11 That is why we always pray for you. We ask our God to make you worthy of the life he has called you to live. May he, by his power, fulfill all your desire for goodness and complete your work of faith.

That is why indicates a very general connection between the previous verses and the aim of Paul's prayer, which he is about to state in a little more detail. The Greek contains an additional word, "also," which does not here imply any kind of contrast, but indicates that Paul is about to make another statement about what he and his colleagues do. Most translations omit it.

In a number of languages it may be necessary to specify what that refers to in the phrase that is why. The content of the following two verses would seem to point clearly to the special glory which the believers are to render to the Lord on that special Day. Certainly that is not a reference to possible punishment. In some instances one may be able to use a very general connective such as "therefore," but where something more specific is required, it may be necessary to say "because of the honor which you are going to give to the Lord, we always pray for you."

We ask our God to make you worthy is literally "that our God may make you worthy." TEV begins a new sentence by repeating in other words the end of the previous sentence. Paul probably means, not "we pray in order that God may make you worthy," but "the subject of our prayer is that God will make you worthy." In a number of languages it is necessary to introduce direct discourse with any expression of asking favors of God or praying to God. For example, it may be necessary to say "we pray to our God, Make the believers in Thessalonica worthy of the life you called them to live."

Make you worthy usually means "consider you worthy," but TEV's translation is justified by the context; the rest of the verse clearly shows that a new kind of conduct is involved. (A similar difficulty was noted in verse 5.) It is difficult in some languages to find an expression which fully translates the term worthy. In some instances the equivalent may be "make you the kind of people who deserve the life." It may even be necessary to use an expression equivalent to "make you good enough to live the life." This is not directly a petition for sanctification; it is a request that the lives of the Thessalonians will come up to the standard expected of those who have been called of God to live in a very special way.

The life he has called you to live is literally "the calling," but this means, not only the act by which God first called the Thessalonians, but the life which he intended they should follow. There are problems involved in the expression the life he has called you to live. It is impossible in some languages to speak of "living a life." However, one can say "worthy of the way in which he has called you to live." But then, there are often difficulties involved in the word called. This must not be rendered in such a way as to suggest "calling to" or "shouting at." The closest equivalent in some languages is an expression relating to the process of inviting or even summoning.

All your desire for goodness is the most probable way of understanding the next words (cf. Brc "that [God] may turn all your good intentions into actions"). Paul is speaking of an activity of God which, he prays, will bring to good effect the Thessalonians' own desire for good. The Seg text understands Paul to mean that the good desires are also God's, and translates "that [God] may accomplish in you...all the benevolent designs of his goodness." This translation is less probable (cf. the footnote to the Seg text). TOB leaves the matter open, producing the vague translation: "that [God] may grant you to accomplish all the good desired."

The request implied in may he, by his power, fulfill all your desire must be introduced in some languages by an expression of prayer or requesting, for example, "we pray to God that he will fulfill."

Fulfill all your desire for goodness may be expressed in some languages as "make it possible for you to do all the good which you want to do," or "...to be good to others in all the ways that you desire to do so."

In the Greek of by his power, the possessive his is understood. Some versions translate by his power as "powerfully." By his power comes at the end of the verse in the original, so it is not quite certain whether this phrase refers only to complete your work of faith or to fulfill all your desire for goodness also. The two phrases introduced by complete and fulfill (one word in Greek) are so similar in meaning and so closely linked that it is best to take by his power as referring to them both. Brc chooses "that he may turn all your good intentions into actions, and powerfully help you to live the life that faith demands." In some languages it is extremely difficult to speak of power as a means by which something is accomplished. Since power is essentially a quality of God himself, and not an instrument, it must be expressed in some languages as cause, for example, "because he is so powerful," or "because he has the power to do so."

The last part of Brc's translation ("the life that faith demands") corresponds to TEV's more literal your work of faith. Your is only implied in the Greek, but many translations add it, and rightly so. Complete your work of faith may mean either (1) "make perfect the activity of your faith" (FrCL), or (2) "complete the things you do because you believe" (cf. JB "complete all that you have been doing through faith"). The difference in meaning is slight, since a purely inward activity of faith would be difficult to imagine, and it is certainly not intended in 1 Thess. 1.3, where a very similar phrase is used. The second alternative would produce a clearer translation.

1.12 In this way the name of our Lord Jesus will receive glory from you, and you from him, by the grace of our God and of the Lord Jesus Christ.

See also the notes on verse 10 and the introductory notes on verses 11-12.

This verse describes what will happen if Paul's prayer in the previous verse is fulfilled. The name of someone is virtually the same, in biblical language, as the person himself, but this way of speaking is not always natural in current speech, and so GeCL omits it: "thereby our Lord Jesus will be honored ...through what he works in you." TEV and some other translations turn the passive verbs of the original (literally "thus will be glorified the name of our Lord Jesus Christ in you, and you in him") into the active. "In you," like "in the saints" in verse 10, may mean either "by you" (cf. FrCL), "among you," (TNT) or "because of you" (Brc). The difference between the first two possibilities is slight, and the third is the least likely. TNT's translation of the second phrase is attractive: "you will be honoured because you belong to him."

In this way may be expressed in some languages as a condition, for example, "if this happens." In other instances one may express the meaning by using a phrase of means, for example, "by doing this."

Since you is really the agent of the activity of causing glory to the Lord Jesus, it may be better in some languages to translate the first clause of this verse as "by doing this you will cause the Lord Jesus to receive glory," "... cause his reputation to be lifted up," or "...cause him to be looked upon with wonder."

The elliptical clause and you from him may be rendered as "and he will cause you to have glory," or "...to be honored."

On the grace of our God, see the notes on 2 Thess. 1.2. The idea that the name of our Lord Jesus will receive glory...by the grace of...the Lord Jesus Christ is complicated for reasons which have nothing to do with language, and it is not the translator's responsibility to resolve this kind of difficulty. TNT (cf. GeCL) makes it less obvious by beginning a new sentence: "May our God and the Lord Jesus Christ graciously make this come true." It may be useful to relate the final phrase of verse 12, by the grace of our God and the Lord Jesus Christ, to the immediately preceding elliptical expression, and you from him, for it is obvious that the honor which the Lord Jesus is to give to the believers in Thessalonica will be a result of the goodness of God. One can, therefore, render this final expression as "this will happen because our God and the Lord Jesus Christ are so good to you," "...are so gracious to you," or "...are so exceedingly kind to you."

CHAPTER 2

In chapter 1 Paul has moved rapidly between greetings (v. 1), prayer (vv. 2, 3, 11), narrative (v. 4), and teaching (vv. 5-10). Chapter 2 consists of a rather long section of teaching (vv. 1-4, 6-12; v. 5 is a narrative aside), followed by a shorter mixed section (vv. 13-17) of prayer (vv. 13a, 16-17) and teaching (vv. 13b-14), together with the first of a series of calls to action (v. 15), which will occupy the central part of chapter 3.

There are various features which show that 2.1 begins a new stage in the development of Paul's thought.

1. The first Greek word in the sentence (literally "we beg you") is one which Paul has used at the beginning of new sections in 1 Thess. 4.1; 5.12.

2. The second Greek word is one which is commonly used to introduce a new subject. Knox, following the Latin (cf. Zur), misleadingly translates "but." Several translations (including KJV RSV Phps cf. NEB SpCL Lu) translate "now," and Brc (cf. TNT) divides the sentence at the end of verse 1, in order to show that "now" does not refer to a point in time. TEV (cf. BJ, also FrCL Seg Syn) omits the word, but TEV's concerning, in its emphatic position at the beginning of the sentence, is sufficient to show that a new subject is being introduced.

3. As in 1 Thess. 2.1 and many other passages, Paul uses the word brothers to start a new section.

4. The rather solemn title our Lord Jesus Christ is often used near the beginning of a section (cf. 1 Thess. 1.3), just as "Jesus Christ our Lord" is often used at the end (e.g. Romans 5.21; 6.23; 7.25).

Despite these indications of a new subject, chapter 2 is not entirely unrelated to chapter 1, especially to verses 5-10. Both deal with the final judgment, the coming of Christ, and the punishment of the wicked. The differences, which will be examined in detail later, may be summed up as follows:

1. Chapter 2.1-12 gives fuller teaching about the events which must take place before the final judgment.

2. Chapter 2.1-12 concentrates almost entirely (with the exception of verse 8b) on the negative aspects of the final struggle between good and evil. It is only in verse 13 that Paul turns to its positive aspects. In other words, Paul was more concerned in chapter 1 with the coming of Christ, and is more concerned in this present section with the coming of the Wicked One, though there is a close link between the two events.

As always, it is important for the translator to convey, not only the meaning of the individual words and phrases, but also the general tone of the passage. As in 1 Thess. 4.13-17, Paul here is speaking of events which lie partly in the future, and therefore outside both his own and the Thessalonians' direct experience. He therefore uses a certain amount of picture language (for example, breath from his mouth in v. 8), and a number of references to Old Testament passages (especially in verses 4 and 8). Mysterious figures such as the Wicked One and the one who holds it back appear, and it is possible, despite verse 5, that they were as mysterious to the original readers as they are to us. It is therefore quite in order for a translator to use rather solemn expressions, on condition that they are not too old-fashioned and/or literary to be understood by the intended readers. The content of this passage is difficult enough (see the detailed notes below, and the general commentaries), without the translator creating additional, purely linguistic difficulties for his readers.

The passage also contains some indications of rather high emotive content. The most important of these are a sentence (verses 3-4) which has no proper ending, and a long sentence covering verses 8-10. Old Testament expressions would also have emotive overtones for Paul and his readers.

TEV

The Wicked One

1 Concerning the coming of our
Lord Jesus Christ and our being
gathered together to be with him, I
beg you, my brothers, 2 not to be
so easily confused in your thinking
or upset by the claim that the Day
of the Lord has come. Perhaps it
is thought that we said this while
prophesying or preaching, or that
we wrote it in a letter. 3 Do not
let anyone deceive you in any way.
For the Day will not come until the
final Rebellion takes place and the
Wicked One appears, who is destined
to hell. 4 He will oppose every
so-called god or object of worship,
and will put himself above them
all. He will even go in and sit
down in God's Temple and claim to
be God. (2.1-4)

RSV

1 Now concerning the coming of
our Lord Jesus Christ and our as-
sembling to meet him, we beg you,
brethren, 2 not to be quickly
shaken in mind or excited, either
by spirit or by word, or by letter
purporting to be from us, to the
effect that the day of the Lord has
come. 3 Let no one deceive you in
any way; for that day will not
come, unless the rebellion comes
first, and the man of lawlessness[a]
is revealed, the son of perdition,
4 who opposes and exalts himself
against every so-called god or object of worship, so that he takes
his seat in the temple of God, proclaiming himself to be God.

[a]Other ancient authorities read *sin* (2.1-4)

The section heading The Wicked One refers to the person whom Paul calls in verse 3 (literally) "the man of lawlessness" and in verse 8 "the lawless one" (the title is not used in the Greek of verses 6 and 9). Despite the literal translation "the man of lawlessness," it is by no means certain that Paul is thinking of a human figure. In this kind of writing, technically known as "apocalyptic," animals are often used to represent human beings, and human figures to represent supernatural beings. There are many examples of this in Revelation and in parts of Daniel and Ezekiel. TEV is therefore right to use a section heading which does not refer specifically to a "man." In a number of languages, however, it is quite impossible to be obscure in referring to The Wicked One. If one must choose between an expression which refers to a beast and one which refers to a human being, it is preferable to employ a term which will suggest the latter, since that would be more in keeping with the idea of lawless and malevolent intent.

2.1 Concerning the coming of our Lord Jesus Christ and our being gathered together to be with him, I beg you, my brothers,

The word translated concerning provides a good example of the dangers of trying to find a one-for-one correspondence between expressions in the original language and in the receptor language. The Greek word huper, translated concerning, has several meanings which can be distinguished by the grammar of the sentences in which they occur and do not concern us here. Two other meanings are (1) "for," "on behalf of," "for the sake of" (as in 1 Thess. 5.10: "Christ ...died for us"); and (2) "of," "about," "concerning." The second meaning, which is almost certainly the correct one here, is quite different from the first meaning of the same word, but very close to one meaning of a different Greek word, peri, which TEV translates "about" in 1 Thess. 5.1 in a similar context (cf. 1 Thess. 4.9, 13). What matters for the translator is not only, or even primarily, the word used in the original, but the meaning which best fits the context.

TEV marks the beginning of a new section by putting concerning at the beginning of the sentence, and many translators make a similar change in the order of the original. GeCL goes further, and restructures the whole verse: "You are waiting, brothers, for our Lord Jesus Christ to come, and for us to be united with him for ever. We beg you, however...." This clearly and attractively separates (1) the statement of the new theme and (2) Paul's urgent request to his readers, which is expressed in verses 2-3a.

In some languages there is a serious problem involved in relating the introductory statement beginning with concerning and what follows in verse 2. It is not that Paul is begging the Thessalonians concerning the coming of the Lord Jesus Christ, but that he does not want them to be confused about that coming. In a number of languages it may be necessary to place the phrases beginning with concerning immediately after an expression corresponding to confused. Another way of handling this problem is to begin this section by saying "Now I wish to speak concerning the coming of our Lord Jesus Christ...." In this way one can introduce in a very normal manner what is essentially a new topic.

On the coming of our Lord Jesus Christ, see the notes on 1 Thess. 2.19. Our being gathered together to be with him recalls 1 Thess. 4.17. The only significant difference is that 1 Thess. 4.17 mentions both the act of being gathered together with Christ (v. 17a) and the state of remaining permanently with him (v. 17b), whereas the present verse speaks of only the first aspect. To be is not explicit in the original.

Since Paul wants to state very clearly that the coming of the Lord Jesus Christ is in the future, it is important in some languages to restructure the statement in such a way as to make this quite evident, for example, "Concerning the fact that our Lord Jesus Christ will be coming back and we will be gathered together with him," or "...he will gather us together with himself." It is often necessary to indicate clearly that this is a reference to the return of the Lord Jesus Christ and not a reference to the first time that he came into the world.

I beg you may be rendered in some languages as "I urge you strongly," "I plead with you," or "I speak to you with my heart."

As in many contexts, brothers may be rendered as "fellow believers" or "you who also believe in Jesus Christ."

2.2 not to be so easily confused in your thinking or upset by the claim that the Day of the Lord has come. Perhaps it is thought that we said this while prophesying or preaching, or that we wrote it in a letter.

Paul states the reason for his concern about the Christians at Thessalonica. They are in danger of believing, on insufficient grounds, that "the Day of the Lord" had already come. This leads Paul to explain in some detail what he believes that Day will be and to speak of the events which must first take place—events so public and dramatic that everyone will know when they have occurred.

The exact meaning of this verse can best be reached by looking at its wider context and at the general situation of the Thessalonians. Like most Christians in the generation following the death of Jesus, they are living in a state of high expectation that Jesus would soon return and the final judgment would take place. Paul shares these beliefs. His only concern is that the Thessalonians do not become so excited that they accept without question anything they might hear or read on this subject.

In this setting, it is possible to define more closely the meaning of the expressions translated be . . . confused in your thinking and upset. Out of context, the most common meaning of be confused in your thinking in English would be "not to reason correctly," but this is not the main element in the meaning of the Greek. Upset suggests sadness and often annoyance, but again this is not the meaning of the original.

Be confused in your thinking is literally "be shaken from (your) mind," (cf. KJV's and RSV's unidiomatic "shaken in mind"). Biblical thought never separates the mind from the rest of human nature, but for Paul the word translated "mind" or thinking normally means "man using his powers of judgment,"* and this meaning fits the context well. The state of mind from which Paul wants to save his readers is not simply one of terror (cf. Knox "do not be terrified out of your senses") nor insanity (cf. TNT "shaken out of your senses"), but neither is it merely logical confusion, as TEV might suggest, still less a change in one's way of thinking, as in SpCL. Seg "shaken in your good sense" and Brc "thrown off your balance" are closer. Note that most translators either remove or replace the metaphor of shaking. NEB (cf. TOB) has "lose your heads." Most languages are rich in metaphors suggesting various degrees of mental disturbance.

The passive expression not to be so easily confused combined with an implication of means (by the claim that) is the basis for some rather extensive changes in some languages involving the introduction of a reference to human agencies, for example, "do not let those who claim that the Day of the Lord has already come easily confuse you in your thinking." This type of construction

---

*W. D. Stacey, The Pauline View of Man, London 1956, quoted in Best, p. 275.

may, however, involve a number of syntactic complications, and therefore it may be necessary to employ a further restructuring, for example, "Some people say that the Day of the Lord has already come; but I beg you, brothers, not to let such people confuse you in your thinking or upset your thoughts."

Upset is a rare and strong word. It is used in a similar context in Matthew 24.6 and Mark 13.7, where TEV translates "troubles." Here the stress falls, no longer on the Thessalonians' judgment, but on their emotions. The context does not explicitly refer to fear, and Brc's "not to get into a state of panic" is too strong and possibly misleading, though fear is certainly involved in the Gospel verses just referred to. An equivalent of upset is in many languages "to twist" or "cause to turn," for example, "do not let them twist your thoughts," or "do not let them turn your thoughts around." This seems to be a far more common expression than the idea of upsetting or turning something upside down. One can in some languages employ "do not let them trouble you in your thoughts," or even "do not let them cause you to worry about whether your thoughts are right."

Commentators correctly point out that the word translated easily (literally "quickly") does not always refer to time. Paul almost certainly does not mean either "so quickly after my last visit" or "so quickly after my last letter." However, in this context the meaning may still include a time element (cf. GeCL). A possible paraphrase would be "as soon as you hear or read some report that the Day of the Lord has come, don't immediately accept it without question, or let it disturb you emotionally." Although the disturbance of judgment is mentioned before the emotional disturbance, the first is probably the result of the second, and it may therefore be preferable in some languages to reverse the order in translation.

So easily is simply "easily" in the original. The addition of so suggests (1) that the Thessalonians have already been led astray and (2) that Paul is blaming them. The first suggestion may be correct; otherwise, why should Paul discuss the subject in such detail? It is possible that the neglect of work mentioned in chapter 3 was linked with a belief that the Day of the Lord had already come. However, Paul may have found it more tactful to speak of a real situation as if it were only a possible danger. For this reason, too, it may be better to avoid the suggestion that Paul is blaming his readers, though some scholars detect a note of impatience in verse 5. Later in this letter Paul makes a clear distinction between the Christian community as a whole, which needs teaching and practical advice (3.6, 13), and certain members of the community, who, though still to be treated as brothers, are directly condemned (3.11-12, 14-15).

On the Day of the Lord, see notes on 1 Thess. 5.2. There is no textual basis for KJV's "day of Christ," though no doubt for Paul the Old Testament "Day of the Lord" had become also the day of Christ, and "the Lord" in Paul's writings normally means "Christ." GeCL has "the day on which the Lord comes," clearly referring to Christ. TNT and TOB add a note to explain "day of the Lord."

In place of has come, a few translators (Knox, following the Latin, cf. KJV) have "is close at hand." The Greek verb can have this meaning in other tenses and in other contexts. In past tenses, however, it means "has arrived," and in Romans 8.38 and 1 Corinthians 3.22 the same verb is contrasted with events still to come. Rigaux (p. 653) describes the translation "is imminent" as "a commentary," having no linguistic basis.

The rest of verse 2 mentions the possible causes of the Thessalonians' disturbance. Most commentators agree that there are three of these: (1) a "spirit," (2) a "word," and (3) a "letter." (2) and (3) are occasionally taken together, to make a twofold contrast between a spoken utterance and a written message contained in a letter. This is unlikely, mainly because the Greek sentence contains three parallel expressions, and also because the term translated "word" often refers to a spoken message, as in 1 Thess. 1.6 (cf. Acts 20.38).

On the other hand, there seems rather to be a contrast of meaning between spoken messages (1) and (2) above and the written message (3). This is emphasized by TEV and FrCL. The two spoken messages, on this interpretation, would therefore be (1) the kind of ecstatic prophecy described in 1 Corinthians 14 (though this is nowhere else described as "a spirit" without qualification), and (2) a nonecstatic message of preaching or teaching. In the New Testament, neither ecstatic prophecy nor teaching is always accepted as coming from God (see 1 John 4.1). The translation of "spirit" as "prediction" (Knox, Phps) is too narrow; TOB has "prophetic revelation." BJ, which had "prophetic words" in its first edition, widens this to "manifestations of the Spirit" in the second.

Most translations take perhaps it is thought...that we wrote it in a letter to mean that a forged letter, falsely claiming Paul as its author, was circulating, and that this letter contained the statement that the Day of the Lord had come. It is true that verse 3 refers to a deliberate attempt to deceive the Thessalonians. However, the Greek (literally "by a letter as by us") can also imply that a genuine letter by Paul (presumably 1 Thessalonians) had been misunderstood to mean that the Day of the Lord had come. (There was probably not much time, either since the writing of 1 Thessalonians or even since Paul's visit, for a forgery to be written and circulated and to come to Paul's knowledge.) Paul may not even be referring to any letter actually in existence, but be putting his readers on their guard against the danger of being influenced by such a letter (cf. Mft Knox Phps "any...letter," Brc "some letter"). TEV is right to leave these various possibilities open.

It is not certain whether Paul means that

1. the "letter,"
2. the "word," and the "letter,"
3. the "spirit," the "word," and the "letter"

were supposed to be "from us" (RSV). Most translations from KJV to TNT choose the first possibility, and this is the simplest solution. Phps and probably BJ agree with TEV in choosing the third, while Knox, Brc, GeCL Zur choose the second. The main argument for this compromise solution is the difficulty of deciding what could be meant by a prophetic utterance wrongly supposed to come from Paul and his companions. The devices used by translators to show which of these three possibilities they have chosen are varied and interesting. They include:

1. In languages where it is possible, a singular (DuCL SpCL Lu Seg Syn) or plural (GeCL BJ) verb equivalent to "come (from us)."

2. Repetition or nonrepetition of such words as "some" and "any" (JB "any prediction or rumour or any letter," contrast Knox "any spiritual utterance, any message or letter"), cf. NEB GeCL.

3. Restructuring, as in TEV, FrCL Zur (whose use of square brackets is however not to be recommended): "...neither through a [prophetic] spirit nor through a supposedly-from-us-coming word or [such] a letter."

4. Punctuation (e.g. KJV "neither by spirit, nor by word, nor by letter as from us," cf. Brc "some message..., or some statement or some letter").

2.3 Do not let anyone deceive you in any way. For the Day will not come until the final Rebellion takes place and the Wicked One appears, who is destined to hell.

Do not let anyone deceive you in any way is equally emphatic in Greek and English. These words sum up the content of verse 2 and make it clear that Paul is thinking, not (or not primarily) that the Christians at Thessalonica might misunderstand something, but that someone might deliberately deceive them. An equivalent of do not let anyone deceive you in any way may be "do not permit anyone to fool you in the least." In some instances an equivalent may be "do not believe at all the wrong words that people are telling you about this."

For the Day will not come until makes explicit, as do virtually all translations from KJV onwards, an idea which is implicit in the Greek, and which Paul would have expressed if he had not broken off his sentence at the end of verse 2. The key clause in verse 3 is literally "unless the apostasy comes first."

The conjunction for would suggest a causal relation between not being deceived by the claims of the Day of the Lord having already come and the certainty of the future event for the Day of the Lord. Therefore it may be essential in some instances to translate "do not let anyone deceive you in any way, for you may be sure that the Day will not come...." It may also be important to render the Day as "that special Day."

In some languages there is a problem involved in speaking about "a day coming." Objects may come, but not time. However, in most instances one may speak of "a day happening" or say "it will be that day."

From this point until at least verse 10, the translator has the difficult but necessary task of distinguishing between the meaning of the language Paul uses and the theological or other realities to which they are intended to refer. The latter aspect is the task of the biblical theologian. For example, general commentaries and many special studies try to answer the question: who is the one who holds it back in verse 7? (cf. v. 6). The translator should be aware of this and similar problems, but he should avoid any attempt to present a particular solution in his translation.

Final Rebellion translates a single word (cf. RSV "rebellion") which in secular Greek meant "desertion," often associated with treason and rebellion against a lawful ruler. In the Greek Old Testament, including the deuterocanonical books (or Apocrypha), the word is used to describe unfaithfulness to God or the denial of God. This is the meaning of the closely related English word "apostasy." Acts 21.21, the only other place in the New Testament where this term is used, speaks of those who "abandon the Law of Moses" (TEV). The element of rebellion is perhaps implied, and is certainly present in later verses of the present chapter, but the central meaning is that of being unfaithful to, abandoning, or denying something or someone. A previous relationship with the person or belief denied is strongly presupposed. The translation should not, however, specify a denial of faith in Christ, since the context does not refer only to people who have been Christians. GeCL translates "first must many fall away from God." As TEV makes clear, "first" means "before the day of the Lord." Paul is not beginning to number a series of points, and the translation should not leave the reader expecting a later sentence beginning "second" or "next."

In many languages Rebellion can only be expressed as a verb, with some type of indication of those who participate in the rebellion. Until the final Rebellion takes place must thus be rendered in some languages as "until the time when so many people rebel against God," "...turn against God," or "... refuse to have anything to do with God."

Appears is literally "is revealed" (RSV). Passive verbs often indicate the activity of God, but this seems rather far-fetched here. "Reveal" in this verse does not have a technical theological meaning; it simply means that someone who had been hidden now comes out into the open, so the translation appears is satisfactory.

The Wicked One is literally "the man of lawlessness," according to the most likely reading of the Greek, though some manuscripts, followed by KJV, have "man of sin." On the meaning of this expression, see the introductory notes on chapter 2.

In 1 Corinthians 9.21, a related form of the word translated here Wicked is used, not with a bad meaning, but to refer to non-Jews who do not know the law of Moses. Almost always, however, this and related words refer to those who actively disobey a law which they do know. Verse 4 shows that Paul is not thinking only of those within the Jewish and Christian tradition.

TEV's the Wicked One, even with the capitals (see 4th paragraph, p. 150), is perhaps not quite as strong as the original. DuCL's tempting "the one...who is lawlessness in person," on the other hand, is a slight overtranslation. GeCL strikes a balance with "the enemy of God," anticipating verse 4, and adds a glossary note. In a number of languages the Wicked One is rendered as "the one who completely opposes God," or "the one who is against everything that God has ever said."

Who is destined to hell is literally "the son of perdition." There is no doubt that this is the same person as the Wicked One, who is described in more detail in verse 4. The literal translation "son of perdition" is unnatural in English. It reflects a Hebrew idiom which describes, first, character (e.g. Acts 4.36 "son of encouragement," TEV "'One who Encourages'"), and second, the group to which one belongs (e.g. Mt. 13.38 "sons of the kingdom," TEV "the people who belong to the Kingdom"). In the present verse, "son of perdition" almost certainly means neither "the perverter"nor "the corrupter" (DuCL); not "the product of all that leads to death" (Phps, a literal misunderstanding of the Hebrew idiom), but "the one who is to be destroyed" ("by God" [implied], therefore "in hell"). In verse 10 he will appear as the leader of others who are also to be destroyed.

In order to make certain that the relative clause who is destined to hell is a nonrestrictive attributive and qualifier of the Wicked One, it may be necessary in some languages to employ a new sentence, for example, "He is the one whom God will destroy" or "...destroy in hell." It may be even useful in some cases to indicate the certainty of the destruction by saying "whom God will surely destroy in hell." Destruction should be rendered, not merely as "killing" or "causing to suffer," but by some such expression as "cause to come to an end" or "utterly ruin."

2.4 He will oppose every so-called god or object of worship, and will put himself above them all. He will even go in and sit down in God's Temple and claim to be God.

The character of the Wicked One becomes clearer in this verse, which is full of echoes from the Old Testament (Daniel 11.36; Ezekiel 28.2, cf. vv. 6,9; Isaiah 14.13-14). Paul is probably also influenced by the tradition later recorded in Mark 13.14 and Matthew 24.15. Jews had vivid memories of the desecration of the Temple in Jerusalem by Greek invaders in 168 B.C., and Paul's language here is therefore heavy with emotive associations which the translator must try to convey—if possible in his text, otherwise by a note. Mft adds "actually" for emphasis before "seating himself in the temple of God." GeCL produces a similar effect by beginning a new sentence with "yes, he will set up his throne in God's temple."

He will oppose may be rendered as "he will speak against," "he will denounce," or "he will regard as nothing."

To oppose every so-called god or object of worship could be interpreted as being a valid and righteous thing for the Wicked One to do, since he would be denouncing all kinds of idols and fetishes. Since this is not what is meant, a more satisfactory rendering may be "every supernatural being which men worship," or "every spirit or god which men worship."

He...will put himself above them all must not be translated in a strictly literal sense of spatial position. What is meant here is that the Wicked One will consider himself to be superior to all supernatural powers or beings. Therefore one may wish to translate "he will consider himself greater than any of these," or "he will assert that he is more powerful than any spirit or god."

Some Greek manuscripts, followed by KJV, add "as God" before sit down in God's Temple, but this addition is not found in the best manuscripts.

And claim to be God is literally "claiming" or "proclaiming himself that he is God." KJV's "shewing himself that he is God" is too weak. These words may either (1) express the purpose for which, or the reason why, the Wicked One sits down in God's Temple (cf. Phps "to show that he really claims to be

God"), or (2), more probably, explain and partly repeat what Paul has said earlier in the verse. Claim to be God may be translated as "announce that he is God" or "tell the people, I am God himself," or "...I myself am God."

TEV

5 Don't you remember? I told
you all this while I was with you.
6 Yet there is something that keeps
this from happening now, and you
know what it is. At the proper
time, then, the Wicked One will appear. 7 The Mysterious Wickedness
is already at work, but what is going to happen will not happen until
the one who holds it back is taken
out of the way. 8 Then the Wicked
One will be revealed, but when the
Lord Jesus comes, he will kill him
with the breath from his mouth and
destroy him with his dazzling presence. 9 The Wicked One will come
with the power of Satan and perform
all kinds of false miracles and
wonders, 10 and use every kind of
wicked deceit on those who will
perish. They will perish because
they did not welcome and love the
truth so as to be saved. 11 And so
God sends the power of error to
work in them so that they believe
what is false. 12 The result is
that all who have not believed the
truth, but have taken pleasure in
sin, will be condemned. (2.5-12)

RSV

5 Do you not remember that when I
was still with you I told you this?
6 And you know what is restraining
him now so that he may be revealed
in his time. 7 For the mystery of
lawlessness is already at work;
only he who now restrains it will
do so until he is out of the way.
8 And then the lawless one will be
revealed, and the Lord Jesus will
slay him with the breath of his
mouth and destroy him by his appearing and his coming. 9 The coming of the lawless one by the activity of Satan will be with all
power and with pretended signs and
wonders, 10 and with all wicked
deception for those who are to
perish, because they refused to
love the truth and so be saved.
11 Therefore God sends upon them a
strong delusion, to make them believe what is false, 12 so that
all may be condemned who did not
believe the truth but had pleasure
in unrighteousness. (2.5-12)

Most translations either treat verses 1-12 as a single paragraph, or start a new paragraph with verse 5. This raises the difficult question of the relation between verses 1-4 and 6-12. (1) According to one view, the two passages give essentially the same kind of teaching, except that the second passage is more detailed than the first. Verses 5 and 6 would then be closely related, and Paul would be understood to be writing throughout verses 1-12 of what the readers already know (v. 6) and should remember (v. 5). The expanded paraphrase in Phps's first edition clearly takes this view: "I expect you remember now how I talked about this when I was with you. You will probably also remember how I used to talk about a 'restraining power'...." In this case, there would either be no break in verses 1-12, or a new section could begin at verse 5. (2) According to another view, Paul makes some kind of a distinction between verses 1-4, which consist of teaching which he gave during his visit to Thessalonica, and verses 6-12, which would contain mainly new teaching. This is how Phps in his second edition understands the passage: "You must surely remember how I talked about this when I was with you. You now know about the 'restraining power'...." In this case, it would seem more natural to start a new paragraph at verse 6 (cf. Rigaux), though Phps does not draw this conclusion. This is the view we shall follow and justify in the notes on verse 6.

For the first time in this letter, Paul distinguishes himself from Silas and Timothy by using the form I. He does not, however, indicate any contrast with them, or any special emphasis on himself.

2.5 Don't you remember? I told you all this while I was with you.

Phillips and some other translations change Paul's rhetorical question, "Do you not remember...?" (RSV), into a strong positive statement. Paul is not, in fact, asking his readers for information; he is saying that they either must or should remember (cf. JB "surely you remember...?"; Brc "you cannot have forgotten..."; NEB "you cannot but remember"; BJ "you remember, don't you...?"). Don't you remember? may be rendered as an emphatic statement, for example, "I am sure you remember," or "you certainly must remember." It may then be necessary to follow the verb remember by the statement which immediately follows, for example, "I am sure you remember that I told you all this while I was still with you." In some instances the reference to all this must be made more specific, for example, "I told you about all that was going to happen."

For the clause while I was with you it may be important to introduce some spatial specification, for example, "while I was still there with you," or "while I was still in Thessalonica with you."

2.6 Yet there is something that keeps this from happening now, and you know what it is. At the proper time, then, the Wicked One will appear.

The Greek sentence begins "and now." "And," common at the beginning of sentences in Hebrew and biblical Greek, is omitted in most translations since RSV, including BJ, but not JB TNT TOB. "And now" here, followed by already in verse 7, suggests a certain amount of repetition between verses 6 and 7. The same Greek words are used more closely together in 1 John 4.3 (TEV "and now it is here in the world already").

Now sometimes has a purely logical meaning, for example, "now let me mention something else" (cf. DuCL "thus"), and this would make good sense, since verse 6 probably begins a new paragraph. However, "now" in Greek usually indicates time, and this seems the more important factor here.

How is now related to the rest of the sentence? Does Paul mean (1) "you know now what is keeping this from happening" (cf. NEB "you must now be aware of the restraining hand"; similarly Mft Phps SpCL Zur); or (2) "you know what is restraining him now" (RSV cf. Knox TEV Brc TNT FrCL GeCL Lu BJ)? It is likely that Paul is moving on to teaching which is at least partly new to the Christians at Thessalonica. However, the main contrast between verses 1-4 and 6-10 lies in the difference of time perspective. In verses 1-4 Paul is concerned to say that the Day of the Lord will not come until certain other events have first taken place. In verses 6-10 he says positively and in more detail what these events are and in what order they will occur. This concern with order in time is shown by the use of such expressions as *now*, *at the proper time* (v. 6), *already* (v. 7), and *then* (v. 8). Paul distinguishes three groups of events: the first group are already occurring; the second are still in the future, but will happen before the Day of the Lord; and the last will take place on the Day of the Lord. However, Paul does not distinguish between the order of events within each group, and probably thinks of them as happening together. The following diagram compares the order in which Paul expects events to happen (first column) with the order in which he mentions them in successive verses. Figures in parentheses refer to verses; the other figures refer to the order in which the events are mentioned.

Group 1: present events				
restraining power		1(6)	4(7)	
mystery of lawlessness at work		3(7)		
Group 2: future events before the end				
the rebellion	2(3)			
restraining power removed			5(7)	
man of lawlessness revealed	3(3)	2(7)	6(8)	9(9)
false signs and wonders				10(9)
Group 3: events at the end				
man of lawlessness destroyed	4(3)		7(8)	
Day/coming of the Lord	1(3)		8(8)	
the wicked perish				11(10)

DIAGRAM 6

This diagram illustrates several points about the development of Paul's thought in this passage. (1) It confirms that he is more concerned in verses 6-10 than in verses 1-4 with the order of events in time. (2) Although there is some repetition, additional details are added at every stage. (3) Paul connects the present, in which the mystery of lawlessness is already at work, through the future period before the end, in which the man of lawlessness will be revealed, to the end, when he will be destroyed. Paul places the Christian hope within the setting of his readers' present experience. (4) Paul is most concerned, not with the restraining power, but with the man of lawlessness.

Languages differ in the way in which they express successions of events. Translators in some languages may need to alter the order in which Paul mentions the various items, to make it agree more closely with the order in which he expects them to happen.

Yet there is something that keeps this from happening now, and you know what it is is much shorter in Greek. Literally it is "and now the restraining (thing) you know." Most translations expand this brief statement in order to make the meaning clear. The "restraining (thing)" (neuter) becomes a "restraing (man)" (masculine) in verse 7, and TEV's something that becomes the one who in the next verse. In both places, Paul uses the definite article "the." This suggests that the readers are supposed to have heard of this power (or person) already. If they had not, Paul would surely have explained in more detail what it was. However, we do not know this today. Best ends a careful seven-page summary of the various theories by saying "we must acknowledge our ignorance" (p. 301).

The verb which TEV translates keeps...from (v. 6) and holds...back (v. 7) is used in various ways in the New Testament: (1) in a good sense, of retaining (Luke 8.15) or holding on to a message (1 Corinthians 15.2, cf. 11.2; see notes on 1 Thess. 5.21), or to one's confidence (Hebrews 3.14) or hope (Hebrews 10.23, cf. Hebrews 3.6); (2) neutrally, of owning possessions (1 Corinthians 7.30, cf. 2 Corinthians 6.10), occupying a seat (Luke 14.9), or of Paul keeping Onesimus with him (Philemon 13); and (3) negatively, of the truth being held captive (Romans 1.18), the Law holding men prisoner (Romans 7.6), or a disease holding someone in its grip (John 5.4). A number of scholars believe that the third sense seems to fit the present context best, though this is not as clear in Greek as in most translations. The Greek verb normally has an object, but not here. There is nothing in the original text corresponding to TEV's this in verse 6 and it in verse 7. The power which holds...back could in theory be an evil power holding men prisoners (as in Romans 7.6), but it is difficult to see why this power should be taken out of the way if another evil power, the Wicked One, is to take its place.

The conjunction yet indicates contrast, but this is not a contrast between the last sentence of verse 5 and the first sentence of verse 6. The contrast is suggested by what Paul affirms will happen, but which has not happened as yet; that is to say, between the contents of verses 3-4 and the statement of verse 6. To express this contrast appropriately, it may be necessary to use a conjunction such as "nevertheless" or "despite what is going to happen."

In some languages a literal rendering of something would suggest a particular object as being the instrument or means which keeps the rebellion and the desecration of the Temple from taking place. Accordingly, some translators render something as "someone" in order to make the statement in verse 6 parallel to what occurs in verse 7. Other translators employ a phrase like "for some reason," in order to indicate that a more general factor is involved in preventing the appearance of the Wicked One. Thus one may translate, for example, "nevertheless for some reason these happenings have not occurred as yet," but it may be better to imply that Paul himself knew the reasons involved and therefore to translate, "nevertheless, for these reasons...."

The words you know seem to state clearly that the Thessalonians knew who or what the power which keeps...from was. Some translators understand the phrase in this way: Mft "you can recall," Knox "(you know what I mean)," Brc "you know about." More probably, the words mean "you are experiencing for yourselves the activity of this restraining power." This is a meaning of know close to that in which Paul spoke of those who "do not know God" (2 Thess. 1.8), indicating much more than that they did not know of God's existence (cf. NEB "you must now be aware of"). If one is to interpret know in the sense of "experience," it may be possible to translate you know what it is as "you know personally what it is," or "...what is doing this," or even "...what is keeping this from happening."

Like the first part of the verse, at the proper time, then, the Wicked One will appear is very concise in Greek. Literally it is "so that he will be revealed in his own time." Some manuscripts have "in his time," which means practically the same thing, unless someone else's time (just possibly, but not likely, God's time) is meant. The pronoun "he" almost certainly refers to "the man of lawlessness," that is, the Wicked One, who is Paul's main concern in this passage.

In a number of languages the proper time must be expressed by some kind of modal element in the verb, for example, "at the time when it should happen." In other instances proper must be expressed as "correct," that is to say, "at the correct time." It may, however, be difficult to speak of a correct or proper time unless there is an indication of the person in whose judgment the time is proper. Therefore one may be obliged to say "at the time that God decides is right."

Since the appearance of the Wicked One is essentially determined by his own initiative, one may say in some languages "the Wicked One will show himself," or "...will cause himself to be known."

If the two halves of this verse are read as a whole, it becomes clear that Paul can only mean: "You are experiencing the power which holds the Wicked One back now, so that he will be revealed at the proper time, and not before." The words "in his own time" are emphasized in Greek by being placed at the end of the sentence. Brc "not...until" is entirely justified: "so that the Wicked One will not burst upon the world until his own proper time" (cf. GeCL "God's enemy can only appear when the time is ripe for him"; DuCL BJ TOB).

2.7 The Mysterious Wickedness is already at work, but what is going to happen will not happen until the one who holds it back is taken out of the way.

Paul continues to express himself in very concentrated language, and it will often be necessary in translation to spell out in more detail some elements of meaning which are only implicit in the text. Moreover, the division between the Greek sentences, which comes at the end of verse 7, does not correspond to the major division in the thought, which comes after already at work. Up to that point, Paul is mainly concerned with present events. From the beginning of verse 8, he is concerned with the future. Verse 7b is transitional, referring backward to the one who holds...back, but is more closely related to the future events which form the subject of verses 8-9. This can be seen more clearly if

Paul's statements are separated from one another and compared with a literal translation:

(1) The Mysterious Wickedness is already at work (v. 7a).

(2) At present someone is holding (the Wicked One) back (v. 7b).

(3) This person will be removed (v. 7b).

(4) His removal is all that is necessary for the Wicked One to appear (v. 8a).

(5) So the Wicked One will then appear (v. 8a).

For the mystery of lawlessness is already at work (1): only the restrainer now until he becomes out of the way (2, 3, 4). And then will be revealed the lawless one (5)....

As already mentioned, verses 6-7 contain a good deal of repetition. In verse 6, Paul was saying that the restraining power was stopping the Wicked One from appearing before the right time. Verses 7-8a say the converse; that is, when the restrainer is taken away, the Wicked One will appear. Paul insists in verse 7, more strongly than before, on what is happening already and "now." (TEV omits this second "now," cf. RSV "he who now restrains it." Unlike the word for now used in verse 6, this word must refer to time.) The Day of the Lord is not yet here, as some think, but events are already taking place which are connected with the end.

The close link between verses 6 and 7-8a is marked by "for" at the beginning of verse 7; but TEV, following current English usage, leaves "for" to be implied. In a sense the relation between the first sentence of verse 7 and the immediately preceding sentence is a contrast in time, and this may be indicated in some languages by the conjunction "but." It may then be useful to transpose the position of the adverb already, for example, "but already the Mysterious Wickedness is at work."

The Mysterious Wickedness* is literally "the mystery of lawlessness." Like the "restraining power," "lawlessness" is sometimes referred to as an abstract power and sometimes as a person. The distinction was probably not absolute for Paul, but he appears to think of the forces of evil as taking on a more personal form as they show themselves more openly in the final struggle. The term "mystery" is almost always used in the New Testament in speaking of truths which are hidden to people generally but which are made known to Christians. The translator should avoid expressions which suggest either (1) something which no one can understand, or (2) a puzzle to which there is a solution which anyone can understand. A mystery, for New Testament writers and for Paul in particular, is an open secret which anyone who becomes a Christian can

*On the use of capitals, see the fourth paragraph on page 150.

come to understand, but which no one can understand apart from faith. TEV does not fully convey the difficult idea of the "open secret," which may need to be explained in a glossary note. The relation between "mystery" and "wickedness" is probably "the mystery which consists of wickedness." TEV shows that it is the wickedness, not directly the mystery, which is...at work, producing the effects to be mentioned in verses 11-12.

The Mysterious Wickedness is already at work may be difficult to translate into some languages, particularly those in which one cannot speak of an abstraction such as wickedness "doing" anything. The closest equivalent in meaning to Wickedness is already at work may be "many people are already doing what is wicked" or "...what is evil." If Wickedness is to be related to the concept of "lawlessness" in the sense of opposition to what God has established as right, one may say "but already many people are doing what is against what God has said." This, however, leaves out of the picture the difficult attributive Mysterious. It would be incorrect to translate this as "and no one can understand this," or to assume that it simply means that "wickedness works in a hidden manner." In a number of languages the closest equivalent of Mysterious would have to be a complete clause, for example, "and we can only understand this because of what God has revealed to us."

Is...at work is the translation most commonly chosen, but some commentators prefer "is...set to work" (Best, cf. Rigaux). The Greek verb used here always speaks of the activity of supernatural powers. If the translation "is... set to work" is chosen, it will be necessary in some languages to state who sets the Mysterious Wickedness to work. The possibilities are (1) Satan, as in verse 9, (2) God, as in verse 11, and (3) the "restraining power," which is the least likely of the three. In verses 9 and 11, the noun which TEV translates power is related to the verb is...at work (or "is...set to work"). It seems most natural to think of the Mysterious Wickedness being set to work by Satan.

The notes on verse 7 suggested reasons for taking the first words of verse 8 with what has gone before. GeCL makes 8a a separate sentence: "When that has happened, God's Enemy will come forward." GeCL also makes a new section of verses 8-17. However, although verses 8-12 contain some important new developments, they have more in common with verses 1-7 than with verses 13-17, and TEV's arrangement of the sections is to be preferred.

The general expression what is going to happen may need to be made more specific and so may be rendered "what I said was going to happen." This will tie the statement to what has already been described in verses 3 and 4. The one who holds it back may be rendered as "the one who prevents it from happening," or "the one who causes it not to happen."

The passive expression is taken out of the way must be made active in some languages, and this would probably require the introduction of an agent. New Testament scholars normally agree that the agent in this instance would be God himself, who arranges events at the proper time. Therefore one may translate until...is taken out of the way as "until God takes out of the way the one who is preventing all this from happening."

2.8 Then the Wicked One will be revealed, but when the Lord Jesus comes, he will kill him with the breath from his mouth and destroy him with his dazzling presence.

Then in New Testament Greek, as in English, may mean either "at that time" or "next, immediately after." The context suggests the second meaning here: "as soon as the restraining power is taken away, the Wicked One will appear." To show the close connection between the temporal elements in these verses, it may be possible to render then as "only then." This will reinforce the relation between the removal of the restraining one and the appearance of the Wicked One.

For the Wicked One, see the introductory notes on 2.1-12 and the notes on verse 3.

The rest of verse 8 has a poetic tone which the translator should try to reproduce, using, of course, the poetic features of the receptor language. There are several poetic features in the original Greek text. To begin with, there is (1) a kind of rhythm and balance of expression: "whom the Lord Jesus will / kill by the breath of his mouth // and / destroy by the appearance of his coming." (2) This is a modified quotation of Isaiah 11.4 (cf. Psalm 33.6), which is poetic in the original Hebrew. (3) The repetition, both between the two halves of the couplet (kill and destroy) and within the second half ("appearance" and "coming") is poetic, as is also (4) the pictorial language, "the breath of his mouth."

Because of the poetic tone of this verse, one should not look for a distinction between kill and destroy. In other contexts, kill can mean "annul, abolish," as in Hebrews 10.9, and destroy can mean "make inactive," as in Romans 3.3; but such a distinction does not need to be made in the present case. (TNT, however, has "take away all his power.") Similarly, "appearance" and "coming" are close in meaning. They are really closer in Greek than in those translations which render "appearance" by such words as "brightness" and "radiance" (KJV cf. Knox Phps NEB TOB). The second edition of BJ correctly changes "resplendence" to "manifestation." Brc, recognizing that parallelism is not a normal feature of English poetry, combines the two lines: "the Lord Jesus will blast him out of existence with the breath of his mouth and with the blinding brilliance of his coming."

There is a serious problem of temporal sequence in verses 8-9. A literal rendering of verse 8 ("and then will be revealed the Lawless One, whom the Lord Jesus will kill...by the appearance of his coming") would seem to imply that immediately upon the appearance of the Wicked One the Lord Jesus will destroy him. However, in verse 9 there is a description of what the Wicked One will do when he comes. It may be possible to suggest a time span between the appearance of the Wicked One and the coming of the Lord Jesus by shifting the order of clauses, as TEV does: then the Wicked One will be revealed, but when the Lord Jesus comes, he will kill...." This order suggests a time span during which the events described in verse 9 can take place. In fact, it may be necessary in some languages to begin verse 9 with a temporal conjunction such as "in the meantime."

When the Lord Jesus comes...with his dazzling presence is literally "by the manifestation of his coming," but this refers to a single event, not (as, for example in RSV) "his appearing and his coming." The poetic use of repetition emphasizes the solemn nature of the event, and GeCL "he will annihilate him by his mere appearing" is rather wide of the mark. The Greek expression translated in TEV as with his dazzling presence is best taken as means rather than simply as a temporal qualification, since it is parallel with the expression with the breath from his mouth. Therefore one may translate this phrase in some languages as "by means of his being present in a dazzling way," or perhaps "by means of his appearing in a glorious way."

For a more detailed discussion of presence, see the discussion of when he comes, page 50 (on 1 Thess. 2.19).

The breath from his mouth is a rather common biblical expression (e.g. Exodus 15.8; Psalm 33.6) which can sometimes be misunderstood in translation. (1) The Greek word for breath also means "spirit" (cf. KJV), but there is no reference here to the Holy Spirit. (2) "Breath" does not mean simply "word," as in Phps "the words from the mouth of the Lord Jesus." (3) God's breath is always thought of as powerful, so the meaning is very different from "a puff of wind will blow him away." A literal rendering of with the breath from his mouth may involve a number of serious complications. In the first place, it is rather redundant to speak of "the breath of his mouth," since the breath is normally regarded as coming from the mouth. Even to speak of someone being killed by this breath may seem either humorous (as a reference to halitosis or bad breath) or as a suggestion of some kind of disease spread by germs carried on the breath. The concept of breath in this verse may be incorporated in the idea of "kill" in some languages by rendering "he will blow him out of this life," or "by blowing he will destroy him." Where it is either misleading or completely unintelligible to speak of "the breath of his mouth," it may be better to drop this aspect of the figurative language and simply say "the Lord Jesus will kill him."

Older translations, such as KJV, followed a text which omitted Jesus and had "consume" instead of kill. Modern editions and translations prefer the text on which TEV is based.

Verses 9-12 raise a general problem of the relation between past, present, and future events, which it is convenient to look at as a whole. If we try to list them according to tense, we reach the not very definite result shown in Diagram 7 (p. 174). The distinction is far from clear-cut. Items 1, 2, and 8 are certainly future in meaning, though the verb in 1 is grammatically present. Item 4 is clearly past. Items 3, 5, 6, and 7 may be present, future, or both in meaning.

However, Greek makes a distinction, perhaps more important than that of tense, between events thought of as (1) taking place over a period of time and now complete, (2) those taking place over a period of time but not yet complete, and (3) those taking place at a point in time and therefore (at least by implica-

2.9

	PAST	PRESENT	FUTURE
1			the lawless one will come
2			he will deceive
3		those who are perishing /	are to perish
4	they refused to love the truth		
5		and so be saved	
6		God sends /	will send on them a strong delusion
7		so that they believe /	will believe what is false
8			unbelievers will be condemned

DIAGRAM 7

tion) complete.* No verbs in group (1) occur in the present verses. "He will deceive" (item 2 in the above list) is not expressed by a verb. Items 1,3, and 6 fall in group (2), and items 4,5,7, and both verbs of 8 fall in group (3).

This distinction, as it has just been applied to these verses, has some interesting though partly tentative implications for the translator. Item 1 does not focus on the event of the coming of the Wicked One, since this has been specified in verse 8. Item 1 focuses rather on the series of events which occur during the period of his coming. Items 3 and 6 overlap present and future: those who are to perish are already beginning to perish. The notes on verse 11 will suggest reasons for the translation "the reason for this is that God is sending...." The other items raise no special problems. Item 4 is clearly marked as occurring at a point in the past. Item 5 focuses on the point of final and complete salvation. The translation of item 7 will be determined by that of item 6, the main verb. The context clearly places item 8 in the future.

2.9 The Wicked One will come with the power of Satan and perform all kinds of false miracles and wonders,

*This is an oversimplification of a complex subject. See J. Lyons, Introduction to Theoretical Linguistics, pp. 314 f.; N. Turner in J. H. Moulton, A Grammar of New Testament Greek, vol. 3, pp. 59 ff.; C. F. D. Moule, An Idiom-Book of New Testament Greek, especially pp. 5 ff.

Here as in verse 8, TEV changes the noun "coming" into an active verb come. But here it is not the Lord Jesus but the Wicked One who comes. TEV and some other translations mark this change by a new sentence.

The grammatical structure of the Greek is not clear. The Wicked One will come may be linked with (1) "by the activity of Satan," (2) "with all power...," or (3) "for (the destruction of) those who will perish." The third possibility is remote. "By the activity of Satan" comes first in the Greek, and it seems more natural to understand it as the basis of the signs and wonders, rather than simply as an aside. This is the view taken by most translators (e.g. NEB "the coming of that wicked man is the work of Satan," cf. Mft Phps JB Brc TNT; RSV "the coming of the lawless one by the activity of Satan will be with all power....")

Will come reflects a present tense in Greek (see the notes on vv. 9-12). Translators must avoid making nonsense of the passage by suggesting that the Wicked One had already come. Yet there is a serious problem involved in the future form of the verb will come since it repeats the beginning of verse 8 and so seems to contradict what has been said in the latter part of that same verse. It may be necessary, therefore, to refer to the coming of the Wicked One as a temporal setting for the kinds of miracles, signs, and wonders which he will perform, for example, "when the Wicked One comes with the power of Satan, he will perform all kinds of miracles...."

On the power of Satan, see verse 7. Satan should be carefully distinguished in translation from his servant the Wicked One. A literal rendering of with the power of Satan might suggest that the Wicked One was merely carrying along Satan's power. It may be necessary to introduce this phrase as a parenthetical and explanatory statement, for example, "Satan himself will give the Wicked One his power," or "he will have Satan's power."

All kinds of false miracles raises two separate questions, one about all, and the other about miracles. (1) All may mean (a) all kinds of (TEV cf. JB Brc NEB TNT), as in Matthew 4.23 (TEV "every kind of disease"), or (b) "to the highest degree," as in Philippians 1.20 (TEV "full of courage," literally "with all courage"). Mft ("the full power") and Phps ("all the force") choose this second meaning of all. (2) When the Greek word dunamis 'power' is used in the plural, it often means miracles. But in this verse, dunamis is in the singular, and Mft RSV Phps NEB Brc accordingly translate it as "power." Combining these two choices, the translator has in practice two possibilities: (1) "all kinds of power" (NEB Brc); (2) "power in the highest degree" (Mft Phps).

TEV, however, combines the expression of power (so frequently used to refer to supernatural force) with the following two Greek terms, generally translated as "signs and wonders." The resulting coalesced expression is perhaps the closest natural equivalent of a rather unusual Greek phrase.

It is also possible to translate "power in the highest degree," leaving the false miracles and wonders to be understood as examples of this power. However, all kinds of fits in better with every kind of wicked deceit in verse 10, so "all kinds of power" is perhaps to be preferred. It may be necessary to translate as "he will demonstrate all kinds of power," or "he will show that he has all kinds of power," and then to bring in the false miracles in an added phrase, for example, "by causing people to see false miracles."

"Signs and wonders" are often linked together, especially by Luke in Acts, in speaking of the miracles performed by the apostles. "Signs" indicates the significance of the event: God is active in a special way, the time of his final victory is near. "Wonders" stresses the astonishment of those who see these events. The combination of the two is so common in principle it would be possible to link them in translation as "miraculous signs" or "amazing and significant happenings."

False miracles and wonders may mean (1) apparent signs and wonders which are really fakes (Knox uses the word "counterfeit," cf. RSV "pretended"); (2) signs and wonders which come from a false source (Mft "the full power, the miracles and portents, of falsehood," cf. NEB); or (3) signs and wonders "calculated to deceive" (Brc). It is difficult to find any parallel to (1) false miracles and wonders in the New Testament, for the New Testament normally takes seriously even those miracles which are performed by evil powers. (2) fits in well with the reference to Satan as the ultimate cause of these events. (3) fits in well with the more detailed description of those who will perish, especially in verse 11, and is perhaps slightly preferable. Accordingly, false miracles and wonders may be rendered as "signs and wonders which deceive people," or "...which cause them to turn the wrong way" (using an idiom which refers to general behavior). It may be possible to combine miracles and wonders as "wonderful events" or "very astonishing happenings."

2.10 and use every kind of wicked deceit on those who will perish. They will perish because they did not welcome and love the truth so as to be saved.

And use every kind of wicked deceit is literally "and with all deceit of wickedness." As with all kinds of false miracles in verse 9, two questions arise: (1) Does "all" mean every kind of or "the highest degree of"? Most translators prefer the first solution, but Mft has "full deceitfulness of evil," Phps "evil's undiluted power to deceive," and NEB "all the deception that sinfulness can impose...." (2) Such expressions as "deceit of wickedness" are a common way of saying wicked deceit in Hebrew and biblical Greek, but a few translations take the expression to mean "deceit which comes from wickedness" (cf. Knox "his wickedness will deceive," also NEB). Deceit is by definition wicked, so the second solution tends to give a stronger translation. Wicked translates a word close in meaning to "lawlessness" in verses 3 and 7, so TEV is right, especially in a common language translation, to use wicked for both of them.

Use every kind of...deceit must be expressed in some languages as "will deceive in every way." In some languages wicked deceit might be misleading since it could suggest that certain kinds of deceit are not wicked. The attributive wicked simply reinforces the meaning of deceit but does not restrict it in the sense of a particular kind of deceit. It may therefore be necessary in some languages to say "in a wicked way he will deceive people in every manner," or even "he will be wicked and deceive people in every way."

On "those who are perishing," see the notes on 2.1-12. TOB's "those who are losing themselves" is too weak. In some contexts the Greek verb may be translated "lose," but the meaning always includes the element of something being destroyed, rather than that of someone losing his way or something being mislaid. (Compare in English "we lost fifty men in the battle.") The idea of a continuous process of perishing is rather difficult to express in some languages, even in English. Many translations use expressions such as "doomed to perish" to link the present and the future (Mft Brc cf. Knox JB TNT). [They] will perish is not repeated in the original; TEV repeats it in order to break a long sentence into smaller parts. Something of the inevitability and certainty of perishing may be expressed in some languages as "those who will surely perish," or "those who will certainly be destroyed." In some instances perish may be rendered as "end up as nothing," but this should not be used as a means of suggesting a doctrine of ultimate annihilation.

Welcome is the word which Paul used in 1 Thess. 1.6 and 2.13 to describe the way in which the Thessalonians had responded to the preaching of the Christian message. The present verse must be understood in a similar way, not as referring to "the love of truth" in any general philosophical sense. The truth (note the definite article) is the Christian message, which is related to salvation. The exact relation may be either (1) one of purpose ("they welcomed the truth in order to be saved"), or (2) one of result ("they welcomed the truth, and thus were saved"). Most translations choose (2), for example, RSV "because they refused to love the truth and so be saved," JB "they would not grasp the love of the truth which could have saved them." NEB SpCL agree with TEV in choosing (1). NEB has "they did not open their minds to love of the truth, so as to find salvation." A similar problem was discussed in the notes on 1 Thess. 2.16, and another will arise in verse 11 of the chapter now under discussion. Paul's main emphasis is probably on the effect of the truth, rather than on the motives for which people do or do not welcome it.

In this type of context did not welcome may often be translated as "were not happy to hear," "did not listen with glad hearts," or "did not accept the words into their hearts."

Love the truth must often be translated by a term which is quite different from one that would express love for a person. For example, love the truth may be rendered as "value highly the truth," or "regard the truth as very important." In some languages one may express this idea idiomatically by saying "put the truth in their hearts." It may, however, be very difficult in some languages to speak of truth as an object. One may speak of "a true message" or "true words," but even then it may be necessary to indicate the content of the true words. In such a case one may need to say, for example, "the true words about our Lord," or "the true message about the Lord Jesus."

Though so as to be saved may be interpreted by some people as implying only purpose, it is often understood by English speakers as suggesting result as well. It may even be linked with welcome and love the truth as means, for example, "and in this way be saved." If the passive expression to be saved must be made active with the agent expressed, it may be important to restructure the final clause as "so that God could save them" or "...would save them."

2.11 And so God sends the power of error to work in them so that they believe what is false.

Paul's main concern in this section has been with secondary powers of evil, and more recently (v. 9) with Satan himself. Now he emphasizes that this whole struggle has its place in the purpose of God.

So (as the same Greek expression, translated differently, in 1 Thess. 2.13) refers backwards (contrast JB), and has a rather general meaning. In order to find the right relation between verses 9-10 and 11-12, it is necessary to look at the wider context. Note first that verse 11 introduces, with the emphatic word God, a factor not mentioned directly since the end of chapter 1, namely, the activity of God. Most translations suggest that verses 9-10 give the reason for the events in verses 11-12, but when we read the passage as a whole, the reverse seems more natural, and is a quite possible meaning of the Greek. In verses 9-10, Paul has been describing events which will take place as the end approaches and (v. 10b) arrives. In verses 11-12, following his usual practice (see Diagram 6), he goes over some of the same ground again, but giving more detail and looking more deeply into the meaning of the events in question. If this is so, the translation should run: "The reason for this (that is, the events described in verses 9-10) is that God is sending a power of error...." Verse 11 would then unfold an aspect of the Christian "mystery" (cf. v. 7), explaining that the events of verses 9-10, summarized in verse 12, are the result of what God is doing.

The power which God sends has not been mentioned directly before, so following normal Greek usage in such cases, Paul does not use a definite article. This power leads unbelievers into error, in order that, or with the result that (the same problem as in v. 10), they will not only accept wrong information, but they will trust what is not worthy of trust. Cf. Mft "put faith in falsehood," Phps "put their faith in an utter fraud." Paul uses here a definite article before "lie," referring back to verse 9, where the "lie" (TEV false) was mentioned for the first time, therefore without an article. The modern reader finds it easier to accept that the power of error produces the result that people believe what is false, rather than that God sends this power in order that people may believe what is false; but both concepts are included in the meaning, and the main clause God sends suggests the translation "in order that they may believe what is false."

In linking verse 11 with verse 10, it is important that the conjunctive element (so or "therefore" or "for this reason") refers to the various events of verses 8, 9, and 10, and not merely to the result or purpose suggested at the end of verse 10, namely, so as to be saved. It may, therefore, be important to introduce a transition in the form of "because of what is going to happen," or "because of all that is going to happen."

Since the activity of God in sending the power of error is something which has already begun to take place, it may be useful to use a verb form which suggests continuous activity, for example, "God is sending."

It may be very difficult in some languages to speak of "sending the power of error," since both "power" and "error" are abstracts, and they really qualify something else. It may even be impossible to speak of "sending" an abstract such as "power" or "error." However, it may be possible to say "God causes them to think wrongly, and this strongly affects their thinking." Or one may be able to say "God causes them to act very wrongly," or "...to be badly mistaken in the way in which they act."

2.12 The result is that all who have not believed the truth, but have taken pleasure in sin, will be condemned.

A problem similar to that of verse 11 exists also in verse 12. Here translations are divided between expressing the idea of purpose (RSV "so that all may be condemned," cf. Mft JB NEB SpCL TOB) and the idea of result (TEV the result is, cf. Phps TNT DuCL FrCL). Knox and GeCL divide the sentence in such a way that neither relation is explicit. Here, as in verse 11, the element of purpose fits the context better. Paul is not only saying that unbelief results in condemnation, but that this is all part of God's purpose. To indicate the concept of purpose, it may be necessary to refer back to the activity of God mentioned in verse 11, for example, "God did that so that all...will be condemned." Result may be expressed specifically as "hence all...will be condemned."

As in verse 11, believed includes an element of personal truth (like love the truth in v. 10). The Hebrew word for "truth," which often underlies New Testament usage, refers to that which is firm and can be relied upon. As in the case of verse 10, it may be necessary to render the truth as "the true words" or "the true message," and even to add something about the content of the message, namely, "about our Lord Jesus."

"To take pleasure in" something does not merely mean to enjoy the object. As in Mark 1.11, there is an element of will and choice. In the present verse, therefore, JB translates "chose wickedness" and Brc has "deliberately chose sin." Have taken pleasure in sin may be rendered as "are happy when they sin," or "sin and are glad that they have sinned." Perhaps the simplest equivalent in some languages is "like to sin."

In a number of languages it may be necessary to reverse the order of the negative and positive statements and say, for example, "the result is that all who like to sin and who do not believe the truth will be condemned."

The Greek word translated condemned by itself means simply "judge," but here the context requires the meaning condemned. Compare Romans 2.12b, where there is a close parallel with "are lost" in verse 12a; cf. also 1 Corinthians 11.31-32. The passive expression will be condemned may be made active by introducing God as the agent, for example, "God will condemn them," "God will pronounce them guilty," or "God will say, You are guilty."

TEV

You Are Chosen for Salvation

13 We must thank God at all
times for you, brothers, you whom
the Lord loves. For God chose you
as the first[b] to be saved, by the
Spirit's power to make you God's
holy people and by your faith in
the truth. 14 God called you to
this through the Good News we
preached to you; he called you to
possess your share of the glory of
our Lord Jesus Christ. 15 So then,
our brothers, stand firm and hold
on to those truths which we taught
you, both in our preaching and in
our letter.
16 May our Lord Jesus Christ
himself and God our Father, who
loved us and in his grace gave us
unfailing courage and a firm hope,
17 fill you with courage and
strengthen you to always do and say
what is good.

[b]as the first; *some manuscripts have* from the beginning.

(2.13-17)

RSV

13 But we are bound to give
thanks to God always for you,
brethren beloved by the Lord, because God chose you from the beginning[b] to be saved, through sanctification by the Spirit[c] and belief in the truth. 14 To this he
called you through our gospel, so
that you may obtain the glory of
our Lord Jesus Christ. 15 So then,
brethren, stand firm and hold to
the traditions which you were
taught by us, either by word of
mouth or by letter.
16 Now may our Lord Jesus Christ
himself, and God our Father, who
loved us and gave us eternal comfort and good hope through grace,
17 comfort your hearts and establish them in every good work and
word.

[b]Other ancient authorities read *as the first converts*

[c]Or *of spirit*

(2.13-17)

For the following reasons these verses are, in a sense, the hinge on which the whole letter turns.

1. They are related to what has gone before. The first part of verse 13 is similar to 1.3, suggesting that Paul is now returning to his starting point, to sum up what he has said up to this point. Faith in the truth (v. 13) recalls the mention of faith (believe) and truth in verses 10-12. The theme of choosing and calling in verses 13-14 was touched upon in 1.11, and glory in verse 14 takes up the theme of 1.12. In verse 15 (cf. v. 17) the appeal to the readers to hold on to what Paul and his companions have taught, in their preaching and in their letter, contrasts with the false or misunderstood teaching and letter mentioned in 2.2. God's purpose for unbelievers, which has been the subject of verses 11-12, is contrasted with his plan for believers, outlined in verses 13-17.

2. These verses also anticipate what is to come. They contain prayers and calls to action similar to those which form the main theme of chapter 3. Verses 16-17 speak of the courage or encouragement which Paul prays God to give the church in Thessalonica. This section and chapter 3 both include also Paul's own encouragement (the same verb parakaleō is used in 3.12). To always do...what is good (literally "in every good work") prepares the way for Paul to insist in 3.6-15 on the obligation to work. This section indeed reads almost like

the beginning of a letter, especially since Paul often begins by striking a positive note, and going on to say harder things (cf. 1 Corinthians 1.4-9 and 1.10-17).

3. These verses form a distinct section. This is shown both by formal features such as transitionals ("but" and the emphatic "we" in v. 13; finally, our brothers in 3.1), and by a change of theme. Paul is now giving thanks, not, as in 1.3-4, for what the Thessalonians have done, but for what God has done for them.

The section heading You Are Chosen for Salvation is a particularly helpful device coming at this point, since it assists the reader in noting the significant shift in content. The preceding verses deal with those who have believed the false signs and wonders and thus are condemned. The contrast, beginning in verse 13, is with those who have believed God and for whom therefore Paul and his colleagues give thanks. The passive form of this title may, of course, be altered into an active form by saying "God has chosen you for salvation," or "God has chosen to save you."

2.13 We must thank God at all times for you, brothers, you whom the Lord loves. For God chose you as the first to be saved, by the Spirit's power to make you God's holy people and by your faith in the truth.

The first two words of the Greek (literally "but we") mark a transition. "But" is the translation of KJV RSV Phps JB NEB GeCL SpCL Lu; Mft translates "now"; and the word is omitted by Knox Brc TNT DuCL FrCL, as by TEV. There is a general change of theme, from the doom of unbelievers to the salvation of believers, but there is no specific contrast such as the English term "but" suggests. Bicknell's attempt (quoted in Morris, p. 236) to see a contrast between the evangelists, who thank God "in spite of the discouragement of some of their converts," and those converts themselves, is not convincing. If the transition is marked in other ways in translation, the word "but" or "now" can be omitted without loss. We is emphatic, but any contrast is between the subjects of verses 1-12 and 13-17 as a whole. For this reason GeCL makes explicit the contrast between unbelievers and believers and so renders "but for you, we must continually thank God." Such an indication of the contrast is especially important at this point, particularly for the oral comprehension of the text. Usually the section headings are not read when one reads a passage aloud to a congregation.

The Greek sentence continues to the end of verse 14. It is not unduly long by Paul's standards, but most translations divide it. In dividing the sentence translators sometimes tend to alter the emphasis on the various statements. These statements may be listed as follows, in simplified form:

1. We must thank God for you.
2. The Lord loves you.
3. God chose you.
4. God called you (v. 14).

KJV RSV Mft do not divide the sentence. JB NEB SpCL TOB divide it at the end of verse 13, thereby linking items 1, 2, and 3 of the above list. Knox Phps DuCL

FrCL, like TEV, make three sentences, linking items 1 and 2 and leaving "the Lord loves you" as a dependent clause. GeCL makes four sentences, not specifying any relation between them. Brc TNT reverse 2 and 1, thereby throwing extra emphasis on 2 ("brothers, you are dear to God, and we can do no other than always thank God for you").

Which are the closest relations, not primarily in grammar, but in meaning, between the four statements? How are they most naturally grouped? Grammar alone would suggest (1) a link between 1 and 2, because 2 is subordinate to 1 in the original text; (2) a link between 3 and 4, because they have the same subject, God, and because 4 is a dependent clause, hanging on to 3, in the Greek text. In meaning, however, 2 is more closely linked with 3 and 4 than with 1. 1 is preliminary; 2 is a general statement which is spelled out in more detail (as Paul often does) in what follows. The possible difference of grammatical agent between 2 and 3-4 is not significant, for Paul constantly links the work of God and of Christ (he does so very closely in vv. 16-17). The general structure of the translation may be given as: "We must thank God for you, brothers. The Lord loves you. God chose you. God called you." The relations between statements 2, 3, and 4 may even be made more explicit in some languages as: "The Lord loves you, which may be seen by the fact that God chose you and called you." However, because of the intervening clauses, one may need to say: "The fact that the Lord loves you is evidenced by God having chosen you," and then, following the intervening clauses: "The Lord's love for you is also clear by God having called you."

Lord may refer to God or to Christ. Though generally in Paul's writings "Lord" refers to Christ, in this context, which speaks of "love," "choosing," and "calling," one may be justified in understanding "Lord" as referring to God.

Loves is a participle whose meaning is not limited to a point in time, and often overlaps both the past and the present. In languages which have a tense structure similar to that of English, the past tense "loved" could imply that God or Christ no longer loved the Thessalonians, so it is best in such languages to use a present or a timeless tense (see 1 Thess. 1.4). Some languages have two quite distinct terms for "love," one suggesting desire to possess and the other implying concern and care for another. Probably the latter emphasis is important in this particular passage. Such terms for "love" are often derived from expressions denoting the concern of parents for their children. In some instances this kind of love is expressed in an idiomatic manner, for example, "his heart goes out to us."

The form of the verb translated chose implies "for himself." This idea is reinforced by God's holy people, but it does not normally need to be expressed here. The tense of the verb chose, like that of called in verse 14, normally indicates an event at a particular point in past time, though the context probably shows that this point is at the beginning of time. However, see the following paragraph. There is always some danger involved in selecting a term to render chose, for this almost inevitably suggests a kind of separation of items. It is important to make certain that the type of choice indicated here means selecting out what is accepted from what is to be rejected. Sometimes this is expressed as "God specially named you," "God put a special mark on you," or "God called out your name."

The textual basis for the phrase as the first is not certain. It is followed by Mft Knox Phps Brc TNT DuCL FrCL, but most commentators, together with KJV RSV JB NEB GeCL Lu BJ Seg Syn TOB, follow a text which reads "from the beginning." Whichever text is used, it is difficult to know exactly what Paul meant. (1) The Greek text followed by the TEV contains a metaphor of harvest, Mft has "the first to be reaped for salvation," and Knox "the firstfruits in the harvest of salvation." Commentators tend to avoid this reading, partly because the Thessalonians were not the first to be converted in Macedonia (Paul visited Philippi first), and also because Paul usually adds some such expression as "of Achaia" (1 Corinthians 16.15 RSV) to explain "firstfruits." It may be necessary in some languages to be even more explicit and say, for example, "among the first to be saved," or "among the first persons whom God was saving." (2) If the text which reads "from the beginning" is followed, the question arises "from the beginning of what?" Some languages will need to specify this. GeCL does this in the most probable way: "Already before he made the world, he chose you."

To be saved is literally "to (or for) salvation." Many languages prefer an active verb to the abstract noun. Since there is a noun in the original, no tense is specified, and the context shows that Paul is thinking of salvation in the widest possible terms, from its beginning in God's purpose to its completion at the last day. In the active form to be saved may be rendered as "whom God was saving." But it may not be possible to find a ready equivalent to the term saved or "salvation." In general, the equivalences of the biblical concept of salvation are of two types: one is based upon the idea of rescuing from danger or imminent death; and the other relates to restoration to health and soundness of body and mind. The latter meaning is increasingly used in translation of the Scriptures, because the concept of rescuing seems to be too narrowly restricted to a particular event, rather than focusing upon the results of such an event and the continuing relationship of the believer to God and his power.

By the Spirit's power to make you God's holy people is literally "in sanctification of spirit," but the TEV rendering is by no means a loose paraphrase. The text could mean simply that the (human) spirits of the Thessalonians are to be made holy, and this is how Mft and Knox understand it; but the great majority of translators and commentators understand Paul to be referring to the work of the Holy Spirit. TEV makes explicit the meaning of "sanctification" as setting (someone or something) apart to belong to God.

By the Spirit's power may be rendered as "by what the Spirit has done." This may be expressed in some languages as a causative relation, for example, "God has caused the Spirit to make you his holy people," or "...caused you to become his holy people." In some languages God's holy people can only be rendered effectively as "people who belong to God." The emphasis is not upon the goodness of the people but upon their very special relationship to God.

Faith in the truth may also mean "faith which is created by truth," that is, "truth which calls faith into being"; but note NEB "the truth that you believe" and also Knox. Verse 12 already linked faith (i.e. believe) with truth (see the notes on that verse). In both verses, truth has the specific meaning of the Christian message, like the Good News in the next verse. TEV's translation fits the context well, since verse 12 has just mentioned believing the truth, and verse 15 will repeat the call to hold on to what has been received.

Note that in the event of salvation the primary agent is God but there are two secondary agents, the Holy Spirit and the person who believes. This relation must be expressed in some languages as cause, for example, "to be saved because of how the Spirit made you God's holy people, and because of how you have put your confidence in the truth," or "... in the true message."

2.14 God called you to this through the Good News we preached to you; he called you to possess your share of the glory of our Lord Jesus Christ.

This verse links God's purpose for men with specific events which happened during Paul's visit to Thessalonica. The verb called refers to a particular point in time, and through the Good News we preached to you (literally "through our gospel," cf. 1 Thess. 1.5) tells us to what point in time Paul is referring. Some difficulties may be encountered in translating called, for this is not the idea of "shouting at" or "calling a person's name at a distance." The closest equivalent in some languages is "earnestly invite" or even "urge."

To this means everything Paul has mentioned as part of God's purpose: salvation, sanctification, and faith. The purpose of to this is explained in the second part of the verse as to possess your share of the glory of our Lord Jesus Christ. Though the implications of to this are spelled out later in verse 14, it may be necessary in the first part of the verse to employ some such phrase as "to this new kind of life" or "to be his people."

He called you is not in the Greek, but is repeated from the beginning of the verse in order to divide the sentence.

On to possess, see 1 Thess. 5.9. Both there and here, the word means "gaining possession of." In other contexts it can mean simply possess, but here the context shows that Paul is thinking of a process rather than a state. BJ "enter into possession" combines both ideas rather effectively.

Your share of is implicit in the original. The idea is not that of dividing something, but of participating in the glory (see 1 Thess. 2.6) which is part of the nature of God himself. Brc has "he wanted you to have as your own the glory of our Lord Jesus Christ." Though it is important to avoid the implication of dividing up the glory of Jesus Christ, it is also important to avoid the implication that one is to take over as one's own the glory of Jesus Christ. The emphasis here is upon participating in the glory. This may be expressed in some languages as "to also be happy because of the glory of our Lord Jesus Christ." In some instances the closest equivalent may be "to have a little of that wonderfulness which the Lord Jesus Christ has."

2.15 So then, our brothers, stand firm and hold on to those truths which we taught you, both in our preaching and in our letter.

So then and our brothers show that Paul is introducing a new thought. After having spoken of God's activity, he turns briefly to what his readers must do. Stand firm (see 1 Thess. 3.8) and hold on refer to action over a period of time. Instead of being "shaken" (v. 2) by false teaching, the Thessalonians must remain loyal to what Paul and his companions taught them, both by word of mouth during their visit and by "a letter of ours," presumably 1 Thessalonians.

It is frequently impossible to use the metaphor stand firm. In some languages it would be taken to mean "defend yourselves." Useful equivalents may be "continue to believe as you have," "do not change your beliefs at all," or "do not let anyone change your beliefs." The two expressions, stand firm and hold on to those truths, are essentially equivalent in meaning. They are simply two different ways of describing how one should remain true to one's convictions. Hold on to those truths may often be rendered as "continue to believe..." or "do not give up believing those truths."

Those truths is literally "the traditions." This word can have a bad meaning, as when Jesus condemns those who "hold fast the tradition of men" (Mark 7.8), but that is not the case in this verse. Paul is referring here to a body of teaching which was not simply his own way of presenting the Christian message (cf. "our gospel," v. 14), but which was shared, at least in general terms, by the church as a whole. This teaching was partly doctrinal (as most probably in this passage) and partly to do with worship and daily life. Paul does not mean only that he handed these truths on to the Thessalonians, but also that the truths had been handed on to him (cf. 1 Corinthians 11.23, 15.3). FrCL (cf. DuCL) has "the teachings which we have passed on to you." Mft's "rules" is too narrow. An equivalent of "the teachings which we have passed on to you" may be in some languages "what we taught and which we in turn had earlier been taught," or "... which others in turn had taught us."

In our preaching may be rendered as "when we were talking to you," or "when we were preaching to you." In our letter may be rendered as "in the letter which we wrote to you." It may, however, be necessary to be more explicit, for example, "in the earlier letter we wrote to you," thus avoiding the suggestion that Paul is referring to the letter he was dictating at that time.

2.16 May our Lord Jesus Christ himself and God our Father, who loved us and in his grace gave us unfailing courage and a firm hope,

In this section Paul returns to his main theme, the activity of God and Christ, who are closely linked here and may also be so in verse 13. The transition is marked by the same Greek word in both places. There is an implied contrast between what the brothers are told to do in verse 15 and what Christ and God are asked to do in this prayer. "Now" (KJV RSV) and "so then" (Brc) mark this transition better than NEB's "and," which gives the impression of introducing an afterthought.

The indirect prayer beginning may our Lord Jesus Christ must be introduced in some languages with a verb of praying or beseeching, for example, "we pray to God that..." or "we beseech our Lord Jesus Christ himself and God our Father that he will...."

It may also be necessary to break this rather involved prayer in verses 16 and 17 into two sentences. This may be done, for example, as follows: "I pray to our Lord Jesus Christ himself and to God our Father, who loved us and who by his grace gave us unfailing courage and good hope. I pray that they will fill your hearts with courage and make you strong to always do and say what is good."

There are many points of similarity between this prayer and 1 Thess. 3.11-13 (see the notes on that passage).

Loved us and gave us refer to events at a point in past time; TEV's translation is better than "has loved" and "has given." When did these events happen? In Paul's writings these verbs in this form are often associated with the death and resurrection of Christ. That interpretation is possible here, though Paul does not say so explicitly, as he does in Galatians 2.19-20. Alternatively, the verbs may refer, like chose in verse 13, to an act of God which, involving an act of his will, is thought of as taking place at the beginning of time rather than at any particular point within human history.

Though the petition is directed to both the Lord Jesus Christ and God the Father, it is only God who is spoken of as loving and by his grace giving unfailing courage and firm hope. It is important, however, in translating not to suggest that only God, and not the Lord Jesus Christ, loves and gives courage.

Best suggests that unfailing courage and a firm hope may mean practically the same thing, unfailing courage being Paul's own phrase and a firm hope an expression in common use. This would give a translation such as "unfailing courage, a 'firm hope'"—without the connective "and," since in English this word normally links two expressions which are somewhat different in meaning.

For courage, many translations have "encouragement" or the equivalent verb "encourage." The word can also mean "exhortation" (cf. 1 Thess. 2.3, 11), but not in this context. Unfailing courage may mean "courage which never fails" or "courage which always continues"; and this is how most translators take it. Best, however, suggests the meaning "God has encouraged in respect of eternity," and this fits the context well. GeCL has "courage for all the future." Gave us unfailing courage must be expressed in several languages as a causative, with unfailing rendered as a type of adverb, for example, "caused us always to have courage" or "...to always be courageous." In some languages courage might be expressed quite idiomatically as "never to run away in one's heart," or even "to have a firm heart always."

A firm hope may be expressed as "to hope well." That is to say, "God made us to hope well." Literally the phrase is "a good hope," and in this type of context the attributive "good" suggests something of the content of hope rather than merely the efficiency with which one hopes. Accordingly, in some languages "a good hope" may be "a patient waiting for what is good."

The translator has to face the question "What did God do in (or 'by') his grace?" To what verb or verbs are these words related? (1) Most older and some modern translations follow the order of the original: God "gave us comfort and good hope through grace" (RSV cf. KJV Knox Phps Brc Lu). (2) Most modern and also the older French translations link grace more explicitly with gave by putting in his grace (or "by his grace") immediately before or after gave us (so TEV cf. JB NEB TNT FrCL GeCL BJ Seg Syn TOB). (3) SpCL, supported by Rigaux and Best,* translates "in his goodness God loved us and gave (us)." (4) Mft alone links grace with verse 17: "graciously encourage your hearts." The Greek phrase (literally, "in grace") is not as common in the New Testament as one might perhaps expect. It occurs in Colossians 4.6, but the meaning there is rather different. In Colossians 3.16, most editions, commentaries, and translations take "in grace" with what follows, as Mft does in the present verse. On balance, solution (3) seems better than (2). Solution (4) is possible, but it requires a punctuation different from that of the UBS Greek New Testament.

Some translations avoid the traditional word for grace, as being no longer part of current language (see notes on 1 Thess. 1.1). Here, TNT has "kindness," and GeCL (cf. DuCL) has "goodness."

His before grace is not in the Greek, but it is clearly implied, and most modern translations except BJ and TOB add it. In his grace may be treated as means, attendant circumstance, or cause, and in many languages it is more normal to treat this phrase as cause, for example, "because he is so good" or "because of his kindness."

DuCL interestingly restructures the whole of verses 16-17 as follows: "We wish that in all the good that you do in word and deed, you may be encouraged and strengthened by our Lord Jesus Christ and God, our Father. He has shown us his love and given us in his goodness unending comfort and good hope." This has the advantage (1) of dividing a rather long sentence, and (2) of avoiding the form "may," which is perhaps beginning to fall out of use in some modern languages, as the corresponding Greek form was doing at the time the New Testament was being written. If restructuring on this scale is attempted, there is something to be said for reversing the two sentences, to give something like: "God our Father in his goodness has shown us his love, and given us a good hope and encouragement for all the future. We pray to him and to our Lord Jesus Christ that he may encourage and strengthen your judgment" (see comments on v. 17) "in every good thing you do and say."

2.17 fill you with courage and strengthen you to always do and say what is good.

The TEV translation of verse 16 leaves one slight difficulty unsolved. It carries into English an ambiguity of the Greek text, in which the pronoun "he" (of "he may encourage") may refer to our Lord Jesus Christ, to God our Father, or to both acting jointly. Verse 17 is a continuation of the sentence begun in verse 16, so that the one who loved us and...gave us courage... is the same one who Paul desires may fill you with courage and strengthen you.

Fill you with courage is literally "encourage your hearts." Any translation

*That is, Best's commentary, p. 320; but the translation which accompanies the commentary, p. 310, does not make this clear.

of "hearts" which suggests mere emotion is to be avoided (see 1 Thess. 2.4, where TEV has "our motives"; cf. 1 Thess. 2.17, where TEV has "our thoughts"). The Greek word for "heart," like its Hebrew equivalent, sometimes means the whole "inner man," as in 1 Peter 3.4. TEV, along with Phps JB NEB TNT DuCL GeCL TOB, accordingly replaces "your hearts" by you. However, "heart" can also refer more precisely to judgment and will, as in Mark 7.21, cf. Jeremiah 5.21 (KJV "without understanding," RSV "senseless") and Job 12.3 (RSV "understanding," NEB "sense"). This would fit in excellently with Paul's appeal to his readers in 2.1-3 to use good sense and judgment. Similarly, strengthen you is the opposite of being "shaken" (see notes on v. 2).

In a number of languages it is impossible to speak of "filling you (or "your hearts") with courage," but one may say "to cause you to be completely courageous," "to cause you to have complete courage," or "to cause you to stand up against any and all dangers."

To always do and say what is good (literally "in every good deed and word") correctly links always and good with both do and say. The implied meaning is not "strengthen you whenever you are doing or saying something good," but "strengthen you so that you can always do and say what is good" (or perhaps, as in vv. 9-10, "so that you can do and say all kinds of good things"). TEV (cf. Brc) brings this out. Knox's "confirm you in every right habit of action and speech" somewhat over-emphasizes the suggestion that the Thessalonians are already (at least in general, cf. chapter 3) doing and saying what is good. However, Paul by no means denies this.

It may be difficult in some languages to combine the concept of "strengthen" with the idea of doing and saying what is good. The basic underlying meaning of strengthen in this context is an increase in "capacity" or "ability." In some instances one may wish to translate this as "make you continually able to always do and say what is good." By the introduction of "continually" and "able," the concept of abiding strength is clearly indicated.

CHAPTER 3

It is difficult to be certain of the exact relation between chapter 3 (especially vv. 1-5) and the preceding part of this letter. In the brief introduction to 2 Thessalonians, we noted that although most translations and commentaries make a major break at the end of chapter 2, there is some overlap between the prayer of 2.16-17 and the further prayer of 3.3-5. Rigaux relates 2.13-17 and 3.1-5 as two groups of "encouragements," which together with 2.1-12 make up the second section of 2.1—3.5.

One way of approaching this problem is to consider the two main subjects of the letter. The first is Paul's teaching about the Wicked One (2.1-12), in which the correct teaching of verses 3-12 is contrasted with the false teaching reported in verses 1-2. The second is Paul's teaching about the obligation to work (3.6-15), which includes a warning against lazy people.

There are several points of similarity between these two important passages. (a) In both, there is a contrast between right and wrong: in 2.1-12 between right and wrong teaching, and in 3.6-15 between right and wrong behavior. (b) The main sentence in each passage (2.8-10; 3.7-9) is comparatively long. (c) The purpose of both passages is similar: 2.1-12 aims to prevent the Thessalonians from being "confused...or upset" by false teaching, while 3.6-15 aims to prevent those who do nothing except meddle in other people's business from disturbing the entire Christian community. Paul does not tell us whether the two problems are related; that is, we do not know whether it was because some people thought the Day of the Lord had come that they stopped working. Perhaps two different groups were involved. However, both problems were contributing to a general atmosphere of restlessness, and Paul's "encouragements," both in 2.13-17 (especially v. 15, stand firm and hold on) and 3.1-5 (especially vv. 3-5; see the detailed notes there), are intended to strengthen the readers' faith in the midst of this confusion.

The entire passage 2.13—3.5 can be viewed, not as a mere transition, but as the hinge on which the whole letter turns, the "joint" or meeting point between two similar and possibly related themes. It is in this setting that the special problem of the place of 3.1-5 in the structure of this letter can best be discussed.

Before doing so, it is worth noting that there are significant links (1) between 2.13-17 and 3.6-15, bypassing 3.1-5, and (2) between 3.6-15 and 1 Thessalonians.

1. Links between 2.13-17 and 3.6-15.

1.1 The theme of "encouragement," announced in 2.16-17 (courage), does not come to an end at 3.5. It is taken up again in 3.12 with the use of the same Greek word, which TEV there translates warn (see the detailed notes on that verse).

1.2 To always do and say what is good in 2.17 is literally "in every good work and word" (RSV), and the use of the word "work" prepares the way for the warning against idleness in 3.6 ff.

1.3 There is some similarity between the general summary statements in 2.17 and 3.13.

1.4 In 2.15, Paul uses the word "traditions" (*those truths*), which is repeated in the singular in 3.6.

2. There is one major link between 3.6-15 and 1 Thessalonians. That is the theme of the obligation to work, which Paul mentioned rather briefly in 1 Thess. 4.11-12, referred to in passing in 1 Thess. 5.14, and now discusses in greater detail and with more severity, no doubt because his earlier teaching had not had the desired effect. Within this obvious and important link, there is a striking similarity of detail between 1 Thess. 2.9 and 2 Thess. 3.8, in which Paul refers to his own example in almost identical words.

TEV

Pray for Us

1 Finally, our brothers, pray
for us, that the Lord's message may
continue to spread rapidly and be
received with honor, just as it was
among you. 2 Pray also that God
will rescue us from wicked and evil
people; for not everyone believes
the message.
3 But the Lord is faithful, and
he will strengthen you and keep you
safe from the Evil One. 4 And the
Lord gives us confidence in you; and
we are sure that you are doing and
will continue to do what we tell
you.
5 May the Lord lead you into a
greater understanding of the love
of God and the endurance that is
given by Christ. (3.1-5)

RSV

1 Finally, brethren, pray for
us, that the word of the Lord may
speed on and triumph, as it did
among you, 2 and that we may be
delivered from wicked and evil men;
for not all have faith. 3 But the
Lord is faithful; he will strength-
en you and guard you from evil.[d]
4 And we have confidence in the
Lord about you, that you are doing
and will do the things which we
command. 5 May the Lord direct
your hearts to the love of God and
to the steadfastness of Christ.

[d]Or *the evil one* (3.1-5)

These five verses consist of four sentences, short sentences by Paul's standards, which produce a slightly staccato effect normally associated with the end of his letters. This impression is reinforced by the repeated use in verses 3-5 of the Greek conjunction *de*, meaning "and" or "but," a word which, at least in verses 4 and 5, serves simply to introduce the next item in a series. Usually it is near the end of his letters that Paul asks his readers to pray for him; verse 1a is similar to 1 Thess. 5.25.

The section is divided at the end of verse 2. In verses 1-2 Paul asks for the readers' prayers, in verses 3-4 (as in 2.16-17) he expresses his confident hope that God will keep the Thessalonians safe, and in verse 5 he prays that this may be so. The two subsections (correctly printed as separate paragraphs in TEV) are linked by a play on words: *believes* in verse 2 and *faithful* in verse 3 stand next to each other in the Greek and differ by only one letter.

It is an open question whether verse 5 should be printed as a separate paragraph. There is a grammatical distinction between this verse and the two that precede it, since verses 3-4 include verbs in the future (will strengthen, will... keep, will continue to do), while verse 5 has the form of a prayer (may the Lord lead...). However, verses 3-5 share the common theme of stability (see the note on these verses), and it is better on the whole to print them as a single paragraph, as in DuCL and GeCL.

It is difficult to be certain whether this passage looks mainly forward to 3.6-15, or backward to chapter 2. The references to stability, faithfulness, confidence, and endurance are equally appropriate to both the main themes of the letter. Verses 1-2 have no close parallel anywhere in this letter, though Paul has written at length in 1 Thessalonians about his own and his fellow apostles' conflicts and difficulties. Verses 3-5 are so general that they do not point clearly either forward or backward, and commentators have sometimes remarked on their inadequacy (Rigaux comments: "Every speaker has his good and bad days," p. 693).

It is tempting to see the very flatness of verses 3-5 as an indirect indication that they belong more closely with what follows. Paul often begins with a general statement, following it by something more specific. He is especially careful to do this when approaching a delicate subject, as here and in 1 Thess. 4.1-8. 1 Thess. 4.1 is likewise a general statement, and it begins almost exactly like 2 Thess. 3.1.

3.1 Finally, our brothers, pray for us, that the Lord's message may continue to spread rapidly and be received with honor, just as it was among you.

Finally, as in 1 Thess. 4.1 (see the note on that verse), does not necessarily imply that Paul is coming to the end of his letter; it means that his last major subject is being approached. This is an additional reason for taking verses 1-5 with what follows. GeCL "we are coming to the end" overemphasizes finally, while DuCL "also" ("pray also for us, brothers") underemphasizes it. Knox and TNT have "and now" (cf. Brc "it only remains," TOB), which strikes a good balance. If finally is too closely related to pray in the translation, it may suggest that the final content of this letter refers to prayer. In a sense, however, finally introduces the whole theme of the obligation of the Thessalonians to work. The equivalent of finally in some languages is "and now for the last part of what I want to say," or "and now to introduce my last point."

Our brothers, as in many previous passages and at verse 6, marks the beginning of a new section. (The function of this word in verse 13 is rather different.)

The form of the Greek verb for pray excludes the idea of offering prayer at only one particular time. However, it is reading too much into the text to make it mean "go on praying, as you are doing already," or "pray continually." The purpose of the prayer or its content—the two ideas are as difficult to distinguish in Greek as in English—is twofold: first and foremost, the spread of the Christian message; and secondly, the rescue of Paul and his companions from their enemies. If "Lord" is understood as referring to God, then it is "the word that comes from God"; but if "Lord" is interpreted as referring to Jesus, then it is "the word is about the Lord."

Pray for us as a command may require in some languages an introductory expression which will make it seem more like a request, for example, "please pray for us." In a number of languages pray is simply "speak to God on behalf of," and therefore pray for us is rendered as "speak to God on our behalf."

The Lord's message is the same in Greek as "the message about the Lord" in 1 Thess. 1.8, but "the message which the Lord gives" is also a possible meaning (cf. GeCL). DuCL has simply "the gospel," and this is what Paul means, but "gospel" in English and some other languages may be a word used mainly in church circles and therefore not part of a common language translation.

May continue to spread rapidly and be received with honor is literally "may run and be glorified." Continue is implicit (see next paragraph). Paul has spoken of the previous rapid spread of the Christian message in 1 Thess. 1.8 ff. What is the literal meaning of this metaphor "to run"? TEV's spread rapidly conveys the essential ideas of progress and speed. In other contexts (e.g. 1 Corinthians 9.24-26) "run" implies effort, but this does not seem to be appropriate here. To speak of the Christian message being "glorified" is unusual. The close connection with "run" makes the reader think of those who win a race and receive a prize, and one almost expects a reference to the "glorifying" of those who receive the message and remain faithful to it (cf. Romans 8.17,30). But "be glorified" has the same subject as "run," and the text cannot be made to mean "pray that the word may spread rapidly, and that those who receive it may be glorified." To glorify the word means to give the Christian message its due honor and to receive it with thanks (cf. 1.10, 12). The first element is brought out in the same way by both TEV and TNT (cf. Knox); the second is brought out by GeCL "may be received with thanks to God." "Run" and "glorify" are closely linked, but Brc weakens both by combining them as "may make the same splendid progress."

Continue is one possible interpretation of a comparison which is not explicit in the text (literally "may run and be glorified also among you"). Knox makes this comparison explicit "may run its course triumphantly with us, as it does with you." However, "with us" might be misunderstood as meaning "pray that we ourselves (Paul, Silas, and Timothy) may honor the Christian message more highly." This would make "run" very difficult to understand, it would have no parallel elsewhere in Paul's writing, and it would not fit in easily with verse 2. Paul is not thinking here of the evangelists themselves, but of their mission. GeCL's way of making the comparison explicit is better: "that the message from the Lord may spread rapidly, and everywhere, as with you, may be received with thanks to God." It would also be possible grammatically to take "as among you" with both "run" and "be glorified," producing the translation: "may spread rapidly and be glorified everywhere, as it did and was among you." The structure of the Greek sentence slightly favors this interpretation, since "run" and "be glorified" are closely linked. On the other hand, it might be argued that "run" suggests movement from one place to another, rather than within a single community.

3.2 Pray also that God will rescue us from wicked and evil people; for not everyone believes the message.

This verse contains Paul's second request for prayer, and both parts of it are expressed in very general terms. Paul was probably referring to particular difficulties in which he and his companions found themselves at the time of writing. The Thessalonians may have known about these problems, but we do not. The Greek has literally "that we may be rescued from the wicked and evil men." It would be unnatural to use here the word "the" in English, since there has been no previous reference to particular wicked men (except perhaps in 2.7, which is an even more difficult verse). KJV has "unreasonable" where TEV has wicked. "Unreasonable" represents an earlier sense of the Greek word, but by the time of Paul its meaning had become more general.

A literal translation of rescue might suggest that Paul and his colleagues were actually in the power of wicked and evil men who had in some way gotten control of them, perhaps even putting them in prison. That is clearly not the correct meaning. Therefore, it may be more appropriate to translate "pray also that God will keep us from suffering because of wicked and evil men," or "...that God will keep wicked and evil men from harming us," or "...causing us great trouble."

It may be impossible in some languages to distinguish between wicked and evil. These are essentially equivalent terms, and may be translated together in some languages simply as "very wicked men." A qualifier such as "very" may be regarded as compensating for the loss of one of the attributes or as representing the closest equivalent emphasis.

The relation between the two parts of the verse is not clear. For rightly indicates only a loose connection, since the second part of the verse does not explain the first, except indirectly in the sense that if everyone believed the message there would be no wicked and evil people. DuCL FrCL GeCL make verse 2b a separate sentence.

The message is implicit, since "believe" in normal English (though not in church language) requires an object. The text is literally "for not of all the faith." Knox interprets this in a footnote as "'The faith does not reach all hearts'; or possibly 'faith is not to be found in all hearts'." However, "faith," even with "the," should not be understood here as a system of belief; rather it is the positive response to the Christian message. "Faith" is therefore often translated by a verb such as "believe." FrCL has "for it is not everyone who accepts to believe," and GeCL "for not all let themselves be called to believe." If one does make the message explicit as the object of the verb believes, it may be necessary to relate this message to what has already been spoken of in verse 14 as the Good News and in verse 15 as our preaching. Therefore one may wish to say "believes the message we have proclaimed," or "believes the Good News." The last word of verse 2, "faith," and the first word of verse 3, "faithful," form the hinge on which Paul turns to a rather different subject, the contrast between faith and stability.

Verses 3-5 cannot be understood without realizing that the basic meaning of the Hebrew concept of faith is "firmness, reliability, or steadfastness."* This is the central idea which is repeatedly emphasized here by the words translated faithful, strengthen, keep you safe, confidence (v. 4), endurance (v. 5), and possibly also lead (v. 5). (The original suggests making a path which is straight and therefore safe.) There is a restless spirit in the air, with people becoming over-excited about the Day of the Lord and busybodies upsetting the life of the community. In addition, there are attacks from outside the church, and even fiercer tests will come before the End. Only the Lord (that is, Jesus) can keep the Thessalonians safe among these dangers (vv. 3, 5), but they must also hold on to the evangelists' teaching (v. 4).

3.3 But the Lord is faithful, and he will strengthen you and keep you safe from the Evil One.

The play on words mentioned above is reproduced in many English translations (from KJV to TNT) and by some translations in other languages (e.g. SpCL). There are, however, two reasons for avoiding it in English, and one or both of them may apply in other languages also. (1) It may be good to follow TEV in replacing "faith" in verse 2 by a related verb like "believe," in order to show that Paul is speaking of an event. (2) Faithful is gradually falling out of nonliterary English, except in a number of set phrases, most of which refer to an inferior's relationship with his superior ("faithful servant," "faithful dog," though not "faithful husband/wife"). This term is therefore not very appropriate in speaking of God's relationship with men. Phps "the Lord is utterly to be depended upon" brings out the meaning well, at a slightly higher language level (cf. Brc "you can rely on the Lord to strengthen you"). In addition to these two factors, the ability to reproduce plays on words in translation depends entirely on the resources of the receptor language, and meaning must have priority over formal and stylistic features.

Most translations, both traditional and modern, translate the Greek conjunction de here as "but," since there is a clear contrast between the faithlessness of the wicked men in verse 2 and the faithfulness of Christ or God. If the play on words is not retained, there is a rather less specific contrast between the wicked men and God. In order to point up the contrast, it may be possible to restructure but the Lord is faithful by rendering this expression as "but you can trust the Lord completely." Here, however, the contrast must be between not everyone and you. It is not between the message and the Lord. In some languages the Lord is faithful must be semantically restructured, since in reality the Lord is the goal of the process of trusting, and people are the ones who

*W. A. Whitehouse in A. Richardson (ed.), A Theological Word Book of the Bible. London, 1950.

trust. In many languages expressions for trust or dependence are quite idiomatic in form, for example, "you may lean on the Lord," "you may put your hand on the Lord," or "the Lord will always hold you up."

A literal rendering of he will strengthen you might suggest mere physical strength. It is better in some instances to render this as "he will cause your hearts to be strong," or "he will strengthen your wills." The strength here is obviously not physical, but psychological and spiritual. On strengthen see 1 Thess. 3.2.

Here as in verse 2 (rescue), the translator must avoid the suggestion that Christ will make it possible for the Thessalonians to avoid persecution completely. Paul knows that persecution is already going on and cannot be avoided, but he is confident that Christ will keep both him and the Thessalonian Christians safe in the midst of these attacks. The expression keep you safe from the Evil One must be inverted in a number of languages, for example, "prevent the Evil One from harming you," or "cause that the Evil One will not harm you," or "... make you suffer."

The last words may mean either the Evil One or "evil." (The same ambiguity is found in Matthew 5.37, and in the Lord's Prayer, Matthew 6.13.) Translations are divided: Mft NEB JB Brc cf. DuCL ("the devil") FrCL Seg Syn BJ TOB agree with TEV, while KJV Knox RSV Phps TNT cf. SpCL have "evil." (German translations, like the original, can have both meanings. RSV TNT JB Seg BJ TOB give the other possible translation in a note.) The arguments for each translation are rather evenly balanced. It is at least clear that the idea of a completely impersonal power of evil is foreign to Paul's thought. The wider context, especially 2.6-9, refers to the Wicked One in clearly personal terms. The narrower context, on the other hand, which has just mentioned wicked men, would support a more general translation "evil," thus covering attacks from either human or supernatural powers. Ancient Jewish writings speak of an "evil impulse." This idea is relevant if Paul is now thinking, not of attacks from outside the Christian community (as in v. 2), nor even of disturbances within it (as in vv. 6 ff.), but of attacks from within the individual. "Evil" therefore seems slightly preferable to the Evil One (cf. Knox "he will strengthen you, and keep you from all harm").

3.4 And the Lord gives us confidence in you; and we are sure that you are doing and will continue to do what we tell you.

1 Thess. 4.1 is the best commentary on this verse. The main problems in translating it concern the tenses of two of the four verbs in the Greek text. The other two are quite clear: are doing and will continue to do (literally "will do"; continue is implied).

The Lord gives us confidence in you is literally "we have-been-and-are-confident in the Lord about you." The confidence begins in the past, no doubt at the time of the readers' conversion, and continues into the present. If, as in English, it is awkward to express both these ideas, it is best to use a present tense. It is not quite clear whether Paul's confidence is in the Lord, in you, or in both, whether "we are confident in the Lord concerning you," or "we as Christians have confidence in you." The two ideas are closely related, and TEV satisfactorily includes both.

The Lord gives us confidence in you actually represents a causative relation. "It is the Lord that causes us to have confidence in you," or "...to be sure about you." To have confidence in someone may be expressed in some languages as "to trust" or "to rely on" someone. Therefore, one may translate this statement as "the Lord causes us to rely on you."

As in a number of contexts, the Lord must often be translated as "our Lord," since those to whom the Lord is related as ruler must often be specified.

There may be a problem in some languages in beginning verse 4 with a conjunction such as and, since there is no obvious and immediate relation between the preceding clause and what follows. It may be better to omit and and begin the sentence as "the Lord also gives us confidence." In this way some indication of the relation between this statement and the beginning of verse 3 may be made explicit.

The translation of what we tell you involves an overlap of past and present, though the tense of the Greek verb is present. In verses 6 and 12, Paul is clearly referring to the particular teaching he is now giving about the obligation to work. In verse 10, he uses the same verb in the past tense. In verse 4, Paul has not yet mentioned any specific teaching. In any case, he states that the Thessalonians are already doing what we tell you, and this clearly implies some earlier instruction, either during Paul's visit or in a letter. The translation of what we tell you should be wide enough to include both past and present teaching. Some translations avoid the problem of tense by using a noun instead of the verb, for example, Brc "our instructions" (cf. Phps GeCL). JB generalizes the statement by adding the word "all": "will go on doing all that we tell you."

The Greek verb means "tell" in the sense of command or order, not in the sense of telling a story. The words are doing and will continue to do emphasize the practical nature of the teaching Paul has in mind. This is another slight indication that verses 1-5 are linked with what follows, rather than with the doctrinal teaching of chapter 2.

In some instances the rendering of are doing and will continue to do may cause confusion, because a verb meaning "to do" may carry the implication of "to work." This would not be entirely appropriate in view of what Paul says beginning with verse 6. The implications here are broader than mere work, and therefore it is more appropriate in some instances to translate "we are sure that you are living and will continue to live in the way in which we tell you," or "...are behaving and will continue to behave in the manner we prescribe."

3.5 May the Lord lead you into a greater understanding of the love of God and the endurance that is given by Christ.

As apostles, Paul and his companions (see 1 Thess. 2.7) have to give directions, even commands, to young churches, but Paul turns immediately to prayer that Christ himself will guide his readers. The central meaning of the Greek word rendered lead is "direct" or "guide."

Expressions introducing prayer, like may the Lord, are falling out of use except in church circles. GeCL (cf. DuCL) has "we ask the Lord." One may also simply say "we pray to the Lord," or "we pray that the Lord will...."

You into a greater understanding is literally "your hearts." (On "hearts," see 1 Thess. 2.4.) It is an open question whether Paul would have thought of this term as a metaphor, but this would be the case in many modern languages. Since "heart" can sometimes mean "mind" and refer therefore to intellectual, not just emotional, activity, TEV interprets "heart" as a person's ability to understand. But that an understanding of God's love and Christ-given endurance involves more than the intellect alone, is clear from the context.

In some other languages also it may be necessary to replace "hearts" with a more literal expression. GeCL has "your thoughts," and SpCL "may the Lord help you to feel the love of God." Since the introduction of "hearts" or even "minds" in this context may be misleading, it is better in some languages to translate "I pray that the Lord will guide you to love God."

The love of God and the endurance that is given by Christ are literally "the love of God" and "the endurance of Christ." Both expressions can have more than one meaning. "The love of God," in Greek as in English, may mean "love for God" or "God's love" (for man). Most traditional translations leave the question undecided, and most modern translations (except FrCL) take the phrase to refer to God's love for man, for example, Brc "the way in which God has loved you," GeCL "the love which God has shown to us" (cf. Mft Phps NEB "God's love"). TEV's translation may appear to allow either possibility, but the expression into a greater understanding is more appropriate if God's love for man is in mind, rather than man's love for God. (Also, the possible parallel with the endurance that is given by Christ points to the former interpretation.) The main argument in favor of the translation "love for God" is that the context seems to speak of a movement of the Thessalonians toward God, for literally the wording is "lead your hearts to" (or "into" or "unto") "the love of God." But it must be admitted (1) that the word translated "to" may also (though more often in John than in Paul) have the meaning "in," and (2) that "the love of God" in Paul usually means God's love for man. If one wishes to translate "the love of God" more explicitly as "God's love for people," one may restructure the first part of verse 5 as "I pray that the Lord may cause you to experience God's love for you," or "...how much God loves you," or "...the fact that God loves you."

The meaning of "the endurance of Christ" is likewise uncertain. The phrase is not used anywhere else in the New Testament. The endurance may either be directed from the believer to Christ or from Christ to the believer. In the first case, the meaning will be "patient waiting for Christ" (KJV). This would fit in well with 2.1-12, and there are many Old Testament texts which speak of waiting patiently for the Lord. "Patient" in modern English suggests a more passive attitude than the Greek, but "endurance" is linked with "hope" in 1 Thess. 1.3, so KJV's "waiting" (implicit, though not printed in italics) may be justified. If one follows this interpretation, it is possible to say "that the Lord may cause you to wait patiently for Christ's coming." It is often not sufficient simply to say "to wait for Christ."

On the other hand, "the endurance of Christ" may mean either "the endurance which Christ gives" (as in TEV and FrCL) or "the endurance which Christ showed (while on earth)," as in Brc "all that Christ triumphantly went through for you" (cf. Phps "the patient suffering of Christ" and GeCL).

Unless there are strong reasons to the contrary, it seems natural to understand "the love of God" and "the endurance of Christ" in the same way, that is, either both as a movement from believers or both as a movement toward believers. FrCL is unusual in taking the first phrase as a movement toward God, and the second as a movement toward believers.

If Christ is regarded simply as the goal of the endurance or reliance, one may translate "that the Lord may cause you to rely completely on Christ," or "...depend completely on Christ." However, if it is understood as experiencing the kind of endurance which Christ demonstrated, then one may say "that the Lord may cause you to remain firm in the same way that Christ remained firm," or "...endure even as Christ endured."

There is a very complicated problem involved at this point in that <u>the Lord</u> (a reference to Christ) is the primary causative agent and <u>the endurance</u> is itself either given by Christ or is something experienced by him. It may be misleading to refer to "the Lord" as the primary agent at the beginning of verse 5 and to introduce "Christ" later in the same verse. If, however, one translates "I pray that the Lord will cause you to have love for God and firm reliance on him," the final pronoun "him" will likely be understood as referring to "God," and not to "Christ." Therefore it may be necessary to invert the order of the petitions so as to read: "I pray that the Lord will cause you to rely completely on him, and to experience love for God."

TEV

The Obligation to Work

6 Our brothers, we command you in the name of our Lord Jesus Christ to keep away from all brothers who are living a lazy life and who do not follow the instructions that we gave them. 7 You yourselves know very well that you should do just what we did. We were not lazy when we were with you. 8 We did not accept anyone's support without paying for it. Instead, we worked and toiled; we kept working day and night so as not to be an expense to any of you. 9 We did this, not because we do not have the right to demand our support; we did it to be an example for you to follow. 10 While we were with you we used to tell you,

RSV

6 Now we command you, brethren, in the name of our Lord Jesus Christ, that you keep away from any brother who is living in idleness and not in accord with the tradition that you received from us. 7 For you yourselves know how you ought to imitate us; we were not idle when we were with you, 8 we did not eat any one's bread without paying, but with toil and labor we worked night and day, that we might not burden any of you. 9 It was not because we have not that right, but to give you in our conduct an example to imitate. 10 For even when we were with you, we gave you

"Whoever refuses to work is not allowed to eat."
11 We say this because we hear
that there are some people among
you who live lazy lives and who do
nothing except meddle in other people's business. 12 In the name of
the Lord Jesus Christ we command
these people and warn them to lead
orderly lives and work to earn
their own living.
13 But you, brothers, must not
become tired of doing good. 14 It
may be that someone there will not
obey the message we send you in
this letter. If so, take note of
him and have nothing to do with
him, so that he will be ashamed.
15 But do not treat him as an enemy; instead, warn him as a brother.
(3.6-15)

this command: If any one will not
work, let him not eat. 11 For we
hear that some of you are living in
idleness, mere busybodies, not doing any work. 12 Now such persons
we command and exhort in the Lord
Jesus Christ to do their work in
quietness and to earn their own
living. 13 Brethren, do not be
weary in well-doing.
14 If any one refuses to obey
what we say in this letter, note
that man, and have nothing to do
with him, that he may be ashamed.
15 Do not look on him as an enemy,
but warn him as a brother.
(3.6-15)

This section raises three general questions, related (1) to the writers, (2) to the readers, and (3) to the smaller group whom Paul is criticizing.

1. Paul is conscious that as an apostle he had the right or authority, not only to be supported by the members of the church, but to issue commands. The Greek verb here translated command and already used in verse 4 (where it is rendered tell), is repeated in verses 10 (used to tell), and 12; see also 1 Thess. 4.2,11. However, Paul softens this use of his authority in various ways. First, he associates Silas and Timothy with himself, and the pronoun "we" or its equivalent should be used throughout. Verse 15, where Brc and TNT use "I," is a direct imperative in the Greek, as in TEV. Second, Paul does not ask his readers in this section to do anything that he and his companions have not done themselves (cf. 1 Thess. 2.9). Third, in verse 12 the word command is followed by a second verb which TEV translates warn, but which is probably rather softer in the original.

2. Paul is writing to the entire Christian community at Thessalonica. This community includes the people whom he criticizes, and Paul does not order them to be shut out of the church, even if they take no notice of his letter. At the beginning and at the end of the section, Paul emphasizes that they are brothers (that is, fellow Christians) and must be treated as such.

3. In the notes on 1 Thess. 5.14, reasons have been given for thinking that Paul's main attack is against laziness rather than disorderly conduct, though both meanings are possible. Verses 7-10 show clearly that the first meaning is primarily intended here. Paul insists, not on the fact that he lived an orderly life in Thessalonica, but on the fact that he worked. However, Paul is also concerned that the "busybodies" shall not upset the life of the whole Christian com-

munity, so the need to lead orderly lives is also in his mind (see the detailed notes on v. 12), and should be fully brought out in translation.

The beginning of a new section is marked by the transitional de, correctly omitted in most modern translations (KJV RSV "now"); by the use of brothers, and by the use of the solemn formula in the name of the Lord Jesus Christ.

The section heading The Obligation to Work must often be restructured in such a way that the necessity for work is expressed by a modal particle such as "must" or "should." One may then have a section heading such as "All persons must work," or "All believers should work."

3.6 Our brothers, we command you in the name of our Lord Jesus Christ to keep away from all brothers who are living a lazy life and who do not follow the instructions that we gave them.

The text of this verse is in doubt at two places. First, KJV Mft Knox RSV Phps NEB TNT Rigaux, etc., use a text which reads our Lord Jesus Christ, while the reading of the UBS Greek text, followed by JB Brc Best DuCL FrCL GeCL, omits our. The manuscripts which omit our are few in number but they are "great authorities" (Rigaux, p. 703). Despite the textual problem, it is not possible in some languages to translate "the Lord"; rather, one must always use our Lord so as to specify the relation which Christ has to those to whom he is Lord.

Second, the text translated we gave them (literally "they received from us") is uncertain. The three main variants are (1) "they received," a difficult reading with good manuscript support, followed by TNT FrCL Best Rigaux as well as TEV and the UBS Greek New Testament; (2) "you received," an easier and therefore less probable reading followed by most translations, including RSV NEB GeCL DuCL; and (3) KJV's "he received," which is not well attested. The difficulty about "they received" is that it does not, strictly speaking, agree with "every brother" earlier in the verse; but "every brother" is clearly plural in meaning, as TEV's all brothers shows.

In the name of our Lord Jesus Christ must be modified in some languages if it is to be comprehensible. One may say, for example, "as representing our Lord Jesus Christ," or "on the authority of our Lord Jesus Christ," or even "because this is what our Lord Jesus Christ would say." In this context Paul is obviously asserting that he is speaking on behalf of the Lord Jesus Christ.

General commentaries discuss what may have been involved in "keeping away from" the brothers whom Paul criticizes, or in "having nothing to do with" them (v. 14). The expression Paul uses in this verse simply means "to put a distance between oneself and someone else." Keep away from is entirely adequate (cf. RSV JB; Mft "shun," Knox TNT "have nothing to do with," Phps "don't associate with," NEB "hold aloof from," Brc "withdraw yourselves from"). It is important to avoid an expression which would suggest "put out of your company," "excommunicate," or "thrust aside." The focus here is not on forceable exclusion of such persons from the fellowship, but on refusal to associate with them. Note that in this statement they are still regarded as brothers, which may be translated as "fellow believers." One may therefore render this expression as "have nothing to do with all of those fellow believers who are living a lazy life."

It may not be possible in some languages to speak of living a lazy life, but it is usually possible to say "who are lazy," though this is not precisely what Paul is saying. A closer equivalent may be "who refuse to work," or "who do not work as they should."

Instructions in Greek is the singular noun "tradition." Paul has used it in the plural in 2.15. The whole phrase is literally "keep (yourselves) away from every brother lazily walking and not according to the tradition which they received from us." "Walk" is a common Hebrew idiom for "behave." "Tradition" in this context does not imply antiquity; it is simply the handing on of something which did not originate with Paul himself. Paul must therefore be referring to the body of teaching (in this context, concerning behavior rather than doctrine) which he shared with the other apostles, and which he no doubt believed went back to Jesus himself. In 1 Corinthians 15.3 the same word for "received" is used, and TEV's I passed on translates the verb which corresponds to the noun used here for "tradition." However, the 1 Corinthians passage consists of doctrinal teaching. The ethical teaching had already been given by Paul to the Thessalonians, either during his visit or in an earlier letter or both (cf. v. 4), and the lazy "busybodies" had heard it together with the rest of the community. This teaching, as Paul will soon emphasize, had been confirmed by the apostles' example. However, it is difficult to include something so personal as an example within the "tradition" itself (though cf. Best, p. 335), especially since Paul insists in verse 9 that he had the right to behave differently. The translation "tradition" (KJV Knox RSV NEB JB Brc TNT) misleadingly suggests antiquity and formality. TEV's instructions (cf. DuCL FrCL GeCL SpCL; Mft "rule," Phps "teaching") does not by itself convey the idea of "handing on," but this is expressed by some translations in other ways (FrCL "the teaching which we transmitted to them"; TNT "the tradition which we passed on to them").

Other key words in this verse have been already discussed. For command, see the introduction to this section and the notes on verse 4. For living a lazy life, see the introduction to this section and the notes on 1 Thess. 5.14.

It may be difficult in some languages to have two relative clauses both attributive to brothers. The second relative clause, who do not follow the instructions that we gave them, is an indirect amplification of the first, who are living a lazy life. The logical relation may be expressed in some languages as "who are living a lazy life; in this respect they do not follow the instructions that we gave them," or "...this means that they are not following the instructions we gave them."

3.7 You yourselves know very well that you should do just what we did. We were not lazy when we were with you.

From here to verse 10, Paul refers back to his conduct while he was in Thessalonica, in order to support the statement in verse 6. The relation with verse 6 is shown in the text by an introductory "for," which most modern translations leave unexpressed.

There is an inherent problem in the first sentence of verse 7, since you should do just what we did could refer to more than one kind of event. It could suggest, for example, that the Thessalonians were to keep away from fellow believers who were lazy, even as Paul and his colleagues kept away from them. However, this sentence refers to what follows and not to what precedes. Such a reference may be difficult in some languages, and therefore it may be better to use a term for do which suggests a general pattern of behavior or living, for example, "You yourselves know very well that you should live in the same way that we lived," or even "...that you should work in the same way that we worked."

Again, we were not lazy may be rendered as "we did not refuse to work." But even this may be somewhat misleading. It could suggest, for example, some forced labor which Paul did not refuse to do. Therefore it may be useful to change the negative statement not lazy to a positive one, for example, "we worked hard."

3.8 We did not accept anyone's support without paying for it. Instead, we worked and toiled; we kept working day and night so as not to be an expense to any of you.

This verse restates in more detail what Paul has said in verse 7 about his own and his companions' example. As often in Paul's writings (e.g. 1 Thess. 1.5, 8), this verse consists of a negative statement followed by a positive one, and the two are contrasted by a strong "but." TEV brings out the contrast by beginning a new sentence with instead. Conversely, we worked and toiled and we kept working day and night (literally "but in work and toil night and day we worked") should be taken closely together.

We did not accept anyone's support without paying for it is literally "nor did we eat bread from anyone for nothing." "Bread" is a common Hebrew idiom for food of any kind (cf. JB "have our meals at anyone's table," TNT "we paid for all the food we were given"). Some translations, like TEV, are even wider; NEB has "board and lodging," and Brc "maintenance." There is a slight contradiction in meaning between accept... support and without paying for it, since to accept someone's support implies becoming someone's debtor. In translation into other languages, it is best to make it clear that Paul did not accept any object (food, or at most board and lodging) without paying for it.

Without paying for it is essentially a negative condition meaning "unless we paid for it," or "if we did not pay for it." The combination of a negative statement, we did not accept anyone's support, with the negative condition may prove misleading in some languages, and a shift to a completely positive statement may be necessary, for example, "we accepted help from people only if we paid for it," or "we let people help us, but we always paid them for what they did." A more specific reference to food might be introduced as "we paid for all the food we received from anyone."

The contrast between the first and second parts of verse 8 may be introduced in a somewhat fuller manner by saying "Instead of receiving something for nothing, we worked and toiled...."

Worked and toiled in Greek are nouns indicating events, which TEV and some other translations therefore render by verbs. The same nouns are used in 1 Thess. 2.9. We kept working day and night so as not to be an expense to any of you is identical in Greek with part of 1 Thess. 2.9, where TEV has trouble for expense. The difference in translation can be attributed to the difference in contexts. Paul's point in 1 Thess. 2 is "we came to you with pure motives, asking nothing for ourselves, but eager to share the Christian message with you." In 2 Thess. 3 Paul is concerned, not only to defend the evangelists' own behavior, but to offer it as an example to his readers. His main interest now is not their behavior in general, but the work they did. In other respects, the notes on 1 Thess. 2.9 apply to this verse also.

It may be impossible in some languages to find two verbs corresponding to worked and toiled. The two words found in the Greek text do not indicate different kinds of activity; they are used simply to emphasize that much labor was involved. Therefore one may say "we worked very hard indeed."

A literal rendering of we kept working day and night can be misleading in some languages, since it might be understood to mean "all day and all night," thus allowing no time for rest or anything else. It may therefore be necessary to use a more general statement such as "we were working almost all the time," or "we hardly stopped working."

The purpose clause so as not to be an expense to any of you may be expressed in some languages as a reason, for example, "because we did not want to be an expense to any of you," or "because we did not want any of you to have to pay something to help us."

3.9 We did this, not because we do not have the right to demand our support; we did it to be an example for you to follow.

Paul expresses himself in this verse in a compressed way, which the translator needs to analyze and to expand where necessary before attempting a stylistically neat translation. The literal translation is: "not that" (or "because") "we do not have a right, but in order that we may give you ourselves an example so that (you) might imitate us." The general meaning is:

1. We had the right (not to work) (see 1 Corinthians 9.4-18).
2. (We did not use this right), because we wanted to give you an example.
3. You should follow this example.

The phrase have the right, which Paul uses repeatedly in 1 Corinthians 9.4-18, means "have (nonphysical) power which comes from legitimate authority," the opposite of brute force. It is often used in speaking of the authority of a particular office. In the present context, it is Paul, Silas, and Timothy who, as apostles, have the right to be financially supported by the churches. Likewise, as apostles, they can give an example to the Christian community (cf. Philippians 3.17). Their authority as apostles comes from Christ, and the word translated right often refers to the power which God possesses or which he gives to particular people (cf. John 1.12: "he gave them the right to become God's children"). No general teaching about "human rights" is in Paul's mind.

Difficulties are encountered in any literal rendering of the double negative in not because we do not have the right to demand our support. In some languages it may be better to reproduce this as a positive statement, for example, "we have the right to demand our support but we did not do it, rather we kept on working in order to be an example for you to follow."

The right to demand our support may be expressed in some languages as "it was perfectly all right for us to ask you to give us food and lodging," or "... to give us food and a place to live." One may also say "it was perfectly proper for us to ask," or "it was the correct thing for us to do in asking."

An example for you to follow partly repeats verse 7 (cf. also Philippians 3.17). The last part of this verse also includes some internal repetition ("give you an example to follow"). The words are thus emphatic, and different languages can convey this emphasis in different ways, without the stylistic heaviness of the literal English translation. "Ourselves" (reflected in the literal rendering of this verse) does not mean "so that we ourselves (and no one else) may give you an example," but "so that we might give you ourselves as an example," (cf. Brc "it was to provide you with ourselves as a pattern and example to copy"; TNT "so that we might offer ourselves to you as a pattern of behaviour"). The translation of both this verse and the context should make it clear that Paul is not saying generally that the Thessalonians should follow the evangelists' behavior at all points, but that they should follow their example in work. TEV made this clear in verse 7 by you should do just what we did.

In many languages one cannot speak of "following an example," but one can "do as others do" or "live in the same way that others live." Therefore one may translate the final part of verse 9 as "we worked as we did, so that you would know how to live as we lived," or "...do as we did."

3.10 While we were with you we used to tell you, "Whoever refuses to work is not allowed to eat."

Used to tell renders a Greek verb meaning "command," "order," or "tell" (in the sense of giving instruction). The same verb is used in verses 4 (tell), 6 (command), and 12 (command). Paul is not referring to a rule in force in all the churches, but to specific instructions given during his visit, which he now repeats as a reminder (cf. JB "We gave you a rule when we were with you: not to let anyone have any food if he refused to do any work"). The form of the verb indicates that the instructions were not given only once, but that they were given continually or habitually, whenever the situation demanded that they be given.

Commentaries discuss whether is not allowed to eat means that fellow Christians would not supply food to those who did not work, or that they would be excluded from the common meals in which the Lord's Supper was celebrated. The text itself does not make the situation clear, and the translation should not be narrower than the text.

The last part of this verse could be misunderstood as a general piece of worldly wisdom, "If you don't work, you don't eat." This is not even a possible meaning of the text, which is literally "if anyone does not want to work, neither let him eat" (a third person imperative reflected in TEV's is not allowed to eat).

Verse 10b, even understood as a command, sounds like a fixed formula, and Paul has mentioned in verse 6 the handing on of a tradition (see the notes on that verse). It is therefore not surprising that commentators have looked for parallels to this saying. No close parallels have been found from New Testament times, but see Proverbs 10.4.

"Will not work" (RSV NEB) should not be misunderstood as a future tense. The Greek is clearly "does not want to work." However, it is important to avoid giving the impression that this includes persons who actually do work but who do not like to do it. It may be necessary, therefore, in some languages to follow the TEV rendering and translate whoever refuses to work. Also, it may be necessary to employ a conditional (as, in fact, the Greek does): "if anyone does not want to work," or "if some persons refuse to work." A literal rendering of "whoever does not want to work" might be taken to include persons who do not like to work but who nevertheless do work. It may be necessary in some languages to indicate clearly, as TEV does, that these are persons who refuse to work. Also, it may be necessary to employ a conditional (as in Greek) "if anyone does not want to work," or "if some persons refuse to work."

It may be difficult to render literally is not allowed to eat, for this type of expression suggests the imposition of authority, and in some languages this cannot be expressed without indicating whose authority. Furthermore, a literal rendering of is not allowed to eat could suggest "you must make him fast," or "you must keep him from eating." This would imply a kind of overt punishment or rigid control by the church, something rather out of harmony with the immediate context and the historical situation. The most satisfactory equivalent in some languages is "you should not give him anything to eat."

3.11 We say this because we hear that there are some people among you who live lazy lives and who do nothing except meddle in other people's business.

After several verses of careful preparation (at least vv. 6-10 and possibly 3-10), Paul comes to the most central and sensitive point in this part of the letter. The first words are literally "for we hear." "For" is a common word, in Greek as in English, often used, as in verse 7, in a weak and general sense. Here, on the contrary, the word has its full force and its strict meaning; it introduces an explanation of what has gone before. TEV (contrast Brc TNT) brings this out very well by we say this because, and secondarily by beginning a new paragraph (cf. DuCL FrCL GeCL [but not SpCL] Syn). JB begins a new paragraph at verse 10, making it relate to verse 11, in the manner that a rule is related to an example of its application. Brc transforms the present "we hear" into "news has reached us." GeCL, on the other hand, emphasizes both the present tense and the change to specific facts by translating "now we hear." The text strongly implies that Paul has recently received news from Thessalonica, either by letter or by a direct oral message. There is no suggestion of hearsay or rumor.

Because of the particular form of this communication (namely, a letter), it may be necessary to render we say this as "we are writing this."

In some languages a literal rendering of we hear would suggest actual listening rather than learning about an event through channels. Therefore it may be more satisfactory to translate we hear as "we have been told" or even "we have learned." Such a shift from a literal rendering of hear may be necessary to avoid the suggestion of "rumor."

Among you (Brc "in your society," TNT "of you") reminds the reader that Paul is still addressing the whole community, including those members of it ("brothers," cf. vv. 6, 15) who are behaving badly.

Live lazy lives (recalling verse 6; see the notes there) is literally "are walking (i.e. behaving) lazily." This is not a reference to a lifelong habit of laziness, but to a refusal to work.

The last part of the verse, literally "not working but being busybodies," contains a play on words which raises difficulties similar to those mentioned in the notes on verses 2 and 3. Mft attempts a play on words with his "busybodies instead of busy." The single word translated meddle in other people's business is the same as the word "work," with the addition of a prefix meaning "around" (GeCL "run around uselessly"). It is a secondary matter, depending on the resources of the receptor language, whether such a play on words can be reproduced in translation. If it can be done naturally, so much the better, but the more important translation problem is how to combine the two ideas of (1) not working and (2) interfering in other people's affairs. The translation of (1) must not imply such total passivity as to contradict (2). TEV slightly undertranslates (1), subordinating it to (2) by the phrase do nothing except. Brc, at a rather higher level of language, keeps a good balance while still linking the two phrases closely together: "idle in their own affairs, and interfering in everyone else's."

The double relative clauses in verse 11, who live lazy lives and who do nothing except meddle in other people's business, may create serious grammatical problems in some languages, and therefore some restructuring may be required. However, the relation between these two relative clauses is quite different from the relation between a similar set of relative clauses in verse 6. Here in verse 11 there is an element of contrast; these people refuse to work but do not hesitate to meddle in other people's affairs. The contrast and the play on words can perhaps be introduced by setting off the final relative clause as a separate sentence, for example, "...who refuse to work. Rather, they are constantly involved in other people's work," or "who refuse to work for themselves but are busy meddling in other people's work." The rendering of "work for themselves" must not be understood in the sense of self-employment, but rather in a sense of "working in order to support themselves."

3.12 In the name of the Lord Jesus Christ we command these people and warn them to lead orderly lives and work to earn their own living.

For a discussion of in the name of the Lord Jesus Christ, see verse 6.

Paul's instructions are introduced by two verbs, both normally used by a superior addressing an inferior. Command clearly includes this meaning. Warn does not, and it is an unusual meaning of the Greek, which, in similar contexts, normally means "appeal to, urge, exhort, encourage." FrCL has "recommend" (cf. SpCL). GeCL (cf. DuCL) takes the two words together and translates "we exhort" (possibly "warn") "them...with all emphasis." Brc, at the risk of anti-climax, differentiates the two verbs rather sharply as "our instructions and our plea." TEV's warn seems rather too strong. It is true that in verses 4 and 6 (cf. 10), Paul has used the same Greek verb without feeling any need to soften it by adding a gentler expression. However, examples of this procedure are to be found elsewhere in Paul's writings (e.g. Romans 1.11-12), and verse 15 fulfills a similar function here. Some such expression as "command and urge" would preserve the balance. Best has the rather less emphatic "instruct and request."

In some languages there is a problem in relating the verbs command and warn to what follows, because what follows is essentially direct discourse. One would expect the second person plural "you" to be used in the direct discourse, so that the latter part of verse 12 would read "we command these people and urge them, You must lead orderly lives and work to earn your own living." A difficulty with the term warn is that it suggests a negative prohibition which might be taken to mean "warn them not to lead orderly lives." A rendering such as "strongly urge" in place of warn would eliminate this difficulty.

RSV's "such persons," for these people, faithfully reproduces the form of the Greek, but sounds too pejorative for a letter partly addressed to the people in question, and for a passage in which Paul insists that they are still "brothers" (v. 15). The Vulgate carefully avoids a common pejorative Latin pronoun, and translates "to those however who are of this kind." Similarly TEV avoids "such."

There are two possible meanings of living a lazy life in verse 6 (cf. v. 11 and 1 Thess. 5.14), but we have already given reasons for suggesting that Paul's main attack is against refusal to work, rather than against disorderly conduct as such. However, the second meaning does lie in the background, and Paul's fear that those who refuse to work may disturb and agitate the Christian community is reflected both in verse 11 (meddle) and here. Orderly is not formally related in Greek to the word for lazy or "disorderly" which has been used earlier, but the meanings are contrastively related. Orderly may mean either "calm" or "silent," but "calm" fits the context better. Lead orderly lives is literally "go-on-working with calm" (FrCL "work regularly," cf. GeCL). TEV separates work and attaches it to the following phrase.

It may be impossible to translate literally lead orderly lives. It may be possible to say "live in an orderly way," but in many languages the concept of "orderly" has nothing to do with proper living. The closest equivalent in meaning may be more appropriately expressed as a type of modal, for example, "live as they should."

Earn their own living is literally "eat their own bread" (see the notes on v. 8). This may be expressed in some languages as "earn money for food and clothes," or "work to feed their mouths." Or the focus may be upon family responsibilities, for example, "work to help their families."

3.13 But you, brothers, must not become tired of doing good.

Paul turns away from the group which is refusing to work and addresses the rest of the Christian community. He also turns from a specific order to a general instruction. The transition is marked in TEV as in Greek by an emphatic but you, brothers, which RSV, usually so close to the form of the Greek, does not reproduce in its "brethren." NEB similarly has simply "my friends." Phps has "and the rest of you, my brothers." Perhaps verse 15 is intended to correct this emphasis by stating that even those who do not work are still to be counted among the Christian "brothers."

The abrupt appositional expression, you, brothers, may seem particularly awkward in this context. Perhaps one can use an expression such as "you, my fellow believers," but it is also possible to say "but, my fellow believers, you must not become tired of doing good."

Some translations (including Mft Phps NEB JB DuCL FrCL SpCL Seg BJ TOB) also mark the transition by beginning a new paragraph with this verse. RSV and Lu make this verse the end of a paragraph. This is less satisfactory, since verse 13 is closely linked to the more specific instructions of verses 14-15.

There is a danger that some may wrongly interpret must not become tired of doing good. This expression could be interpreted to mean that the believers should refrain from doing good so that they would not become tired. The meaning is, of course, that the believers should keep on doing good, even though they might be tired. The correct meaning is more appropriately expressed in some languages as "you must never give up doing good."

3.14 It may be that someone there will not obey the message we send you in this letter. If so, take note of him and have nothing to do with him, so that he will be ashamed.

This is not the first time Paul discusses the need to work, and in verses 14-15 he turns to the problem of what should be done if this repeated order is not obeyed. TEV makes explicit the fact that Paul is referring, not to earlier teaching, but to the teaching contained in this letter. A possible, but much less natural, alternative translation would be "but if someone does not obey our message (contained in) the (earlier) letter." TEV's more probable interpretation involves changing the present "obey" into the future will...obey, inserting a present verb we send, and inserting this before letter. Similar procedures may be necessary in other languages (cf. GeCL "but if someone does not want to follow the instructions in this letter").

In 1 Thess. 2.13, "word" (TEV message) clearly referred to a spoken word (cf. 1 Thess. 1.5, 8), but the present context makes no contrast between "word" and letter, and a general term such as message or even "teaching" should be chosen in translation. The translator should avoid any term which would suggest a single word rather than a message consisting of a number of words. Greek-speaking Jews, following Exodus 34.28, referred to the Ten Commandments as the "Ten Words" of the covenant, and the meaning is similar here. For once, Paul's message is not (at least not directly) "good news" in the form of a narrative about Jesus, but instructions intended to correct an error.

The possibility suggested by it may be that someone there may be made a conditional clause, for example, "if there is anyone." Will not obey may be more precisely described in some languages as "refuse to do" or "refuse to conform to."

Take note of him is so rendered by JB and TNT. Mft has "mark him," Knox "he is to be a marked man," NEB Brc "mark him well" (cf. GeCL). DuCL has "hold him in view." A simple equivalent may be "name him" or "recognize who he is."

Have nothing to do with him is, more literally, "do not mix with him." The meaning of this verb is similar to that translated keep away from in verse 6. The same verb is used in 1 Corinthians 5.9, 11.

The problem of deciding how the Thessalonians were to have nothing to do with the disobedient member and still treat him as a brother (v. 15) involves both translation and exegesis. The translator should avoid expressions which suggest (like FrCL) that the Thessalonians were to have no contact with the disobedient brother. Brc has "refuse to associate with him" (cf. Best). Seg and Syn "have no relationship (relation) with him." TOB has rapport. DuCL has "do not go around with him." In some instances this may be expressed as "treat him as though he didn't exist"—which is almost equivalent to "make him a nonperson"! In other cases an equivalent may be "do not talk with him," or "do not invite him to your house." All of these expressions may be simply various ways of describing what is essentially a kind of ostracism.

So that he will be ashamed may be spelled out in some detail in some languages as "so that he will know that what he has done is wrong." Shame is often expressed idiomatically as "so that he will become red," "so that he will become pale," or "so that his real name will be found out" (in which case "name" is a reference to real character).

3.15 But do not treat him as an enemy; instead, warn him as a brother.

The main problem in translating this verse is stylistic. It is caused by the fact that the verse contains a double contrast (1) between verses 14 and 15, (2) between 15a and 15b. The Greek avoids awkwardness by using one word for "but" at the beginning of verse 15, and another and stronger word in the middle. These correspond neatly to TEV's but and instead, KJV's "yet" and "but," and Best's "however" and "but." The first "but" is expanded, legitimately but not very neatly, by NEB into "I do not mean" (cf. Phps JB Brc TNT). Verse 15b is a positive statement which holds the balance between the negative statements of verses 14b and 15a.

Do not treat him as an enemy may be rendered as "do not act toward him as you would act toward an enemy." This may be treated idiomatically in some languages as "do not name him as an enemy," or "do not call him your enemy."

Warn (a different word from warn in verse 12) may also mean "teach" or "instruct." The more specific idea of warning fits the context better here. The

Greek suggests repeated warnings. Warn him as a brother must be rendered somewhat more explicitly in some languages, for example, "warn him about doing such things in the same way as you would warn your own brother." On the other hand, the term brother in this context may refer specifically to a fellow believer, and therefore one must say "warn him not to do as he has done, as one who is a fellow believer," or "...one who also believes in Christ."

TEV	RSV
Final Words	
16 May the Lord himself, who is our source of peace, give you peace at all times and in every way. The Lord be with you all. 17 With my own hand I write this: *Greetings from Paul.* This is the way I sign every letter; this is how I write. 18 May the grace of our Lord Jesus Christ be with you all. (3.16-18)	16 Now may the Lord of peace himself give you peace at all times in all ways. The Lord be with you all. 17 I, Paul, write this greeting with my own hand. This is the mark in every letter of mine; it is the way I write. 18 The grace of our Lord Jesus Christ be with you all. (3.16-18)

These verses consist of a short prayer and blessing (v. 16) and Paul's personal postscript (vv. 17-18), which includes a blessing (v. 18) partly repeating verse 16. It seems more natural to take verses 17-18 as a single paragraph (along with the UBS Greek New Testament RSV NEB Brc TNT Lu SpCL), rather than to separate verse 18, as do Phps and other common language translations. (See also the note on 3.17.)

In place of the rather prosaic Final Words, it may be possible to use as a section heading a phrase such as "Paul says goodbye to the Thessalonians," "Paul closes his letter to the Thessalonians," or "With these words Paul ends letter."

3.16 May the Lord himself, who is our source of peace, give you peace at all times and in every way. The Lord be with you all.

On the form may the Lord, see the note on verse 5. Here, as in verse 5, GeCL has "we ask the Lord." Normally a request to God must be introduced by an expression such as "we pray" or "I pray."

The Lord...who is our source of peace is literally "the Lord of peace," a Hebrew idiom rather like Barnabas's nickname "Son of Consolation," that is, "he who consoles." The meaning is not that the Lord (Jesus) is himself at peace, but that he gives peace (cf. FrCL "who gives peace," GeCL "from whom all peace comes," DuCL "from whom peace comes"). TEV's our source of peace perhaps narrows the meaning too much. If our is expressed at all, it must be inclusive in meaning, that is, including the Thessalonians as well as Paul and his companions. Our source of peace must be rendered in some languages as a causative expression, for example, "he is the one who causes us to be at peace," or, expressed idiomatically, "...causes us to sit down in our hearts," or, expressed negatively, "...causes us no longer to worry."

On peace, see 1 Thess. 1.1.

There is no difficulty in at all times (cf. JB "all the time"), but the text corresponding to in every way is uncertain. Some manuscripts have "in every place," as in 1 Corinthians 1.2; 1 Thess. 1.8; and other passages. In every way, less common in Greek, is more likely to be correct and is followed by virtually all translators. At all times may be rendered as "always," but it may also be appropriately rendered as "under all circumstances" or "in every situation."

3.17 With my own hand I write this: Greetings from Paul. This is the way I sign every letter; this is how I write.

It is not quite clear in what the greetings consist. There are at least three possibilities: (1) verse 16 (Best), (2) verse 17, (3) verses 17-18. Best thinks that it was at verse 16, and not at verse 17, that Paul took the pen from his secretary's hand. This would, of course, be necessary if verse 16 were to be the greeting. Parallel passages in other letters suggest that Paul's personal greeting does not refer backward to earlier verses, but usually includes later verses. For example, see 1 Corinthians 16.21 (v. 22 is scarcely a "greeting," vv. 23-24 are); Galatians 6.11 (not a greeting, but a reference to Paul's own handwriting); Colossians 4.18 (cannot refer to preceding verses). Philemon 19 is not relevant since it probably means that the whole letter was written in Paul's own handwriting.

The Greek of the first few words is very concise, and will often need restructuring in translation. Literally it is "the greeting in my hand of Paul," that is, "in my (Paul's) own hand" (cf. GeCL "I, Paul, write the greeting with my own hand"). This may be rendered as "I am writing these words with my own hand," "these very words I am writing with my own hand," or "I myself am writing these words."

Greetings from Paul must be rendered in some languages as "I am greeting you," equivalent in some languages to "I am saying to you hello."

This is the way I sign every letter may be expressed as "this is how I write my name at the end of every letter." Such an expression would include the final clause of verse 17, this is how I write.

On the matter of possible forgeries, see the notes on 2 Thess. 2.2.

3.18 May the grace of our Lord Jesus Christ be with you all.

This verse is the same as 1 Thess. 5.28, except for the addition of all (cf. GeCL "Jesus Christ our Lord keep you all in his grace," DuCL "our Lord Jesus Christ be gracious to you all").

The final blessing must be expressed in the form of a prayer in many languages, for example, "I pray that our Lord Jesus Christ may be kind to you all."

"Amen" and the final note included in KJV are not part of the original text.

BIBLIOGRAPHY

BIBLE TEXTS AND VERSIONS CITED

(Unless otherwise indicated in the text, references are to the most recent edition listed. CL = Common Language Translation.)

Bibel, Die...nach der Übersetzung Martin Luthers. NT revised 1956. Stuttgart: Württembergische Bibelanstalt. Cited as Lu.

Bible, La. Traduction par Louis Segond. NT revised 1964. Paris, etc.: Les Sociétés Bibliques. Cited as Seg.

Bonnes Nouvelles Aujourd'hui. Le Nouveau Testament traduit en français courant d'après le texte grec. 1971. Paris, etc.: Les Sociétés Bibliques. Cited as FrCL.

Dios Llega al Hombre. El Nuevo Testamento de Nuestro Señor Jesucristo: Versión Popular. 1st edition 1966; 2nd edition 1970. Asunción etc.: Sociedades Bíblicas Unidas. European edition 1971. Madrid: Sociedad Bíblica. Cited as SpCL.

Good News for Modern Man: The New Testament in Today's English Version. 1st edition 1966; 3rd edition 1971. New York: American Bible Society. 1st British edition 1968; 3rd British edition 1972. London: Collins. Cited as TEV.

Groot Nieuws voor U. Het nieuwe testament in de omgangstaal. 1972. Amsterdam/Boxtel: Katholieke Bijbelstichting and Nederlandsche Bijbelgenootschap. Cited as DuCL.

Gute Nachricht, Die: Das Neue Testament in heutigem Deutsch. 1971. Stuttgart: Bibelanstalt. Cited as GeCL.

Heilige Schrift, Die: Zürcher Bibel. 1949. Berlin: Evangelische Haupt-Bibelgesellschaft. Cited as Zur.

Holy Bible, The. Authorised or King James Version. 1611. Cited as KJV.

Jerusalem Bible, The. 1966. London: Darton, Longman & Todd. Cited as JB.

Letters to Young Churches, translated by J. B. Phillips. 1st edition 1949. London: Bles. 2nd edition in The New Testament in Modern English. 1972. London: Collins. Cited as Phps.

New American Bible, The. 1970. Paterson, N. J.: St. Anthony Guild Press. Cited as NAB.

New English Bible, The. 1st edition of NT 1961; 2nd edition 1970. London: Oxford University Press, and Cambridge: Cambridge University Press. Cited as NEB.

New Testament, The: a new translation by William Barclay. Volume II: The Letters and the Revelation. 1969. London: Collins. Cited as Brc.

New Testament, The: a new translation by James Moffatt. 1922. London: Hodder & Stoughton. Cited as Mft.

New Testament in English, The, by Ronald A. Knox. 1944. London: Burns Oates and Washbourne. Cited as Knox.

New Testament, The: Revised Standard Version. NT 1946. London, Edinburgh, and New York: Thomas Nelson & Sons. 2nd edition reprinted 1972 as part of The Common Bible. Cited as RSV.

Sainte Bible, La: Version Synodale. 7th edition, revised, 1952. Paris: Alliance Biblique Française. Cited as Syn.

Sainte Bible, La: traduite en français sous la direction de l'Ecole Biblique de Jérusalem. 1956. 2nd edition 1973. Paris: Les Editions du Cerf. Cited as BJ.

Traduction Oecuménique de la Bible: Nouveau Testament. Paris: Sociétés Bibliques/Les Editions du Cerf. Cited as TOB.

Translator's New Testament, The. 1973. London: British & Foreign Bible Society. Cited as TNT.

GENERAL BIBLIOGRAPHY

Text

The Greek New Testament, edited by K. Aland, M. Black, C. M. Martini, B. M. Metzger, and A. Wikgren. 1966; 2nd edition 1968. Stuttgart: United Bible Societies.

Metzger, B. M. A Textual Commentary on the Greek New Testament. 1971. London and New York: United Bible Societies.

Grammars

Moule, C. F. D. An Idiom-Book of New Testament Greek. 1953. Cambridge, England: Cambridge University Press.

Moulton, J. H. A Grammar of New Testament Greek. Vol. 1, 1906, 3rd edition 1908. Vol. 2, by J. H. Moulton and W. F. Howard, 1920, 2nd edition 1929. Vol. 3, by N. Turner, 1963. Edinburgh: T. & T. Clark.

Commentaries

(Commentaries of special value to the translator are marked *.)

*Best, E. The First and Second Epistles to the Thessalonians. 1972. London: A. & C. Black.

Denney, J. The Epistles to the Thessalonians. 1892. London: Hodder & Stoughton.

Dobschütz, E. von. Kritisch-exegetischer Kommentar über das Neue Testament, Band 10: Die Thessalonicher-Briefe. 7th edition, 1909. Göttingen: Vandenhoeck & Ruprecht.

Frame, J. E. A Critical and Exegetical Commentary on the Epistles of St. Paul to the Thessalonians. 1912. Edinburgh: T. & T. Clark.

Grayston, K. The Letters of the Philippians and Thessalonians. 1967. Cambridge, England: Cambridge University Press.

Morris, L. The Epistles of Paul to the Thessalonians. 1956. London: The Tyndale Press.

------. The First and Second Epistles to the Thessalonians. 1959. Grand Rapids: Wm. B. Eerdmans Publishing Co.

Neil, W. The Epistles of Paul to the Thessalonians. 1950. London: Hodder & Stoughton.

*Rigaux, B. Les Epîtres de saint Paul aux Thessaloniciens. 1954. Paris: Gabalda.

Whiteley, D. E. H. Thessalonians in the Revised Standard Version. 1969. London: Oxford University Press.

Special Studies

Giblin, C. H. The Threat to Faith. 1967. Rome: Biblical Institute Press.

Hartman, L. Prophecy Interpreted. 1966. Uppsala: University Press.

Henneken, B. Verkündigung und Prophetie im 1. Thessalonicherbrief. 1969. Stuttgart: Katholische Bibelanstalt.

Trilling, W. Untersuchungen zum zweiten Thessalonicherbrief. 1972. Leipzig: St. Benno-Verlag.

GLOSSARY

abstract refers to terms which designate the qualities and quantities (that is, the features) of objects and events and are not objects or events themselves. For example, "red" is a quality of a number of objects but is not a thing in and of itself. Typical abstracts include "goodness," "beauty," "length," "breadth," and "time."

active voice. See voice.

adjective is a word which limits, describes, or qualifies a noun. In English, "red," "tall," "beautiful," "important," etc. are adjectives.

adverb is a word which limits, describes, or modifies a verb, an adjective, or another adverb. In English, "quickly," "soon," "primarily," "very," etc. are adverbs.

adversative expresses something opposed to or in contrast to something already stated. "But" and "however" are adversative conjunctions.

agency, agent. In a sentence or clause the agent is that which accomplishes the action, regardless of whether the grammatical construction is active or passive. In "John struck Bill" (active) and "Bill was struck by John" (passive), the agent in either case is "John." See secondary agency.

ambiguous describes a word or phrase which in a specific context may have two or more different meanings. For example, "Bill did not leave because John came" could mean either (1) "The coming of John prevented Bill from leaving" or (2) "The coming of John was not the cause of Bill's leaving." It is often the case that what is ambiguous in written form is not ambiguous when actually spoken, since features of intonation and slight pauses usually specify which of two or more meanings is intended. Furthermore, even in written discourse, the entire context normally serves to indicate which meaning is intended by the author.

aorist refers to a set of forms in Greek verbs which denote an action completed without the implication of continuance or duration. Usually, but not always, the action is considered as completed in past time.

apposition is the placing of two expressions together so that both identify the same object or event, for example, "my friend, Mr. Smith."

attribution, attributive. An attributive is a term which limits or describes another term. In "the big man ran slowly," the adjective "big" is an attributive of "man" and the adverb "slowly" is an attributive of "ran." Attribution, therefore, is the act of assigning a certain quality or character to an object or an event. See adjective, adverb, qualifier.

benefactive refers to goals for whom or which something is done. The pronoun "him" is the benefactive goal in each of the following constructions: "they showed him kindness," "they did the work for him," and "they found him an apartment."

causative (also causal relation, etc.) relates to events and indicates that someone caused something to happen, rather than that he did it himself. In "John ran the horse," the verb "ran" is a causative, since it was not John who ran, but rather it was John who caused the horse to run.

classifier is a term used with another term (often a proper noun) to indicate what category the latter belongs to. "Town" may serve as a classifier in the phrase "town of Bethlehem" and "river" as a classifier in "river Jordan."

clause is a grammatical construction, normally consisting of a subject and a predicate. See predicate.

components are the parts or elements which go together to form the whole of an object. For example, the components of bread are flour, salt, shortening, yeast, and water. The components of the meaning (semantic components) of a term are the elements of meaning which it contains. For example, some of the components of "boy" are "human," "male," and "immature."

concessive means expressing a concession, that is, the allowance or admission of something which is at variance with the principal thing stated. Concession is usually expressed in English by "though" ("even though," "although"). Example: "Though the current was swift, James was able to cross the stream."

conditional refers to a clause or phrase which expresses or implies a condition, in English usually introduced by "if."

conjunctions are words which serve as connectors between words, phrases, clauses, and sentences. "And," "but," "if," "because," etc. are typical conjunctions in English.

connotation involves the emotional attitude of a speaker (or writer) to an expression he uses and the emotional response of the hearers (or readers). Connotations may be good or bad, strong or weak, and they are often described in such terms as "colloquial," "taboo," "vulgar," "old-fashioned," and "intimate."

construction. See structure.

context is that which proceeds and/or follows any part of a discourse. For example, the context of a word or phrase in Scripture would be the other words and phrases associated with it in the sentence, paragraph, section, and even the entire book in which it occurs. The context of a term often affects its meaning, so that it does not mean exactly the same thing in one context that it does in another.

contrastive means adversative.

copyists were men who made handwritten copies of books, before the invention of printing. They were also called "scribes." See manuscript.

culture is the sum total of the ways of living built up by the people living in a certain geographic area. A culture is passed on from one generation to another, but undergoes development or gradual change.

dependent clause is a grammatical construction, consisting normally of a subject and predicate, which is dependent on or embedded in another construction. For example, "if he comes" is a dependent clause in the sentence "If he comes, we'll have to leave."

direct discourse. See discourse.

discourse is the connected and continuous communication of thought by means of language, whether spoken or written. The way in which the elements of a discourse are arranged is called discourse structure. Direct discourse is the reproduction of the actual words of one person which are embedded in the discourse of another person. For example, "He declared, 'I will have nothing to do with this man.'" Indirect discourse is the reporting of the words of one person which is embedded in the discourse of another person in an altered grammatical form. For example, "He said he would have nothing to do with that man."

distributive refers to the members of a group individually and without exception. "Each," "every," "none," etc. are distributive adjectives.

epistolary "we" is the use of the pronoun "we" ("us," "our") instead of "I" ("me," "my") in writing by a single person, for the purpose of achieving a more formal or impersonal effect. Also called "editorial 'we'."

event is a semantic category of meanings referring to actions, processes, etc., in which objects can participate. In English, most events are grammatically classified as verbs ("run," "grow," "think," etc.), but many nouns also may refer to events, as, for example, "baptism," "song," "game," and "prayer."

exaggeration (rhetorical exaggeration) is a figure of speech which states more than the speaker or writer intends to be understood. For example, "Everyone is doing it" may simply mean "Many persons are doing it."

exclusive first person plural excludes the person(s) addressed. That is, a speaker may use "we" to refer to himself and his companions, while specifically excluding the person(s) to whom he is speaking. See inclusive first person plural.

exegesis, exegete, exegetical. The process of determining the meaning of a text (or the result of this process), normally in terms of "who said what to whom under what circumstances and with what intent," is called exegesis. A correct exegesis is indispensable before a passage can be translated correctly. Excgetes are men who devote their labors to exegesis. Exegetical refers to exegesis.

explicit refers to information which is expressed in the words of a discourse. This is in contrast to implicit information. See implicit.

figurative extension of meaning, figurative language, or figure of speech is the use of words in other than their literal or ordinary sense, in order to suggest a picture or image or for some other special effect. (See literal.) Metaphors and similes are figures of speech.

finite verb is any verb form which distinguishes person, number, tense, mode, or aspect. It is usually referred to in contrast to an infinitive verb form, which indicates the action or state without specifying such things as agent or time.

first person. See person.

first person plural includes the speaker and at least one other person: "we," "us," "our," "ours." See exclusive first person plural and inclusive first person plural.

first person singular is the speaker: "I," "me," "my," "mine."

footnotes. See marginal helps.

generic has reference to all the members of a particular class or kind of objects. It is the contrary of specific. For example, the term "animal" is generic, while "dog" is specific. However, "dog" is generic in relation to "poodle."

goal is the object which receives or undergoes the action of a verb. Grammatically, the goal may be the subject of a passive construction ("John was hit," in which "John" is the goal of "hit"), or of certain intransitives ("the door shut"), or it may be the direct object of a transitive verb ("[something] hit John").

idiom or idiomatic expression is a combination of terms whose meanings cannot be derived by adding up the meanings of the parts. "To hang one's head," "to have a green thumb," and "behind the eight ball" are English idioms. Idioms almost always lose their meaning completely when translated from one language to another.

imperative refers to forms of a verb which indicate commands or requests. In "go and do likewise," the verbs "go" and "do" are imperatives. In most languages imperatives are confined to the grammatical second person; but some languages have corresponding forms for the first and third persons. These are usually expressed in English by the use of "may" or "let." For example, "May we not have to beg!" "Let them eat cake!"

implicit refers to information that is not formally represented in a discourse, since it is assumed that it is already known to the receptor. This is in contrast to explicit information, which is expressed in the words of a discourse.

inclusive first person plural includes both the speaker and the one(s) to whom he is speaking. See exclusive first person plural.

indirect discourse. See discourse.

infinitive. See finite verb.

literal means the ordinary or primary meaning of a term or expression, in contrast to a figurative meaning. (See figurative.) In translation, literal is following the exact words and word order of the source language.

locative refers to a grammatical form or term which indicates a place in or at which an event occurs or an object or person is located.

manuscript is the original or a copy of a discourse written by hand. Thousands of manuscript copies of various New Testament books are still in existence, but none of the original manuscripts. See copyists.

marginal helps in Bible Society usage are notes, normally occurring on the same page as the text and providing purely objective, factual information of the following types: alternative readings (different forms of the source-language text), alternative renderings (different ways of rendering the source-language text), historical data, and cultural details, all of which may be necessary for a satisfactory understanding of the text. Notes which are doctrinal or homiletical interpretations of the text are excluded from Scriptures published by the Bible Societies.

metaphor is likening one object to another by speaking of it as if it were the other, as "flowers dancing in the breeze." Metaphors are the most commonly used figures of speech and are often so subtle that a speaker or writer is not conscious of the fact that he is using figurative language. See simile.

middle voice. See voice.

modal refers to forms of verbs in certain languages which indicate the attitude of a speaker to what he is saying; for example, wish, hesitancy, command, etc. The various categories of verb forms are called "moods" (or "modes"). In English they are expressed by such auxiliary verbs as "can," "do," "may," "shall," etc.

nonrestrictive attributives. See restrictive attributives.

noun is a word that is the name of a subject of discourse, as a person, place, thing, idea, etc. See proper noun.

object. See semantics.

optative means expressing desire or choice. This is indicated in some languages by certain verb forms.

participle is a verbal adjective, that is, a word which retains some of the characteristics of a verb while functioning as an adjective. In "singing waters" and "painted desert," "singing" and "painted" are participles.

particle is a small word whose grammatical form does not change. In English the most common particles are prepositions and conjunctions.

passive voice. See voice.

pejorative means having a disparaging effect or force. For example, the suffix "-ish" in "childish" is pejorative.

perfect tense is a form of a verb which indicates an action already completed when another action occurs.

person, as a grammatical term, refers to the speaker, the person spoken to, or the person(s) or thing(s) spoken about. First person is the person(s) or thing(s) speaking ("I," "me," "my," "mine"; "we," "us," "our," "ours"). Second person is the person(s) or thing(s) spoken to ("thou," "thee," "thy," "thine"; "ye," "you," "your," "yours"). Third person is the person(s) or thing(s) spoken about ("he," "she," "it," "his," "her," "them," "their," etc.). The examples here given are all pronouns, but in many languages the verb forms distinguish between the persons and also indicate whether they are singular or plural.

phrase is a grammatical construction of two or more words, but less than a complete clause or a sentence. A phrase may have the same function as the head word of the phrase. For example, "the old man" has essentially the same functions as "man" would have, or it may have a function which is different from the function of either set of constituents, for example, "to town," "for John."

play on words in a discourse is the use of the similarity in the sounds of two words to produce a special effect.

pluperfect means, literally, "more than perfect" (see perfect tense) and refers to a verb form which indicates an action already completed when another action occurred. For example, in "The meeting had already ended when the speaker arrived," the verb "had...ended" is a pluperfect.

plural refers to the form of a word which indicates more than one. See singular.

predicate is the division of a clause which contrasts with or supplements the subject. The subject is the topic of the clause and the predicate is what is said about the subject.

preposition is a word (usually a particle) whose function is to indicate the relation of a noun or pronoun to another noun, pronoun, verb, or adjective. Some English prepositions are "for," "from," "in," "to," "with."

progressive is an aspect of an event which refers to its continuation or duration. For example, "the bird is singing" is the progressive aspect of "the bird sings."

pronouns are words which are used in place of nouns, such as "he," "him," "his," "she," "we," "them," "who," "which," "this," "these," etc.

proper noun is the name of a unique object, as Jerusalem, Joshua, Jordan. However, the same proper noun may be applied to more than one object, for example, "John" (the Baptist or the Apostle) and "Antioch" (of Syria or of Pisidia).

qualifier is a term which limits the meaning of another term. See attributive.

qualitative and quantitative are terms which are frequently used in contrast to each other. Qualitative has to do with quality, and quantitative with quantity. Certain words ("great," for example) are sometimes used qualitatively ("a great man") and at other times quantitatively ("a great pile").

receptor is the person(s) receiving a message. The receptor language is the language into which a translation is made. The receptor culture is the culture of the people for whom a translation is made, especially when it differs radically from the culture of the people for whom the original message was written. See culture and source language.

relative clause is a dependent clause which qualifies the object to which it refers. In "the man whom you saw," the clause "whom you saw" is relative because it relates to and qualifies "man."

rendering is the manner in which a specific passage is translated from one language to another.

restrictive attributives are so called because they restrict the meaning of the objects which they qualify, while nonrestrictive attributives do not. In the expression "the soldiers who were retreating were commanded to halt and regroup" (no commas), the clause "who were retreating" indicates that the command was restricted to a particular class of soldiers, namely, those who were retreating. But in the expression "the soldiers, who were retreating, were commanded to halt and regroup" (attributive set off by commas) means that "who were retreating" qualifies all the soldiers referred to in the discourse and simply provides supplementary information about them.

restructure is to reconstruct or rearrange. See structure.

rhetorical refers to special forms of speech which are used for emphasis or to create an effect on the receptor. A rhetorical question, for example, is not designed to elicit an answer but to make an emphatic statement.

second person. See person.

secondary agency (agent) involves the immediate agent of a causative construction. In the sentence "John made Bill hit the man," John is the primary agent and Bill is the secondary agent. John may also be regarded as the "responsible agent" and "Bill" as the "immediate agent." Similarly, in the sentence "God spoke through the prophets," God is the primary agent and the prophets are the secondary agent. They do the actual speaking, but the responsible agent is God. See agency.

semantics is the study of the meaning of language forms. In contrast to grammar, which classifies words as nouns, verbs, etc., according to how they are used, semantics classifies words according to their meaning. Semantic categories (or classes) include objects, events, abstracts. See abstract, event, object.

Semitic refers to a family of languages which includes Hebrew, Aramaic, and Arabic.

sentence is a grammatical construction composed of one or more clauses and capable of standing alone.

Septuagint is a translation of the Old Testament into Greek, made some two hundred years before Christ. It is often abbreviated as LXX.

simile (pronounced SIM-i-lee) is a figure of speech which describes one event or object by comparing it to another, as "she runs like a deer," "he is as straight as an arrow." Similes are less subtle than metaphors in that they use "like," "as," or some other word to mark or signal the comparison.

singular refers to the form of a word which indicates one thing or person, in contrast to plural, which indicates more than one.

source language is the language in which the original message was produced. For the New Testament, of course, this is the Greek of that particular period.

specific implies the precise or individual designation of an object. The term is used in contrast to generic.

structure is the systematic arrangement of the form of language, including the ways in which words combine into phrases, phrases into clauses, and clauses into sentences. Because this process may be compared to the building of a house or a bridge, such words as structure and construction are used in reference to it. To separate and rearrange the various components of a sentence or other unit of discourse in the translation process is to restructure it.

style is a particular or characteristic manner in discourse. Each language has certain distinctive stylistic features which cannot be reproduced literally in another language. Within any language, certain groups of speakers may have their characteristic discourse styles, and among individual speakers and writers, each has his own style. Various stylistic devices are used for the purpose of achieving a more pleasing style. For example, synonyms are sometimes used to avoid the monotonous repetition of the same words, or the normal order of clauses and phrases may be altered for the sake of emphasis.

subjunctive refers to certain forms of verbs that are used to express an act or state as being contingent or possible (sometimes as wish or desire), rather than as actual fact.

substitute passive is a form which is passive in meaning, though active in form. For example, in the expression "they received punishment," the subject "they" is really the goal of the activity of the "punishment." The same is true of such expressions as "he got kicked" and "they obtained mercy."

synonyms are words which are different in form but similar in meaning, as "boy" and "lad." Expressions which have essentially the same meaning are said to be synonymous.

taboo refers to something set apart as sacred by religious custom and is therefore forbidden to all but certain persons or uses (positive taboo), or something which is regarded as evil and therefore forbidden to all by tradition or social usage (negative taboo).

tense is usually a form of a verb which indicates time relative to a discourse or some event in a discourse. The most common forms of tense are past, present, and future.

third person. See person.

transitionals are words or phrases which mark the connections between related events. Some typical transitionals are "next," "then," "later," "after that," "the day following," "when this was done."

verbs are a grammatical class of words which express existence, action, or occurence, as "be," "become," "run," "think," etc.

voice in grammar is the relation of the action expressed by a verb to the participants in the action. In English and many other languages, the active voice indicates that the subject performs the action ("John hit the man"), while the passive voice indicates that the subject is being acted upon ("the man was hit"). The Greek language has a middle voice, in which the subject may be regarded as doing something to or for himself (or itself).

INDEX